Team Coaching: Artists at Work

Team Coaching: Artists at Work

South African coaches share their theory and practice

edited by
Helena Dolny

with contributions from
Maryse Barak
Lloyd Chapman
Michael Cooper
Helena Dolny
Tim Goodenough
Marti Janse Van Rensburg
Khatija Saley
Ray Sher

PENGUIN BOOKS

PENGUIN BOOKS

Published by the Penguin Group
Penguin Books (South Africa) (Pty) Ltd, 24 Sturdee Avenue, Rosebank,
Johannesburg 2196, South Africa
Penguin Group (USA) Inc, 375 Hudson Street, New York, New York 10014, USA
Penguin Group (Canada), 90 Eglinton Avenue East, Suite 700, Toronto, Ontario,
Canada M4P 2Y3 (a division of Pearson Penguin Canada Inc)
Penguin Books Ltd, 80 Strand, London WC2R 0RL, England
Penguin Ireland, 25 St Stephen's Green, Dublin 2, Ireland (a division of
Penguin Books Ltd)
Penguin Group (Australia), 250 Camberwell Road, Camberwell, Victoria 3124,
Australia (a division of Pearson Australia Group Pty Ltd)
Penguin Books India Pvt Ltd, 11 Community Centre, Panchsheel Park,
New Delhi – 110 017, India
Penguin Group (NZ), 67 Apollo Drive, Mairangi Bay, Auckland 1310, New Zealand
(a division of Pearson New Zealand Ltd)

Penguin Books (South Africa) (Pty) Ltd, Registered Offices:
24 Sturdee Avenue, Rosebank, Johannesburg 2196, South Africa

www.penguinbooks.co.za

First published by Penguin Books (South Africa) (Pty) Ltd 2009

Copyright © The authors of individual contributions 2009

ISBN 978 0 143 02582 5

Typeset by CJH Design in 10.5/14 pt Charter
Cover design: Flame Design, Cape Town
Printed and bound by Mills Litho, Cape Town

For Nancy Kline, with appreciation
The Thinking Environment™ prevailed for the authors
as a way of being and working with one another

CONTENTS

Preface   1
Helena Dolny

PART ONE: PERSONAL STORIES
Introduction – *Helena Dolny*   7
Helena Dolny   8
Maryse Barak   13
Lloyd Chapman   20
Michael Cooper   25
Tim Goodenough   29
Marti Janse Van Rensburg   34
Khatija Saley   39
Ray Sher   43
Closing Words – *Marti Janse Van Rensburg*   49

PART TWO: SEVEN INTERVENTIONS: SEVEN STORIES
Introduction – *Marti Janse Van Rensburg*   53
Input, Throughput, Output – *Marti Janse Van Rensburg*   54
Coaching Sporting Sceptics – against the clock! – *Tim Goodenough*   63
Be prepared . . . and then prepare to let it all go! *Ray Sher*   70
Meta-Coaching™ – *Michael Cooper*   78
Transforming Team Meetings – *Helena Dolny*   88
Team Coaching with the Integral-Experiential Coaching
Model – *Lloyd Chapman*   99
Facilitating Reconciliation – *Maryse Barak* as told to *Helena Dolny* 114
Closing Words – *Marti Janse Van Rensburg*   123

PART THREE: A REPERTOIRE OF TOOLS
Introduction: Tools to create self-awareness, reflection, energy
    and conversations – *Helena Dolny*   127
So where to? The need for shared vision to map a way forward –
    Helena Dolny   130
GOALS: Options, Testing, Rating Progress, Accountability and
    Celebration – *Helena Dolny*   134

Mental Development for Coaching – *Tim Goodenough* 140

Building the Container – *Maryse Barak* 144

Learning Styles Preferences: Honey and Mumford contrasted
    with Kolb – *Marti Janse Van Rensburg* 149

The Myers-Briggs Type Indicator® – *Marti Janse Van Rensburg* 157

The Enneagram – *Marti Janse Van Rensburg* 164

What is the relevance of Archetypes in Team Coaching? – *Ray Sher* 174

The 'Six Criteria' of Productive Work: Self-Rating – *Helena Dolny* 180

Productive Work: The Six Criteria 182

Teams dealing with Stress: Heart Maths and the Thinking
    Environment™ – *Lloyd Chapman* 186

Diversity: The Barnga Card Game – *Marti Janse Van Rensburg* 191

Games for Team Building – *Michael Cooper* 194

Building and Benchmarking Coaching Conversation Skills
    – *Helena Dolny* 207

Using image cards to spark reflection – *Marti Janse Van Rensburg* 217

The Power of Narrative – *Helena Dolny* 219

Journalling – *Marti Janse Van Rensburg* 223

The Effective Use of Video and Sound in Team Coaching
    – *Michael Cooper* 224

Closing Words – *Helena Dolny* 227

PART FOUR: SUSTAINABILITY, MEASURABILITY AND DESIGN GENERICS

Introduction – *Helena Dolny* 231

1. Sustaining Team Performance: the Teamwork Guide – Robert
    Rehm's guide, adapted by *Helena Dolny* 232

2. Measurability: Team Coaching: Approaches to Assessing
    Business Benefits and the Return on Investment (ROI)
    – *Khatija Saley* 242

3. Exploring the idea of a generic design – *Helena Dolny, Khatija
    Saley* and *Marti Janse Van Rensburg* 247

Epilogue – *Helena Dolny* 260

Recent Releases and other suggested reading – *Marti Janse Van
    Rensburg* 262

About the Authors 270

Index 275

Acknowledgements

Pam Thornley, who edited this book, created a spreadsheet to track working with eight different authors. We want to appreciate the way she did this with ease, and to say a special thank you for the compliment she paid us as a group. She said that this had been a 'happy book' to work on, that the authors were responsive, pleasant and relaxed, that she'd enjoyed herself enormously, and that the end product is 'handsome'.

I wondered what it would be like to be an editing coordinator. Did I need to be fearful? Could I not recall overhearing painful comments from academic relatives and friends involved in book writing, as they lamented the tardiness of contributing authors? This was not my experience. Team, you were a pleasure to work with. The birthing of this book was remarkably easeful.

A very special thank you is needed which singles out one of us for going the extra mile, and that's Marti Janse Van Rensburg. The time of bringing the book to closure coincided with competitive time pressures for me. Marti stepped up her participation with a graceful generosity and dynamic energy to make sure that all the unfinished loose ends and follow-ups were completed to schedule.

And, finally, thank you to Alison Lowry for having confidence in the project and giving the go-ahead.

Helena Dolny

Acknowledgments

Preface

Once upon a time in June 2007, at the foot of the Magaliesberg hills, a place steeped in South African history, an eclectic group of people gathered at an eclectic venue called Quiet Mountain, and on the turn of the winter solstice this book was conceived. There was a magic to the gathering. As the group dispersed to re-enter their separate lives they were no longer the same. There was cohesion; they had become a team. They were pregnant with the excitement of future collaboration.

Most of the group who worked together at Quiet Mountain were familiar with Nancy Kline's Thinking Environment™ approach: 'The mind works best in the presence of a question'. The overarching question and motivation for our gathering was: 'What learning could we share that would result in a co-created design outcome for working with teams in large institutions and also enhance our own practice?' That question sat in our minds throughout.

Furthermore, we knew that we required the presence of a certain composite of ten components which Kline has identified in her work. When these are fully present and constant, they contribute to our doing our best thinking.

What made the Quiet Mountain gathering so special was our collective maintenance of these ten components. We had chosen the (1) Place carefully, knowing of the thatched reading room upstairs, with views of the mountains, comfortable furniture and space appropriate to our needs. We knew food would be beautifully provisioned by our hosts. We gave each other (2) Attention, carefully respectful not to break thought through interruption at critical moments. We created our climate of (3) Ease quickly and intentionally, celebrating our (4) Diversity and confident of our commonality of values in spite of not knowing one another well at the outset. Our start-up sharing of stories was full of (5) Feeling, giving others an insight into our vulnerabilities and strengths. (6) Equality, (7) Appreciation, (8) Encouragement, and (9) Information were manifestly present.

And our finale was the answer to the unwritten (10) Incisive Questions™ that emerged, 'If we knew that what we have shared is the sum of a whole which exceeds the sum of the parts, and that we have pooled a body of knowledge and generated a debate that is bigger than us, and should be shared beyond us, then we can commit to writing a book together!

The earlier part of this story begins in the blue-grey buildings of a financial services corporate in downtown Johannesburg. Number 5 Simmonds Street, in 2007, housed a small unit of individuals driven by a passion to make a difference, to ensure that their work would contribute to a transformational culture shift in their institution.

Business units within the corporate were requesting team coaches. Those requests initiated a debate. The corporate had in place a screening and hiring process for one-on-one executive coaches. So is anything different about team coaching? And if the answer is yes, then what is the different skill set required by the team coach? A Google search revealed a paucity of writing on team coaching once you stepped outside the sports arena.

The unit opened up their discussion to include some external coaches who were known to work with groups and teams. The first meeting was conventionally productive. We began to identify a set of skills and drew up a matrix; for example, team coaches need specific group facilitation skills which a one-on-one executive coach does not need.

In our second meeting we intended to identify a screening-selection process. The corporate need for consistency, quality assurance and measurability came into play. But, as importantly, we wanted to identify what, if anything, would be desirable as a common basis for team coaching, and what room there was for flexibility, creativity and individuality of style.

At our second meeting, however, two new lines of thought emerged. The first was the realisation of how prevalent the temporary nature of corporate teams was. Continuous restructuring, promotions, new hires and resignations mean never-ending team changes, both in composition and leadership. This resulted in the questions: Is there something more that we would want to achieve besides the generally desired outcome: the 'optimisation of team performance'? What could we include in the coaching intervention that would increase individual self-awareness and enhance people's ability to adapt to others' styles, and hence their capacity to be effective team members wherever and whenever?

The discussion on style adaptation progressed to Lloyd Chapman sharing a hypothesis which, if validated, has considerable significance for South Africans. Lloyd's proposition is that mixed race teams often think that the reason they are not working well is because of race-culture differences. Lloyd has doubts about this reasoning. His hypothesis, which he intends to research, is that the quest for employment equity has resulted in hiring pressures wherein business needs to meet race and gender targets against timelines. Hence a prior and possibly less conscious practice of recruiting for sameness of style no longer prevails because of time pressures, and hence teams are more diverse not only in colour and gender but also in their learning style preferences, which determines the way they work and how they interact with others.

At this juncture, our energies soared; we were intellectually exhilarated, and felt that we were in motion towards a possible edge of new and socially relevant learning.

Our decision was to extend the group, create the possibility of sharing our knowledge and practice, and explore the possibility of a common approach. A retreat to Quiet Mountain was chosen to create that opportunity. The book is an unintended consequence!

Part One of the book is a set of short stories. They are about the writers of this book. When we created a circle on our first morning at Quiet Mountain and deliberated how to start, we discussed the power of personal storytelling and how we used that in team coaching, and therefore how appropriate it would be to do this ourselves.

Part Two is an offering by each of the writers in which they outline the process they use that consistently works well for them, and the theoretical underpinning of their work.

Part Three describes the tools we often use which we chose to share and demonstrate. We didn't just describe to one another how the 'tool' works, we tried it out for ourselves as a group.

Part Four outlines what subsequently emerged as a distilled framework, a vanilla design for a team coaching intervention which can form the basis for customisation according to the specific needs of the client. It also explores the usefulness of putting in place Memoranda of Understanding, the need to identify outcomes, pre-work, measurability, and evaluation.

The composition of the Quiet Mountain group was accidental. There were interconnections, but there was neither inclusivity nor exclusivity as an operating ethic. Several of those invited could not make the dates. Should we wait? We went with the Harrison Owen tenet for open space thinking:

> Whenever it starts, it's the right time
> Whoever comes are the right people
> Whatever happens is what can happen
> When it's over, it's over

But in this case the being 'over' as a gathering became a metamorphosis into a book-writing team.

South Africa is endowed with many talented team coaches. Our grouping at Quiet Mountain represents only a small number of them. We discussed involving more people in the book-writing project, bearing in mind race and gender representivity. However, we took the option to work with the flow of energy created to bring our project to fruition more quickly. There will be valuable books to come from others; we don't aspire to write THE seminal book on the subject. Our aim is more modestly to start the ball rolling, and encourage other South Africans to write and contribute to a body of work on coaching as a component of societal and cultural transformation, work that knows no national boundaries. Our unique national heritage of apartheid and struggle, of conflict, reconciliation and transition has created 'edges' that propel us into zones of discomfort, but which also equip us to more readily step on to the 'high wire'.

The 'high wire' in this case is pooling our shared learning, and our learning-in-progress, our unanswered questions and hypotheses. We are opening ourselves and our practice to public scrutiny. We look forward to interacting with readers' responses and queries; the engagement we generate will be our measure of success.

Helena Dolny

PART ONE

Personal Stories

Introduction

Helena Dolny

The power of storytelling has been with us since time began or Noah set sail, so to speak. Oral history was conveyed through stories. There is a genre of age-old children's stories and fables that convey educational messages: so the moral of the story is ... Between friends and family, bonds are often renewed through recounting old stories of shared experiences epitomised in a now old pop song, 'Do, do, do you remember? Do, do, do you recall?' And so the power of personal storytelling can be used to create bonds during team coaching and team building experiences.

Our Quiet Mountain grouping shared how we have used personal storytelling when working with teams. Lloyd often asks people to recount their personal story, in the evening, around a fire, if possible. Marti sometimes asks people, early in a team gathering, to share a light story from their childhood. This is safer, less threatening than being asked to be comprehensive, and often gives rise to stories that contribute to creating the shared sense of ease that a group needs to be able to work at its best. Ray sometimes asks team members to bring a possession that has personal significance in their lives, and that they are willing to share with others the story attached to that possession. Marti occasionally uses I Ching cards that are predominantly abstract in design (see Part Three, page 217). Participants are asked to choose a card that speaks to them as to where they are in their lives right now and is then invited to talk about what thoughts the imagery on the chosen card sparks off for them. Helena often uses an opening drawn from her training with Nancy Kline, 'What is your name and what is the meaning of your name?' The story of the name is often spontaneously shared, and again provides a light, non-threatening beginning that creates ease. A next round can venture to 'What is a value that you hold that you seek to express in the work that you do?'

In our Quiet Mountain setting, pregnant with expectation, we were, as a group, more willing to share ourselves at our edge. It was as though we had a common unspoken thinking that if we can share our own stories so that we create a shared insight into what has shaped us, what drives us, then we will be able to work at our best as a group. We get others to do this as part of our craft, so we need to practise with each other what we preach!

As we all spoke in turn, the implicit understanding was to present both the personal and the professional. At one point when one person had told their story, focusing only on their professional trajectory, we invoked the South African proverb, 'umuntu umuntu ngabantu ...', 'a person is only a person in relation to other people', and thus gently reminded them to share who is and has been of significance in their personal life.

We hope you will enjoy getting to know us as much as we enjoyed getting to know one another.

Helena Dolny

Seven pink tulips in a frosted glass vase. They stand erect, bending their heads only slightly. Their petals unfold. It is as if they are being gently filled with air, as though with their swelling, the intensity of their colour fades, just a fraction of a shade. As the days pass, they stretch their necks like swans towards the light that falls from the bay window into the room. Gradually they lean forward and bow. I am held by their changing beauty, quietly enthralled.

'Mum, why is it that when you buy tulips, you always buy the pink ones?' my teenage daughters ask me over an autumn supper in Johannesburg. Why indeed? Pink tulips have always been there, from my beginning.

A man pushes a bicycle up the steep hill, the last leg of his journey after his night shift at the factory. The headlamp cuts through the fogginess of the icy winter morning. Lights are already on at home, number 5 Argyle Street, Accrington, Lancashire. 'Regina?' he calls softly to his wife. She answers, 'I think the baby is coming.'

He washes quickly; the sturdy arms of his stocky body moving swiftly to towel himself dry. He puts on his brown striped suit: the one with two pairs of trousers; always better to buy two, pants wear out more quickly than the jacket. He steps out carrying his son, and in five steps he's at the neighbour's front door. They will look after Roman while he takes Regina to the nursing home.

Rough Lee Maternity home, a Victorian structure, is a couple of miles away. The hours go by, not too many of them, and just before midday, Regina pushes her baby into the world. 'It's a girl, healthy, eight pounds five ounces,' the nurse comes to tell the waiting husband. 'Four o'clock: visiting time.'

A girl. He is happy. He wanted a girl. He walks back home down the cobbled streets, row after row of terraced housing. The streets are now busy with people walking. On Sundays there are hardly any buses. Church spires and chimneys of mines and mills shape the skyline; cotton, coal and religion crowded into a northern English Pennine valley overlooked by moors.

Sunday, the shops are closed. Flowers? If it were summer he could cut flowers from his own allotment, but there's nothing there now. The cemetery! That's it, the other side of town and the only place on a Sunday where flowers can be bought. He's never been there yet. As newly arrived immigrants his and Regina's ancestors are buried in Poland and Czechoslovakia. If he hurries, he will just make it, to let his neighbours know the good news, grab a bite to eat, walk to the cemetery, and get back to Regina by four!

He is the father of a newborn girl. Does she have his brown eyes, or the blue eyes of Regina's family? He doesn't yet know. He chooses pink tulips over blue irises and returns, back down the valley and up the other side.

He enters the ward. Gladness shines through the tiredness of the women's faces and the shadows under the eyes that tell of the strain of pregnancy and birth-giving.

'Toni. She's the only girl born here today. There are seven boys,' murmurs Regina, 'and she's a Sunday's child of a Sunday's child.'

The pink tulips are placed to stand erect and proud in a vase. My mother feels loved and special. She is the only woman in the ward who has fresh flowers on this February Sunday afternoon.

I love my birth story, and my naming. Apparently there had been some talk about using old family names. My mother is Regina Maria Mathilda, and Mathilda Lamburta were possibilities for me. I'm not sure how it came to pass, but my father registered me as Helena Maria, a good Eastern European Catholic name. Helena means light. I like it.

So I grew up on the margins of mainstream England. I sometimes laugh telling others that I didn't really know any English people until I went to university! North East Lancashire is a melting pot of immigrants: Irish, Polish, Ukraine, Caribbean, and Pakistani. Schools are not secular. On St Patrick's Day, at the Catholic school I attended, more than 90 per cent of the children wore shamrocks as the proud symbol of their Irish lineage. My classmate Mary Carnevale, Italian, and I looked on, feeling excluded.

My coaching studies prompted me to consider my history of being on the margins. A first-generation immigrant, a girl in a world ruled by men, a Catholic in an England dominated by Protestants, a child whose father was a factory worker. In terms of what's going for me: I'm the wrong sex, the wrong class, the wrong religion. And later I will make choices which lead me to wonder whether I'm the 'wrong colour'! But my coaching studies take me to another place, a place of appreciation, that my 'gift' of having been on the margins has given me a sensibility; an ability to observe, adapt and connect that serves me well in my profession.

My parents' history influenced my choices. My mother had the best secondary school education on offer, but when the Second World War destroyed their lives, she had the legacy of education, language skills and confidence to study and remould her life. My father remained a factory worker. He had only ever been to primary school and the challenge of writing in a foreign language led to fears of studying that were insurmountable. He was a gifted engineer who designed gadgets for household use (such as a cabbage press for making sauerkraut) which he and his mates surreptitiously made up in the factory tools workshop. He won bonuses for innovative suggestions, but he never formally made it beyond the status of 'semi-skilled labourer' as indicated in the box of my United Kingdom marriage certificate which requests 'rank or profession of father'.

A continuing thread throughout my working life has been to create opportunities for people to study, learn, and discover what it is that they can excel at. That discovering of 'Who am I at my best?' and 'How can I be this best in my personal and professional life?' is part of what I now bring to my coaching. It is deeply rooted in my sense of opportunities denied to people I grew up with.

A further childhood legacy that serves me derives from family history that the essence of 'being' is internal and not derived from rank, profession or material wealth. Family history showed me that war is a leveller so the key question becomes, 'Who are you when you have been "levelled"?' My mother came from a wealthy farming family in what is now the Czech Republic. They lost everything material, and their place in society, their social status, their identity. This has made me look for what is the core of a person, as being more important than their position and wealth. And it's made me realise that people in authority, those who command, need to earn respect because of the way they lead, their being and doing, not because they occupy rank. My tolerance for command and control leadership that does not engage the thinking of those around them is zero. The berating Irish Catholic priests of my early childhood, preaching hellfire, precipitated a first conscious awareness of antipathy towards their leadership style; unfortunately, many other figures of similar authoritarian leadership have peopled my political and professional life.

It is unsurprising that I'm drawn to the work of Nancy Kline, author of *Time To Think,* and the practice espoused with regard to leadership coaching. Kline's visionary work is applicable to one's own self-leadership, that of others, or the teams we work with. How is it that we lead? How can we create the environment in which we listen as we lead and enable people to do their best thinking?

Years of deliberate observation indicates that people think well when they are being treated well by others; the ability to think well is not determined by background, IQ or experience. The importance of this finding cannot be overestimated; it must be shouted from the rooftops because, as Kline says, 'There isn't much we can do about the above (background, IQ, and experiences), BUT we can do something about the way we behave with each other.' Over thirty years, Thinking Environment™ work has identified ten components which, when they are present, contribute to a way of being with one another that is catalytic for people to think well.

My journey towards coaching becoming my full-time professional activity has been circuitous but consistent. When the time came to leave secondary school and apply for university places, I felt resistant to the educational conveyor belt that I seemed to be part of. A teacher showed me a leaflet for Voluntary Service Overseas (VSO); it was the tail end of VSO using school-leavers; graduates were the norm. I was sent to be an assistant teacher at Lwitikila secondary school in Mpika, Northern Zambia.

At the end of my time there I travelled through South Africa from Johannesburg to Durban and along the garden route to Cape Town to catch a boat to Southampton. Those ten days of reflective time on the boat were life-changing. I decided to abandon my university place to study literature and philosophy and rather undertake a practical subject that might contribute more directly to improved livelihoods. I wanted to return to Africa. I found myself studying agricultural economics at Reading University.

I fell in love with and married a South African exile. I became involved in politics. Mozambique became independent in June 1976, the month I graduated. I worked for the Committee for Freedom for Mozambique, Angola and Guinea-Bissau. In October that year my husband and I travelled to Maputo. I worked there for ten years, with agricultural cooperatives.

In 1986 I moved to Lusaka. I had support from the African National Congress (ANC) to pursue PhD studies. The land question would be an issue in post-apartheid South Africa. I was part of setting up the ANC's Land Commission and when government changed after the democratic elections I became adviser to the Minister of Land Affairs. A big issue was finance for black farmers. Nelson Mandela set up a Presidential Commission on Rural Finance, and I was appointed as a commissioner. One of the institutions scrutinised by that commission was the Land Bank. In 1997 I became its MD; my predecessor was retiring after forty-seven years of service.

The Land Bank was the job that most directly influenced my decision to change my career. The job challenge was one of institutional transformation. How would the bank service a new clientele with new and more appropriate financial products? But the bank was almost entirely staffed by whites who had never dealt with black customers. Moreover, the bank had been run by a hierarchy with a dictatorial style. On what basis were they now to bring their best thinking selves to work when neither staff nor managers had ever before been expected to think creatively in the workplace? And shouldn't they expect to be replaced in the near future by black professionals? Shouldn't they look for alternative employment opportunities?

Workplace transformation, in the true sense of transformed relationships, beyond the cosmetics of race and gender statistics, is one of the deepest challenges South Africa faces. This issue is made more urgent by the country's socio-economic legacy and the healing need for black professionals to move quickly and effectively up the career ladder.

Within this scenario is the universal challenge to us all: the quality of relationship, irrespective of hierarchy, race, gender, religion and/or culture. Coaching, at its best, offers enhanced relationship, with self, and/or between self and others. It is an honour to accept a coaching assignment. It is a responsibility to conduct the assignment with integrity, with skill, with artistry. To be the best coach I can be is an aspiration that fills my heart and soul.

Maryse Barak

This story is about some of the key learnings that have shaped my life and have created the foundations upon which I build my work.

As far back as I can remember, I have always had a sense of belonging to 'something larger'. As a small child, when I looked up at the sky and the stars, I didn't think *'puny me'*, I felt *'stars-sky-and-me'*.

I suppose that now I would call it 'a sense of purpose'. Reflecting back, I think it may have come from my father who always held fiercely to his political perspective of equality for all. Because he was a member of the Communist Party, his political activities caused us to be unceremoniously kicked out of Egypt in the late 1950s and, ironically, we came to South Africa where he was offered work.

Dad kept his head down and didn't join any political group here. But I received the gift of his awareness. He made sure that his eight-year-old daughter would notice things, like the benches for whites only, and other much harsher inequities. He would engage me in interesting conversations on our walks to the library every Saturday morning. He would listen to my young views with respect, while he gave his with passion and verve!

So I found myself always involved in issues around social justice and though my dad was always *way* to the left of me, he always supported me in my student political activities. As a university student in the 1960s when I protested against apartheid outside St George's Cathedral with my flaming torch, it was marvellous and unusual to have a parent come and stand beside me! It has been a source of power of my core identity that I have always felt hugely respected by my parents. This lesson of genuine respect for individual thought and expression was and remains very meaningful to me.

I graduated with a psychology degree from the University of Cape Town and then hurried off to Paris to study further at the Sorbonne, believing it to be the 'bastion of FREEDOM'. I learned that disillusionment is useful if it reveals reality! The Sorbonne did not live up to my expectations. When Steve, who is now my husband, came to Paris, he brought with him a mind-changing audiotape of Baba Ram Dass' *Be Here Now*. I had never before heard such a perspective on change. Listening to it over and over again, I began to understand how spiritual and emotional change has to happen first in people's hearts. I began to understand that if I could demonstrate the qualities I was 'fighting for' then change could happen. This was my first awareness that internal change is required before external change can happen and take root.

At the age of twenty-one, in 1971, I found myself in London as a remedial teacher. My teaching work was at a secondary modern school in King's Cross (often seen as a school for failures) where students had a 70 to 80 per cent illiteracy rate. At high school level, that means a reading age of six. It was challenging working with those adolescent boys, one-on-one. I was just a few years older than they were. Beyond the teaching were side experiences, such as having to wear band-aids over my nipples in winter to hold the boys' comments at bay: 'Hullo, Miss. Cold, eh, Miss.'

These boys were from extremely poor and deprived families, abused and angry. We worked in a team of specialist teachers, collaborating and sharing our learning in a field that was very new and unexplored at the time.

I had the added responsibility of working a couple of days a week in the junior school as the single remedial teacher, while attending a course in remedial education at the famous Tavistock Clinic. I was supported by a headmistress who was trusting and respectful. The premise on which the remedial programme was based was that the capability to read comes out of *relationship*. If you can create a *relationship* with a child, he will be highly assisted to explore and learn. The key was not to drill, but to play. Create the relationship and learning will follow.

I had to learn the hard lesson of choosing which children to work with. I wanted to help all the children who were in need of individual attention. It was neither possible nor practical. I needed to choose. I first tried working with some of the most abused, most needful kids. It didn't work. But when I engaged with the kids who responded, it worked. It was a revelation for me to learn to make the tough call to work where there is genuine response, no matter how deeply I felt about the needs of all the others.

Steve and I picked up and moved to the States and found ourselves on a 'spiritual shopping spree'. Still driven by the original message of 'be here now', we searched for a spiritual community. After roaming ten thousand miles around America, we ended up in an educational community called Twin Valleys in Ontario, Canada.

Twin Valleys comprised a student population of ninety. They had all found themselves in court for drugs, violence, prostitution and other anti-social behaviour. The judge ruled that instead of sending them to gaol they were to go to Twin Valleys School. TVS was a self-sufficient educational community where staff, staff families and students all lived together, built their own homes and grew their own food. The approach was that education was a privilege only achieved by the student *after* responsible work to secure shelter and food for the community. All teaching was integrated into the doing, building, and growing of the community.

Twin Valleys School was run on this spiritual premise – that human beings are inherently 'perfect, upright, and beautiful'. We held that true education was to learn *how to live* while learning how to make a living. Students and 'communitarians' together learned the principles of 'The Art of Living', which included living to one's highest vision and integrity, no matter the circumstance.

I was appointed to head the primary school for the children of the staff members. I was twenty-four years old. The school had thirteen children and three teachers. Radically, the curriculum was devised by the students through the subjects that caught their imagination and interest. This approach was, amazingly, supported by the Toronto

Board of Education.

I taught the seven-year-olds. How completely wonderful it was to study volcanoes for a whole month! As a teacher, the challenge and stimulation of having to learn all about the topic myself and bring to it various perspectives, stories and information was always enlivening. I will never forget Adam, a bright and curious seven-year-old. He demanded that he present his volcano learning to the whole community at dinner one night. Proudly, he demonstrated his volcano model erupting with chemicals he had mixed, while someone played the drums for effect! The 280 members of the community applauded with delight, and this little boy learned so much more that night than how volcanoes behaved! The next morning he appeared at school and said, 'Now I want to learn about Canada's history.' As the teacher, I was the constant learner!

Steve and I spent a very engaged couple of years at Twin Valleys. It was a stimulating and challenging place to live. Because we were learning everything together, sometimes we had to live through big mistakes. One deep Canadian winter we had no heating because the students had failed to sort it out. It's insanely cold in Canada in winter! But, in retrospect, it was a fabulous experience. Everything was seen through the lens of enabling the best from each person. It established a powerful spiritual foundation for my life, built around a small number of spiritual principles that demand consistent expression. These principles – accepting circumstances as they are, expressing gratitude, withholding judgement, being true to my own integrity and vision – remain as a compass and measure.

As a result of a strange set of circumstances, I had to return to South Africa or lose my citizenship. So, seven years after leaving the country as a young student radical, I returned with my husband Steve seeing purposeful action from a very different perspective. We returned in 1976, the year of the Soweto uprising, when other whites were leaving in droves.

Our work in South Africa was deeply connected to the continuation of the teaching of the spiritual principles on which Twin Valleys was based. We were delighted to collaborate in Johannesburg in the setting up of a community based on those principles. Steve and I gave lectures, and slowly a community gathered around us. We were part of the larger

Emissary community in South Africa, with other centres in Durban and Cape Town. I discovered a talent for lecturing and was on the faculty for all the residential courses. My passion and focus was always the empowering of people. I was really adept in making people feel that they were seen and welcome.

My work was all voluntary and Steven supported us financially until 1990 when his art business went into liquidation. When that happened, clearly I had to begin to earn money. The natural step was to use all that I knew and adapt it to the corporate market. A door opened for me to co-facilitate programmes based on Peter Senge's work. His book *The Fifth Discipline* had just been published and I resonated with his tone and the learning principles. My entry into the world of corporate executives was nerve-racking. I almost had to learn a new language – self-reflection and personal responsibility were not yet key aspects of corporate learning!

I was continuing my voluntary work, which brought me to Planned Parenthood – a Johannesburg family planning clinic. It was the 1980s in South Africa – a state of emergency had been declared and violence was part of daily life. The Family Planning Clinic was a doorway into communities of exceptional nurses and social workers, volunteers and young people. My work was primarily to act as support to the staff through the intense emotional upheavals of the time. I was a naive white woman who held certain life principles to be true. Engagement with these brave women catapulted me into areas of community and work that I had never yet known, and it tested all that I believed in. I think I passed the test because of the love and support of many of these people. Together we designed workshops about respect for self and the courage to establish personal boundaries. Although the entry was through 'family planning education' the possibilities and territory covered with young people in the townships was immense. I learned a lot about my own assumptions, about engagement with what really matters to the people one is working with, and mostly about listening.

Many of the women I worked with influenced me deeply by their courage and their indefatigable work, as well as their spirit of generosity. Being accepted into their community and having a contribution to make opened my heart and my eyes. Now I was really doing what I thought I could achieve as a student radical! It had taken much personal internal change to enable me to contribute meaningfully.

Many images appear as I remember these times: being escorted by 'comrades' through Soweto to visit men who had recently been released from Robben Island; offering addresses to huge congresses of black women's organisations, travelling from Johannesburg to Cape Town with a group of women of all colours at a time when wherever we stopped we were stared at with everything from curiosity and interest to disgust and rejection.

After the 1994 elections I joined Ray Sher and Ros Solomon to co-create an organisation called 'Look Again'. Our idea and vision was to work with lower order workers. Our intention was to deliver self-empowerment workshops and in this we worked with Paul Seseko. We worked with black workers in both English and Zulu and got a fabulous response but it turned out that employers were just not prepared nor ready to spend money on employee empowerment.

'Look Again' taught me about workshop design and the flow of how learning occurs. We learned how to enable people to learn through their whole selves: minds, hearts and bodies. The challenge was to create experiences which would be inclusive, not dependent on literacy or even on English. What made it work? Certainly the combination of the friends who created the organisation, as well as creating an atmosphere of respect, listening, engaging physically with the ideas, having fun and, most of all, sustaining the idea that everyone is worthy and capable. 'Look Again' gave me the gift of confidence to begin working for myself.

I love working with large organisations because of their dynamics and power. The idea that through my engagement with leaders I can have a beneficial impact on the people with the power and so others in the system, is inspiring. I love the fact that when people walk in at the beginning of any of my processes, they are cautious, a little sceptical, but unfold themselves as they experience greater safety. I am also always moved when I see how naturally people respond with their best thinking and contribution when the environment is genuinely respectful.

So, what drew me to coaching? In 2002 I was ready to learn more formally again. Coaching piqued my interest. I wanted to study, be immersed in a learning environment while learning something new. I loved the approach of the I-Coach Academy: the assumption that we already each have a coaching model. This meant that I could make explicit all the theories and principles that guide my work and my life. The highlight of that programme was the personal learning and the community created between the student coaches.

I still find it hard to coach. It keeps me on my own learning edge, and even though this year has been rewarding, it's not easy to continually strengthen the assurance that the client is the expert of their own life and that it is my listening that is the true expertise that will most enable the client to move successfully towards what they want.

My personal forte is to create context and atmosphere, where people can begin to know who they are. That's why I took so strongly to the Thinking Environment™, because that is exactly the process that Nancy Kline designed, enabling people to become more and more in touch with their own brilliance and capability. It is a most superb and elegant way of empowering people to think. It has given me a way of demonstrating all that I hold dear and true through the gateway of corporate work.

Most of my work is not directly about how to 'increase productivity', or 'how I can achieve my (professional) goal(s)'. It is more about, 'Who am I at work?' and 'How can I bring all of me to the workplace and into what I do?'. I carry the assumption that the individual's answers to these questions will lead to collaboration and productivity.

My story of learning is not complete without acknowledging my community of friends over the last thirty years, and especially my community of women. Together over the years we have experienced a place of learning, creating rituals, rites of passage, hearing and telling healing stories from each other. What I do now has come in great measure from this group of women friends.

And equally my story is incomplete without the powerful surround of Steve's love.

In reflection, I began at quite a young age to articulate my sense of purpose, and it has remained much the same throughout. The work I do, all the different bits of it, are about serving this sense of promise – to deliver and demonstrate what I learned so long ago from Ram Dass in a crackly audiotape in Paris: be here now and be fully present.

My experience has been about keeping that promise to myself – to continue learning, keep emerging, so that when I die people will be able to say, 'Maryse was fully herself'.

Lloyd Chapman

I was born in Heidelberg in Gauteng in 1963. My father was a fitter and turner by trade and my mother worked in the post office. When I was a few months old, my parents moved to a mining village called Blinkpan and then later to Komati Power Station. And that is where I spent my youth and went to primary school. Given that there was only one English high school within a radius of 100 kilometres, Witbank High was the only choice we had. So off I went to boarding school.

I enjoyed my years there, played sport, socialised and did everything except apply myself academically. In fact I found school totally boring; I could find no relevance to life in what I was being taught. Anyway, my dad had never had the opportunity to study, so he was determined that my brother and I should have. But he had a condition attached to our going to a university. And it was simply this: we had to go to a university as far away from home as possible. His first career was in the merchant navy and he wanted to instil in my brother and me the fact that there was a much bigger world out there and one that we should explore.

Years later he told me that he was terrified that we would get stuck in small town mentality. So my brother went to the University of the Witwatersrand to study medicine and I went to Rhodes University in Grahamstown to study theology. To this day I do not know how or why I was accepted at the School of Divinity with such a bad academic record. My hypothesis is that I was accepted on the grounds that there were not too many applications for theology so they took what they could get.

Be that as it may, divine intervention or karma, I was accepted and the School of Divinity turned out to be the best thing that ever happened to me. I was fortunate to have some of the best teachers I have ever been exposed to. They opened up a whole new world for me. They made me question everything, and they wanted to know why I took the stand I did. In short, they instilled in me a love of learning that has served me well to this day. They taught me to think critically and question everything. More importantly, they taught me how to do research and how to work on my own. To this day I am grateful for the education I received at Rhodes. The training was so successful that by the end of my third year I even questioned whether I wanted to remain in the ministry. I had serious questions about the model being used in and by the church. However, I still needed to do my internship year before I could graduate. I volunteered to go to Cape Town (even further from home) where I was the assistant minister at Parow Methodist church. (I must just add I was accepted as a probationer with some serious reservations. The panel that interviewed me, I later found out, felt very uncomfortable with my tendency to question the 'Ultimate Truth' or fundamentals of the faith.)

During my probation year I decided to leave the ministry and enter the world of business. My interest in business arose through my interaction with executives during that year. I had the fortunate privilege of working with executives in a number of settings. The interactions from which I learned the most, however, was when I ministered to executives dying of cancer or having had double or triple heart bypass operations. It gave me a perspective on life that has never left me. It also developed a strong empathy within me for these giants of industry. Most people only see the successful sides of executives; I got to know them when they were at their most vulnerable. Despite their outward success and enormous wealth, in the end it actually meant nothing. The awareness that life is more important than our work has never left me.

On completing my National Service I worked in a bank for three months and then joined the Investments Division of Old Mutual. Initially I provided administrative support to the portfolio managers and later I worked in marketing. Here my function was to analyse unit trust performance and write all the marketing material. The five years in investments taught me a great deal about the financial markets and their complexities. I gained a good working knowledge of economics and its impact on various industries and the financial markets. It taught me to look at business in a more holistic way. I gained a working knowledge of macro and microeconomics – macro in the sense that I had to write reports explaining the investment returns achieved, given the existing macroeconomic climate; micro in the sense that I had to analyse the funds' performance based on stock selection and the portfolio manager's ability to time the market correctly. During this time, my ability to do quantitative research and my analytical skills grew exponentially.

Given this strong research and analytical experience I decided to do my MBA thesis on 'The viability of index funds for the Republic of South Africa'. This research has been invaluable in assisting me in my coaching practice. The research was in financial management, which again provided me with an excellent theoretical and experiential knowledge base for executive coaching. Financial sustainability of any organisation is the ultimate measure of an executive's success. I gained a good understanding of what executives have to deliver to shareholders in terms of financial sustainability. At the time, however, undertaking research that proves your employer cannot do what it claims it can was a little naive or arrogant. Needless to say it brought my career in the organisation to a grinding halt.

In 1992 I moved to Norwich Life. The late 90s was a very interesting time in South Africa. The ANC had been unbanned and the first democratic elections in the history of the country had taken place. No doubt about it, the country was a political miracle. The same could not be said of the business environment. Prior to the elections many industries had grown and survived in a protected environment. This was especially true in the case of the financial services industry. The most protected of all were the Life Assurance companies. They had grown and thrived in an environment where there were exchange controls, high inflation and effectively no competition. Given the high rates of inflation, banks could not compete. Furthermore, these Life Companies effectively controlled the unit trust industry.

Norwich Life realised that the market was going to change radically and that they needed to respond to those changes. Roger Le Crerar recruited me to help him re-engineer the business processes to make the company more cost-effective and competitive. We first designed the business processes in a computer simulation and then implemented them. I was then put in charge of the workflow project, which we had up and running in eighteen months. During this time I developed a good working knowledge of systems thinking and business processes. To this day, business process design is a critical element of my integrated coaching model. I learned that process design could make or break any strategy. To my amazement I still find senior managers, whom I coach, who do not understand this. My analysis skills improved substantially during this time as a result of my having to analyse all the business processes. This in turn gave me a good awareness of the operational context. I understood the business from A to Z. To this day I find it very difficult to coach an executive or senior manager if I do not have a good understanding of their strategic business processes. Without that, I cannot help them define the critical competencies that they need to run their business.

In September 1996 Mike Brewis, the managing director of Norwich Life, approached me and invited me to become the company strategist reporting directly to him. In October 1996, at the age of thirty-three, I was appointed company strategist and secretary to the Executive Committee of Norwich Life. By early 1997 the Executive realised that we did not have the skills or knowledge to manage large-scale change interventions. As a result, RGA Consulting was contracted to help us transform the culture of the company. RGA was the first company we found that had a process which involved the whole company in strategy formulation and implementation. The process was basically a combination of Future Search Methodologies and Participative Re-design workshops and was known as the 'Transformation Process'. The former was a process developed by Emery and Trist at the Tavistock Institute in the 1960s. In the 80s it was developed further and popularised by Marvin Weisborg. Robert Rehm designed the latter. I was taught these methodologies and my job was to facilitate all the workshops.

I began to realise that many of the executives and senior management were being overwhelmed by the complexity involved in large-scale change initiatives. I found myself spending more and more of my time coaching the executives on a one-on-one basis. It was then that I started to read the work of Ken Wilber. In Wilber I found an author who provided me with a more holistic framework for my thinking. It had slowly dawned on me that systems thinking was not as holistic as I originally thought. He introduced me to the concept of levels of consciousness and that there is a world view associated with each level.

Subsequent to that, I stumbled upon the work of Elliot Jacques on Stratified Systems Theory. Jacques' work complemented Wilber's very well. Finally I had found in these two individuals a theoretical framework that fitted my experience. For the first time I started to understand why the complexity was overwhelming many of the executives and management.

BOE Bank bought Norwich and averted a hostile takeover. However, the victory was short-lived. Within a month BOE sold Norwich to Fedsure Life. Fedsure then employed Towers Perrin from the United Kingdom to do the initial research and recommend a way forward. In August 1998 Towers Perrin presented their findings and made their recommendations. What came out very strongly in their findings was the depth of understanding and commitment of the Norwich people to the Norwich culture and strategy. Based on these findings, I was offered a position along with the Norwich managing director and the operations director. Fedsure wanted me to help them with the merger of the two companies. I did this for three years but, once again, I was spending more and more time coaching the executives on a one-on-one basis, as well as coaching the executive team on how to manage the complexities involved in large organisations.

It was at this time that a friend alerted me to the growing trend of executive coaching. I then realised that this was what I was actually doing most in my day-to-day work. So when Fedsure asked me to relocate to Johannesburg I opted for unemployment in Cape Town, with the intention of starting an executive coaching practice.

I eventually enrolled for a professional doctorate in coaching through Middlesex University and the National Centre for Workbased Learning in the United Kingdom. I was the first person in the world to qualify with a professional doctorate in executive coaching. For my doctorate I developed the Integrated Experiential Coaching Model which was a phenomenological exploration of executive coaching as an experiential learning process within the context of the Integrated Experiential Coaching Model. This model proposes that executive coaching is about facilitating integrated experiential learning in individuals in order to facilitate personal growth and development with the aim of improving individual and organisational performance.

It is not therapy. It is integrated in that it caters for E F Schumacher's Four Fields of Knowledge and Wilber's Integral Model which cater for personal development through various levels of consciousness, especially in the personal and transpersonal levels. It is experiential in that it uses David A Kolb's Experiential Learning model as the injunction and uses Sheila Harri-Augstein and Laurie Thomas' concept of Learning Conversations as the primary learning tool.

The model and research were initially designed for one-on-one coaching. However, once we had completed the research and presented the findings, my biggest client, who was the basis of the research project, asked me to expand the model to include coaching teams.

It was about this time that I met Helena Dolny, who was interested in introducing team coaching at Standard Bank. She invited a number of us (the contributors to this book) to start developing a team coaching intervention for the Bank – hence my involvement with this project. I now earn my living completely from doing individual and team coaching.

Michael Cooper

One of the hardest questions for me to answer is: 'What is it that you do?' I am often inclined to say 'executive coach' as this is where my passion lies, but how do you include in that author, sports mental conditioning coach, researcher, facilitator, speaker and trainer? I am also keenly aware of my role as a preacher, as well as that of husband, father and counsellor. So I have come to realise that to define my identity by something I do is a mistake. I am none of these things. These are things I sometimes do, they are roles I play and hats I sometimes wear. I 'am' only one thing and that is me. This is not semantics but is quite critical as I have found this search for me, the *me* apart from the roles I play, to be the search I have conducted for ten years now. It is also the key question I try to help all my clients answer. Who are you when you are doing nothing?

When I left school in 1988, like most young men in South Africa, I had two options: I could go to university or I could go the army for my compulsory military service. If I went to university I would have to go to the army after I graduated. I had strong moral and religious objections to being in the army. It was something I felt I could not, in all conscience, do. So instead of going to university I found myself with most of my peers facing a judge in a court in Bloemfontein and hearing, as he slammed down his gavel, that I was to do six years of community service. I would receive R800 a month to live on. Six years seemed like a lifetime to an eighteen-year-old, but I was convinced I was doing the right thing and, in retrospect, I would make exactly the same decision today.

I spent three years working for the Sandton Town Council as an

administrative assistant in the valuations department. After three years
the rest of my sentence was commuted when mandatory conscription
was abolished. I found myself suddenly free to do what I wanted for the
first time in my life. I chose to enter the missionary service and served
for eight years in this capacity. During this time I learned a number of
key lessons, one of which was that you can learn to do anything you
put your mind to. One day I would be rebuilding a car's gearbox, the
next day I'd be building a brick wall, and the day after that I would be
addressing two hundred people. This experience helped tremendously
when I had to make changes in life at a later stage. It has also helped
me to work with clients, because so many in the corporate environment
are driven by the fear of change. They over-identify with their careers
or their specialties and fear having to learn or do something outside
their comfort zone. The other key lesson I learned was to get along
with and work with teams of people. I was exposed to many cultures,
languages, educational backgrounds and personalities. I learned to put
aside judgements and preconceptions and deal with each individual as
unique. It is a critical skill in South Africa today with its diverse teams
and workforce.

When my daughter came along I found myself needing to earn an
income for the first time. Over the years I had always been a trainer
and facilitator in groups as well as in one-on-one situations, and so
I started work for an International IT company as a trainer. For the
next few years I learned and trained many IT systems and languages,
eventually becoming the manager of the training and development
division. I also qualified as a project manager.

It was a very difficult time for me. The duplicity and lack of values
dismayed me, especially in the personal development arena where
CEOs and managers would speak about the worth of people and
how to empower and develop them, but it was usually just window
dressing. I knew I had to get out of the large corporate environment.
I had learned some very valuable things, though: selling, putting
large corporate deals together and presenting them, designing and
developing complex business systems for organisations, work flow and
productivity, budgeting and management techniques. I feel that having
experience at the top of the corporate game gives a coach a unique
insight into the pressures and concerns of the people you deal with. I
also realised that while I had a passion for the softer side of business

and the people issues, the financial drivers are also key, and success lies in balancing both.

During this time I had become a certified project manager and had started designing and training many soft skills courses, and then I took the plunge and left corporate life to go on my own as a freelance trainer and facilitator. After getting over the fear of not knowing where next month's pay cheque would come from, I realised that I truly loved working for myself. One of my main priorities in life is keeping things simple so that I can spend time and energy with my family and on personal pursuits. When you work for yourself you have freedom to decide on your level of involvement and how much time you will spend on any one thing.

My biggest concern at this time was that even though my training was excellent and the programmes were world class, very little of what I presented to my students resulted in a change in behaviour back at the workplace. After some research I found that this was in fact quite normal; statistics revealed that in your normal classroom environment type training less than 15 per cent of what is learned is incorporated back in the workplace. This is shocking! Who would invest in something if there was only a 15 per cent return on it? Yet businesses were and are pouring millions of rands into classes just like this. There had to be a better way!

I started reading and researching heavily in the area of change processes and how people were making real long-lasting change in their personal lives and professional environments. I read all the major thinkers of the time on personal development. I studied and became a Master Practitioner in Neuro-Linguistic Programming (NLP) and Neuro Semantics. I found that the movement of Neuro Semantics as developed by Dr L Michael Hall and Bob Bodenhamer had taken NLP and added to it. In my mind it is the most versatile model for making quick and permanent change in yourself and others. One of the principles I firmly believe in is that you should constantly apply what you teach to yourself first. How can you be coaching people to build healthy, balanced lifestyles if yours is unhealthy and unbalanced and you are not trying to do anything about it? How can you coach honest professionalism if you make a habit of hiding what you really are and offer a less than professional solution to your clients? I am regularly coached myself and try to attend two weeks of training courses each year so that I can continually improve myself.

Out of my study of Neuro Semantics I came across coaching as a change method. Here was an intervention that really worked! The reason coaching was so effective was, firstly, that you work with the change makers in an organisation. Secondly, you work only with people who really buy into the process, not those who have been press-ganged into attending a course. Thirdly, you work with individuals at a uniquely personal level and support them over the change period instead of just seeing them on a once-off basis. This allows them to receive feedback on the change and integrate in an ecological way into their environment. Here was a change mechanism that really worked for me and I knew I had found my ideal career. I had always been a coach by nature, but now I knew it had a name and I could make a good living out of it while maintaining my goal of a simple and spiritual lifestyle.

At my coach training I met Tim Goodenough and we became friends. A year later, at another training programme, I proposed a book and research project to Tim. We were both keen sportsmen and were interested in seeing whether the coaching principles we were applying in business could have a useful application in sport. The existing model used by sports psychologists did not seem to be having much of an impact. We spent the next three years interviewing and researching the mental mindset of elite athletes. We developed a model called the 'Zoning Pyramid'. Using the pyramid, an athlete could consciously measure and develop specific mental skills. The results were published in our book *In The Zone with South Africa's Sports Heroes*. This led to the two of us doing a lot of work with professional athletes in many different sports, as well as having the unique privilege of speaking to the Springbok team just before they won the 2007 World Cup. Tim and I are now partners in a coaching and training business called Coaching Unity.

I consider myself to be part of the Human Potential Movement of psychology. It is led by Dr Michael Hall and is, I believe, the key theoretical psychological underpinning for all the coaching we see today. It includes multiple psychologies such as NLP and Neuro Semantics as well as positive psychology, but predates all these as it goes back to the work of Abraham Maslow. The fundamental belief is that as human beings we are all born with unlimited potential. We are designed to aspire to our highest frames. These frames include the need for self-actualisation. We are also our own worst enemies and any limitations we have are usually to be found in our thinking and not in our environment. I try to maintain this belief in all my work. People are aspiring to be their best and any behaviour I encounter is their system trying to do the best at their current level of understanding. My function is to help people self-actualise, in order to become all that they want to and can be.

I still believe the most efficient tool for great teams is open and honest communication. I try my best to get teams OK with honest and open dialogue. Once a thing has been said it can be dealt with. In the unuttered words of people lie many of the problems of teams and organisations. I am driven by an insatiable curiosity to understand what these thoughts are. I want to understand people, systems and companies. I want to understand myself.

I live in Pretoria with my wife Lynn and daughter Cassidy. They are my greatest friends and assets. They constantly remind me of my weaknesses and are my reasons for everything I do.

Tim Goodenough

I am the third of three boys, with a gap between me and my brothers such that I was always trying to be older – trying to fit in with an older crowd, a trait that still surfaces from time to time today. I had severe allergies as a child; I was allergic to numerous medicines and food groups, including anything with sugar or dairy, as well as being severely asthmatic. The allergies dictated that a natural segregation occurred between me and children my age, simply because socially I couldn't participate fully. I was not able to eat my friends' birthday cake or sweets. This isolation created other social isolations; being different can be difficult. These conditions and several difficult experiences with my peer group started a process that led me to become incredibly curious about people – what drives their behaviour? Why are they like they are? And how can I understand them?

I was very fortunate to have this kind of developmental mindset early on because it meant that I got to observe and try to understand people from childhood. I was watching and learning before, during and after sophisticated personalities emerged and these insights and instincts have become an important part of my job and life.

Sport has also played a big part in my life; in junior school it was a way to be accepted, to connect and to experience being valued. In high school it was a way to compete and push myself. At university it was a way to find myself again, and after university it was a way to relax and unwind. My parents have always been very supportive of me; my dad watched almost every sports game I played at school, and my mom has a gift for listening. My brothers have been absolute pillars of support and belief.

High school was an important time for me; I started to find a bit of confidence and experience a sense of connection with others. I also discovered Neuro-Linguistic Programming (NLP). While surfing the net, I came across some articles written by someone called Carmine Baffa. Carmine claimed to have qualified as a pilot in a really short space of time, a few weeks if I remember correctly, instead of the many long months that is the standard, using a NLP process called modelling. (This is a process where you discover the 'mental recipe' of how someone performs a certain skill, and apply that to yourself.) As someone interested in short cuts, I was fascinated. I read everything I could on the subject of NLP, and made a decision that by the time I was thirty, I was going to have at least become a Practitioner of NLP (the first of three developmental levels of training). At that stage I could only find details of training in the United States, and so I worked out how much it might cost, including flights and accommodation and the amount was incredibly high – high enough to think I would only be able to afford it in my thirties!

After school I attended Rhodes University to study a BSc (Inf Sys) degree. I have always been good with computers, and so a career in something I was good at, as well as positive prospects of subsequent employment, was a natural place to start. I strongly considered studying psychology because the subject fascinated me, but was put off by the idea of working with unhappy people all day long, as well as the many years of study involved.

At Rhodes I moved into a very small residence called Matthews House that accommodated thirty-four men. There I met some amazing and special people. I loved the culture of *'debate anything, always have a good time, work hard, party harder and play good sport'.* I managed to do all of those things, except the *'work hard'* part. Res helped me rediscover my love for sport. Playing Res rugby was a privilege and a responsibility.

By third year, I realised that my up-until-then strategy of photocopy a file per subject during swot week and cram as manically as possible wasn't going to work any more. In fact I realised that I was going to fail, and had a moment lying in a puddle during the middle of a Sunday night on the Rhodes Great Field where I chose not to phone my parents and give up, chose not to drop out. Instead I chose to fight for it, to cram as hard as I could, and try to regain permission to write exams from my lecturers, and pass my majors. I gave up partying and didn't see much of anything or anyone for several weeks. In the end I failed my major with 44 per cent, passed everything else, and was absolutely devastated. I felt I was a failure. That set me up for a fourth and final year, where I picked up another major, but most of all it nurtured my fighting spirit and never-give-up attitude. I learned that the very first time I went for the impossible, I had missed it by only 6 per cent and I knew I was in with a good shout the next time I decided to do something crazy.

During my fourth year I realised that the job market was looking for anyone but a white male with average marks; I had to have something extra, something different. Through a friend I managed to get a job as a part-time teller at the local Standard Bank. I believed that if I worked hard, the bank manager would be a great reference for when I applied to work at Standard Corporate and Merchant Bank (SCMB). For me, that was the gift of affirmative action – it forced me to become more dynamic so that I could compete for a job. I went flat out with my application form for the SCMB graduate programme. Aside from the usual information, applicants were asked to create an advert of themselves using any method or material they liked. I designed a movie using Flash Animation, and worked hard at applying for other jobs to develop my interview skills. A combination of all of the above got me flown to Johannesburg for final interviews. I got the job.

Soon after I arrived to work at SCMB in Jo'burg in early 2003, I signed on to an Internet mailing group that had something to do with NLP. Like all good computer science students who value their online privacy, I used a pseudonym I had created for the purpose of newsgroups and mailing lists. Much to my surprise, I was invited to meet the director of this NLP company, someone named Anne, who happened to be based in Pretoria just 50 kilometres away. I was in a massive quandary. I really was interested in meeting Anne, but she thought my name was Andrew something-or-another, and my friends feared that the whole situation was going to be something crazy, like a bad movie or a Nigerian 419-scam.

However, I decided to set up an appointment, arrived, announced my name was in fact Tim, and spent the next hour or so talking to one of the most incredible women I have ever met – someone who would change my life profoundly. Anne Renew had come out of retirement to become an NLP trainer, except this wasn't NLP any more; this was now Neuro Semantics (NS), an extension of NLP. She had not let age, or even deafness, stand in the way of delivering her message and sharing a powerful vision.

During that hour with Anne, she made me an astonishing offer. After she had done some values elicitation with me, and got to know me a bit better, she informed me that her next NLP Practitioner course started in a month's time, and she would like me to attend free of charge. She also spoke of the emergence of a new field called Coaching, and told me that the NS co-developer, Dr Michael Hall, had developed a coaching course with an Australian named Michelle Duval. They were coming to South Africa in October, and I needed to be ready! I was astonished. At twenty-two I was going to achieve my vision for myself that I had set years before, all because a special lady had chosen to believe in me, to give me a chance.

A challenge for me was that I had no funds for courses, and had no time to attend them, because they weren't 'related' to my work. Fortunately, at the first NLP course I attended, I met someone who needed a website developed. I offered to do it, and earned enough capital to pay for my next course – where, again, I met someone else who needed some web development done. While making mistakes (big and small) and learning all along the way, this pattern continued for the next three years. With some very fortunate breaks, I was able to fund all my trainings and eventually emerged as a NLP Trainer in 2005, and a Meta-Coach (the NS coaching style) Faculty member, attending four Meta-Coaching[1] trainings in five years.

---

[1] Meta Coaching™

I solved the problem of lack of time by taking leave to attend trainings. This resulted in my not having much personal time, and not much capital to play with as everything went into the training budget. In 2003 I was sleeping on one of those foam camping mattresses – I didn't want to spend money on a bed, in case I couldn't afford my next course! I used my intermittent backache to reinforce my resolve to do the impossible, to learn as much as possible and get my qualifications. I had caught a vision, and had developed one for myself, and now the work ethic followed naturally.

During my Meta-Coaching training in 2003 I realised that the philosophy, style and tools of Meta-Coaching were ideally suited for professional sport. My thoughts immediately turned to rugby. I remember rushing home one evening and telling my digs mate that I would one day be the Springbok Mental Guy – an impossible goal. He was too polite to laugh in my face. Immediately after the training I phoned all the provincial rugby unions and told them excitedly about the power of coaching. They responded with a 'Who are you? Who have you worked with?' and eventually with 'We have one of those guys.'

I realised I needed to develop a reputation and wondered for many weeks how I would do that. During my NLP Master Practitioner training in 2004, I got to chatting seriously to a guy called Michael Cooper, whom I had met at a previous NLP training. We got on like a house on fire and had similar interests, including sport. A large part of our training was focused on Modelling, how to successfully identify the 'mental recipe' of an individual's specific skill. Eventually, after many discussions and debates we decided we were going to model professional athletes, to create something unique in the market. We then realised that if we wrote a book on the modelling project, we could not only create an in-depth business card, a product and IP (Intellectual Property), but that all three of those elements would support us in breaking into the existing South African sports market. Thus the vision for *In the Zone with South Africa's Sports Heroes* was born. It took us three and a half years to write, and a lot of patience and hard work, but the project was a success. We interviewed twenty athletes, identified thirteen unique mental skills they had in common, and through that exposure we got our first contract to work for the South African Rugby Union. The book was published in July 2007.

In June 2006 I joined the Standard Bank Personal and Business Banking, Coaching and Mentoring Unit as the Mentoring Manager. It was a dream job; working in the coaching and mentoring field and making a difference, not to mention all the massive learning and very special people I got to work with. Since 2003 I had kept my coaching business running as a private practice, specialising, although not exclusively, in working with athletes, working after hours and at weekends. Now I had the opportunity to immerse myself in coaching both in and out of office hours! After a while my job expanded and I became the Senior Talent Support Manager, looking after Mentoring, PDP-Soft (a self-coaching programme) and Executive Coaching, with a specific emphasis on the top talent in the bank, and what support they were getting in terms of coaching and mentoring. I got to design and co-design coaching and mentoring programmes, adapt and revise them, train and assess facilitators for these programmes and even to deliver them myself, using a coaching style, of course. I also got to evaluate other executive coaches, a rare treat that catapulted my learning into orbit. I couldn't have learned more in eighteen months if I had tried. I also couldn't have been stretched more, and had more of my weaknesses exposed. Being coached has always been *the* critical component of my personal and professional development, and this was never more true than during the time I was part of this amazing team. I am who I am today because of the coaching I have received, imperfect and still learning and growing.

I left the bank in December 2007 to pursue the most passionate part of my passion – working as a coach with elite athletes. I joined the Sharks Super 14 rugby team as their mental coach for the 2008 campaign, and had the privilege again of being stretched and challenged, learning every day and trying to make a difference through living my dream.

Marti Janse Van Rensburg

As was typical with Afrikaans families in the sixties, Marti is not the name on my birth certificate; rather, I was given two names, Martha and Johanna. Tradition dictated that these should be the names of my maternal grandmother as I was the firstborn girl. Not only was

I the firstborn girl, I was also my parents' firstborn child, and the first grandchild on both sides of the family. My biological maternal grandmother died when my mother was only four years old and my grandfather married again shortly afterwards. This, the only maternal grandmother I knew, had the first name of Martha. Her second name was not Johanna though. The decision was that I would take my second name from my biological grandmother – hence Johanna. No thought was given to the meaning of the words.

It is fascinating to me, though, that this balancing act became a recurring theme in my life. The balance between the two grandmothers and the names is also a bit of a balancing act. Martha is about being of service, and I do that, and Johanna, as in Joan of Arc, is about taking up a crusade and doing battle, and I do that too, usually when I sense an injustice.

I grew up in big family (my mother was the oldest of five girls and my paternal grandmother one of ten kids) and have happy memories of big family get-togethers, concerts, family cricket and soccer games, and generally much noise and fun. It was a very stable upbringing. We moved into a house in a new suburb in the eastern part of Pretoria when I was about two years old and I lived there until after I had completed my undergraduate studies. I went to two primary schools, only because one was being built around the corner from us and it was only completed in time for me to go there from my second year of school. I went to only one secondary school.

In spite of the stable childhood in a loving family, my earliest memories of school especially were about not fitting in and being different. I was shy and withdrawn and the more I was teased about wearing specially built-up shoes (to correct knock knees) the more I withdrew into books. I still am a very avid reader and still find myself withdrawing into books when in doubt. I am also still shy, but I often hide that well. Most of my memories of my school years are of being the odd one out, drawn to the other odd characters in school and generally not fitting in.

By the time I got to matric, or my final year of school, I was sixteen and didn't know what I wanted to do, other than the general assumption that I would go to university because my grades were generally rather good. I had toyed with the idea of studying archaeology for a while, mostly because I was fascinated by history and understanding things.

My father assisted me in exploring the possibilities, and on realising that I would not be able to work on sites outside South Africa (this was mid to late 70s) and would probably end up in an archive, I decided to give the idea a miss. My father then took me to the Council for Scientific and Industrial Research (CSIR) for a day-long battery of tests, which indicated that I could do anything I wanted to. This vague answer was followed with the recommendation that I should probably look at something that combined left and right brain, creativity and analysis, such as architecture.

I decided architecture was not a good idea. My excuse was that I did not want to design houses for people with too much money and too little taste, and they were usually the only ones who could afford an architect. It was only later, with perfect hindsight, that I realised that my latent creativity was a sensitive subject and not something I was ready to be measured on.

My father was a scientist and my mother a fashion designer (after both started out as teachers), and I ended up doing both. I thought this was a good way of following the advice to use both sides of my brain – just not in one career. I studied chemical engineering, with the aim of doing research, which I did eventually at the CSIR for about five years. And I also did the fashion bit. We were a family of three girls, but I was the only one really interested in the fashion world. I designed and made clothes from an early age, and from time to time I was involved in my mother's fashion school (training designers). I also designed for and took part in fashion shows both in South Africa and Europe.

My father died suddenly of a heart attack when I was twenty-one and still at university, and a few years later my mother and my youngest sister died in a car accident. I was working at the CSIR at that time. I took over my mother's business while continuing my research work. After an uneventful and happy upbringing (other than an inordinate amount of teenage angst), it suddenly felt as if my world was falling apart. My beloved father – my rock – had died suddenly at the age of forty-eight and now my mother and my baby sister (and we shared a birthday) were gone. It was a very difficult two years and a steep learning curve. After about two years of balancing my mother's business and my research, as well as wrapping up a complicated estate, my health was suffering and I decided to do something drastic.

I took unpaid leave from the CSIR and went travelling for two months. We were brought up with the travel bug. My father always said that a holiday starts the moment you leave home and a typical December trip (from Pretoria to the Cape coast) was always something of an adventure. We would take different routes, stop in small places, learn some geology and astronomy along the way (although we probably didn't always appreciate all of it as we mostly just wanted to get to the ocean). My parents also took us to Europe which, in the mid 1970s, wasn't all that common for middle-class, suburban families.

So here I was, in my late twenties, exhausted and running away. It did me the world of good. I came back and decided to change my life. I sold the home I had grown up in, got rid of my mother's business, resigned from the CSIR, ended a two-year relationship that had begun to resemble a soap opera, and moved to Cape Town. My one other sibling, my dearly beloved sister, lived there.

In Cape Town, I organised my sister's wedding. The family always spoke about the amazing weddings that my mother, as a designer and excellent hostess, would organise for her daughters. I decided that the only way to give my sister the wedding she wanted was to do all of it myself. I made her wedding invitations by hand, made her dress, her husband's suit, did the flowers, did her hair and make-up, escorted her to church and made the only speech at the reception – typical of a real control freak. I do believe she enjoyed it, though, and by close to midnight I was praying for her to leave so that I could leave as well and get some rest.

I decided to open a couturier salon, feeling that I was far enough away from where I had been my mother's daughter or, in science circles, my father's daughter. As is often rather typical of couturier salons, it was a disaster and after two years I decided to find a real job. Most famous designers are bankrolled and make their money from attaching their name to all kinds of things, like sunglasses and cosmetics, as opposed to the one-off designs. The latter are there to create fanfare and build the name.

I considered going back into science, but eventually I did something rather different and went into fashion retail. For me, that was radical. My family consists of academically trained professionals. There are scientists, doctors, pharmacists, lawyers etc and general business was never part of my milieu.

I ended up spending ten years in fashion retail, working for three different companies in Cape Town, Johannesburg and Durban. I had a wonderful time. It was a wonderful way for me to do what had been recommended at the age of sixteen, namely use left and right brain simultaneously. I ended up being merchandise director and managed to prove what I wanted to – and that was that one person can be responsible for planning, distribution and buying, or looking back, looking at the present and guessing the future simultaneously. The last retail company I worked for was sold and (perhaps the stuff of another book?) ended up in liquidation.

Feeling that I had proved what I set out to, I was considering a career change and had enrolled for an MBA. Within six weeks of starting the MBA, the company was put into liquidation and I found myself being forced to make a decision that I had anticipated only having to make eighteen months down the line. As this process came after twelve months of difficulty, due mostly to the sale of the company and a forced relocation, I again found myself facing a turbulent time and decided I couldn't run away again. So I had a midlife, or existential, crisis.

I started looking at my life and what mattered and I realised that the bottom line of financial successes and turnarounds that I had been involved in was great, but that I knew I was good at it. What really stood out for me were the people I had come into contact with over time, and especially during the ten years in retail where I played a managerial role. Those years taught me a lot about people and human behaviour and about myself. I realised that I had an aptitude for acting as a bridge between opposing departments – such as the computer department (very analytical and precise) and the buying department (very creative and un-precise). I could understand both sides and also get both sides to understand each other. In the process I found that people started to come to me to talk about all kinds of problems and intuitively my first reply to 'what do you think I should do?' would be 'what do *you* think you should do?'

The process involved getting individuals to understand themselves and their own reactions better, as well as trying to understand the other person's situation and rationale, in the event of the problem being relationship driven. People would often thank me for helping them to understand things better, for sorting their lives out and dealing with difficult situations. I found myself perplexed that I managed to do this by listening and asking questions, rather than necessarily formally assisting or giving advice.

My general rationale for following this kind of approach was that in the short term it might take longer, but the alternative was that in the longer term they would continue to come back for more advice, making them dependent on me – something I wanted to avoid.

In the process of contemplating my navel, I realised that the people who came to me and thanked me for making a difference in their lives meant more to me than the measurable results I had achieved. I wanted to make this my next career – do full-time what I had done from time to time in my role as manager and leader.

I had been involved in several consulting projects over the years and was often told that I made, or would make, a very good consultant. This therefore became an obvious option. It did concern me, though, that consultants mostly give advice, something I did not want to do all the time.

I stumbled on the term 'coaching' and decided that this was the next career I was looking for. That was in 2000 and even though it was a bumpy ride to start a new career from scratch at the age of forty, I don't regret a minute and, in spite of the bumps, it has been a wonderful journey. I did my MBA research project on coaching in South Africa and as a principle relating to Ubuntu, and started coaching in business in 2001.

In the intervening years, I have expanded my work to include training programmes, designed and given, and group work – and who knows where this might yet lead me?

Khatija Saley

I was born in what is now Mpumalanga province in the eastern part of South Africa, not far from the border with Mozambique. My parents chose what is quite an old-fashioned name for me – Khatija. Khatija was the wife of the prophet Mohammed. She was a strong woman, of noble birth, and supported the prophet and their family financially to allow him to preach. She is regarded as the first Muslim. When I was born I was apparently very alert, with wide-open eyes, inquisitively looking at everything and everyone. The backdrop to my growing up is the Indian suburb of Lenasia, south of Johannesburg, where I did all my schooling.

My father loved animals and I often accompanied him to various farms. It was my father's dream to own a farm. He grew up in a small town in the North West province. The area is recorded in South African history as one where Afrikaner apartheid was born. Being of Indian descent, my father was not allowed to attend any of the schools in the area, as they were for whites only. His family owned land in the town, but lost it when they were relocated to an 'Indian' area outside the town. The result was that my father never got the chance to farm the land his family had once owned.

My mother has a quiet, determined manner and offered her children the freedom to make up their own minds about things. As a result, she has four very strong-willed daughters and a son. I cannot recall her shouting or ever getting a hiding from her, or her ever judging us; she supported each of us in our decisions from as early as I can recall.

I shared my father's love of animals and decided at a very young age that I wanted to become a vet. My high school principal was horrified and said that it was an inappropriate career for an Indian female. He was no stranger to being horrified by me. Our annual ritual was that he would place special restrictions on me every June 16th (the day that commemorates the 1976 Youth Uprising) hoping to discourage me from what he referred to as the *'politics spoiling your life'*. Little did he know that I had learned the South African freedom song *N'kosi sikelel' iAfrika* when I was only three years old.

I applied to study veterinary science at the University of Pretoria. The response I got was that they did not enrol black students. I registered for a year at Wits University to do a BSc and reapplied to the University of Pretoria. I was granted an interview and told that all lectures were given in Afrikaans and that no special provision could be made to accommodate me. I was also advised that I could attend lectures only and not participate in any other campus activities. I found these conditions to be disrespectful and made the decision to forgo my dream; accepting these conditions was against my principles.

Instead, I completed a BA degree, majoring in psychology and philosophy. My love of reading and philosophy started at a young age when I was introduced to Dostoyevsky and Tolstoy and the works of the Renaissance painters. Reading about the life of Van Gogh left a huge impression on me. As a child I carried a book everywhere I went.

I worked part-time at a bank while I was doing my undergraduate studies, and two years after finishing university they offered me a full-time position in the field of human resources. Later I moved into the systems environment for a few years in the role of a systems analyst and business analyst. The projects that I worked on gave me exposure to working with senior teams, in addition to collaborating with international consultants who were working in the bank at the time.

Having been actively involved at school and varsity meant that I took on a leadership role in progressing transformation in the workplace. I trained to become a Lifeline counsellor, working in the areas of rape and Aids. I had always planned to do a master's degree in clinical psychology. Working in the role of analyst resulted in my changing my mind. I felt an MBA would better support me in my consulting role to business. I went on to complete an MBA and a master's in human resources at Wits Business School. My dissertation was on the experiences of female managers in the bank; I was curious to research what the enabling factors were for the women who succeeded.

The bank I was working for was undergoing massive transformation which created opportunities for young black people. I was offered an opportunity to work with the CEO, setting up a unit offering financial products to the low income market. I was then offered a role to oversee strategic HR projects for the biggest unit in the group. I questioned how transformation was being dealt with; as a result, the CEO offered me the role of heading up transformation for the unit. Transformation focused on offering individuals and teams experiences and skills to start understanding and working with leading diversity in the workplace and in the communities in which they lived.

The strategy was successful in that awareness was raised and employment equity targets were being met and, in some cases, exceeded. Being passionate about the work meant that I was constantly looking for ways to better support and sustain change. I realised that for this kind of change to happen work had to be done at an individual level, rather than the particular focus we had at that time.

It was during this time that I met Helena Dolny at one of the transformation workshops. Later, she and I worked on a project together and formed a close and creative working relationship. She left that company, but two years later she contacted me to invite me to work with her in developing a coaching and mentoring framework for the financial services institution. The work was done with the view that humans are unwell, and did not offer support for the individual to move forward.

It was for this reason that I made the decision to work in a field that would provide me with an opportunity to further my interest in work that was being done at an individual level, and where there was opportunity for a more sustainable shift, and where individuals would themselves be able to continue on a journey once started. Hence my reason for being drawn to the profession of coaching.

The opportunity to work in the area of coaching also offered me the chance to live and express my philosophy through my work. In addition, I was being given the chance of a second career. I worked with Helena on developing the Coaching and Mentoring framework, designing an executive coach assessment process, and developing and designing six coaching programmes. We have also developed a facilitator development and assessment programme. We went on to set up a unit to deliver the programmes in the bank, which is where I am currently in a role of senior manager.

I completed a non-accredited six-month introductory executive coach programme designed by a Johannesburg company, The People Business. I then completed a six-month certificate programme with i-coach academy, which at the time delivered its programme through Stellenbosch University. I also do executive coaching.

I am currently completing my master's degree in coaching at Middlesex University. My research focus is to tackle the measurability issues, which are a serious challenge in the area of soft skills development. Yet I work in an industry in which measurability means credibility. Hence my thesis will deal with the 'Return on Investment on the Acquisition of Coaching Skills by Managers'. I have been party to the design of a coaching training programme which focuses on the coaching skills for leading others (performance coaching), leading teams, leading meetings, and personal development planning self-coaching skills. The programme is called Leader as Coach. I am currently training and will soon qualify as a Time to Think Consultant. I was introduced to the work of Nancy Kline at the Standard Bank of South Africa. It has been a life-transforming experience for me.

There is a lot of transformation work that still needs to happen in South Africa. Being an observer and a participant in a world in which there are huge numbers of conflicts and wars going on, and the ongoing abuse of human rights and threats to the sovereignty of countries, is disheartening. What is happening in the world makes me think about Martin Luther King and Mahatma Gandhi, and so many other courageous individuals like them. They dedicated their lives to wanting to leave behind a better legacy than their predecessors had done. Their lives provide an example to live by and I believe their ideals live on, more in the heart than in the behaviour of individuals. It would be our role to try to live and leave behind a better legacy too. I believe strongly that this can happen only when people come together and offer each other respect and dignity. I believe that the work of coaching and Nancy Kline is what will offer the world an opportunity to do this.

Conversations with family and friends offered me the possibility of making the choices of how I responded to my experiences and history of why I did not become a vet, and the choice of an alternative. In my various roles in the corporate world, I have found that very few individuals actually put thought into the choices they make around their careers, the jobs they take on, or how they respond to things. Most of them fall into whatever comes up that offers a promotion and a salary increase.

The decisions I have made and continue to make are the result of support received from family and friends. Through coaching, I want to offer others the support to be able to make the best possible choices they can make, in whatever circumstances they find themselves.

We cannot control the beginning or the end, we can choose what happens in between by making a choice of how we respond and face these ontological limitations.

Heidegger

Ray Sher

This story begins in February 1993. The view from where I sit is breathtaking. The third day of my solo fast on this vision quest; no distractions and I feel euphoric. I wonder at the marvel of these rock formations, a giant moonscape, majestic statues, one of an ancient man facing a very old woman. In this sheer beauty, my fears evaporate.

1993 – the year I turned sixty. I watched the auctioneer banging the gavel, 'Going … going … GONE!' Our twenty-two-year-old business was sold. Next day I woke with that sinking feeling; for a while I found it hard to get up most mornings. As much as we enjoyed the business it had become a huge responsibility. Now I was free to discover more of who I am and what I can do. Now I could take the time for this quest – a journey in search of adventure.

So here I am, halfway through the Vision Quest programme in the nature reserve of the Grootwinterhoekberge, near Cape Town. Alone and fasting in the wilderness, I wait for vision, new direction, experiencing a quiet, long forgotten.

In this rich moment, I review the influence of ancestors. The disjointed memories cascade randomly like a psychedelic movie. My ancestral legacy drifts in – strong survival instincts, creativity, pioneering spirit. Life was tough and they endured.

A purple-throated lizard pops his head up over a rock; the cast of characters appears.

My mother Esther was born in Johannesburg in 1898, when it was but ten years old. Her first husband had died, leaving her with an infant son. I was the child of her second marriage to Ben. I was born in the 1930s, the depression years. Food was scarce. We had no telephones, electricity, radio or motor cars. My father had a bicycle, and we relied on neighbours for the rare ride to Ventersdorp or Johannesburg.

Ben, my father, was a pogrom refugee and struggling Ventersdorp highveld farmer, deep in Land Bank debt after years of continual drought and dwindling mealie crops. Some twenty years later he was forced to sell the farm. He smoked fifty Springbok cigarettes a day as well as a Meerschaum pipe with Boxer tobacco and died of throat cancer: a lonely old man in the back room of a Doornfontein house at age seventy.

Jacob Louis Rosenberg was my maternal Grandpa, a Bolshevik conscription refugee, and early Johannesburg pioneer when it was part of Die Zuid Afrikaanse Republiek. He made the epic journey from Cape Town to Kimberley on Cape Railways and the rest of the journey by ox-wagon, taking months to get there. Many years later, he took the impressionable thirteen-year-old me on a journey of nostalgia, showing me what he remembered of old Johannesburg. He pointed out the block on which the original OK Bazaars stood. 'You see this stand,' he muttered, 'this stand I could have bought for "*a span oxen*"!' 'Why didn't you buy it, Zaida?' I ask. *'Kein oxen gehadt'* ('I had no oxen'), he replied.

The lizard scurries off and I shift, following the moving shade in search of coolness. I wipe my forehead with my shirt sleeve, writing in my journal as the memories flow:

Lali and I married in 1956. I was working in my father-in-law's business – a miserable year as the soft-target son-in-law. Then I started my own glass business. In 1971, a moment of serendipity led to the creation of Granny's Cupboard, an antique and collectibles store in downtown Johannesburg. The wizardry of our interior design, the nostalgia of antique display cabinets and the mix of the merchandise, all contributed to the magic of the atmosphere. Granny's Cupboard was the place to find rare and beautiful objects.

From my vantage point on the mountain, I recognised that after twenty-two years, we had lost our passion for the business. It was time for a career change. That was a serious challenge, me being white, male and sixty years old in the 'new South Africa'.

On a trip to the USA in 1975, I discovered what I really wanted to do. We travelled to Esalen Institute in Big Sur, California. This was the centre of the Human Potential movement, a place where the leading lights of the time presented transformational workshops, and indeed the place where I had my first enlightening experience.

The idea of transforming my own life and inspiring others excited me. The notion of working with people, facilitating personal growth – theirs and mine – set me alight. Inspired by the mastery of the leaders and what I had witnessed, I returned home intending to become a facilitator and make the difference possible for people open to change. All over the world people were awakening and taking conscious charge of their own evolution. They were seeing the possibility of development, harmonising their inner conflicts and aligning themselves with higher human purpose.

While continuing to work in the business, I carried on my search, reading whatever I could find on the subject, getting practical experience. I attended workshops to learn as much as I could. I asked questions and sought guidance. There were those with the generosity of spirit who had the patience to guide and encourage me; I seemed to have a natural talent for this work.

In the coolness of the evening I recalled how I had struggled up the mountain three days before treading heavily, convinced my life was coming to a sad ending. One of the tasks I had been given on my quest was *to tread lightly upon the earth.*

This poem by Rumi, 12th century Persian mystic, had drawn me in:

Today, like every other day, I awake afraid.
Don't go into the study and take down a book.
Rather ... take down the Dulcimer ...
Let the beauty of what you love, be what you do,
There are a thousand ways to kneel and kiss the ground.

Yes! I thought. Let the beauty of what I love, be what I do.

Now, I realised that my life wasn't coming to an end ... it was coming to a fresh new beginning. A new vision appeared. I visualised myself, in a circle of people, leading the process. In that solitude, my gifts and skills greeted me and I realised that I had choices: I could continue on the hopeless downward spiral, or spin up into open space.

Early the next day I came down the rock-strewn path with fynbos in full bloom and a fresh breeze in my face. I was full of renewed energy and ideas that felt like giant bubbles that I was joyfully juggling as I descended. I had laboured up feeling hopeless, and now I was floating down with vision and purpose.

Of the bubbles I bounced, one was teaching Life Skills to young people and as that one circled over my head, the second, a coaching system drawn from the ancient Chinese wisdom of I Ching, or Book of Changes, bounced around. The third bubble, 'Time of Your Life' for retired people, awaited its turn. I could hardly wait to get going.

My first venture into corporate work was as part of a team presenting a diversity programme for staff of a local authority. The process was designed to give people the experience of discrimination in diverse groups. Rather than using the obvious examples of racial or gender differences, we had made height the differential. The Tall ones were given the experience of discrimination. The members of the Short group enjoyed the discomfort of their Tall colleagues and were amused at the turnabout. This process generated powerful insights.

During this period I read a research document describing the challenges facing South Africa, especially the youth between the ages of seventeen and thirty. The thirty-year-old group was part of the study because they would have been seventeen – school-leaving age – in 1976. This was a significant date for learners (Soweto riots). The research had revealed that 77 per cent of the estimated twelve million young people in South Africa at that time had not received an education that would support them in the work environment. They were marginalised.

Sheila Sisulu, who was CEO of the Joint Enrichment Project (JEP), discussed with me the need for the young people coming to JEP to acquire life skills as well as trade and other skills.

We designed a Life Skills programme which included instruction on how to draft a CV, how to create a vision, and some of the basic skills needed to navigate through life and achieve one's dreams. Participants on our course enjoyed browsing through magazines looking for pictures that described their dreams and building the story of their future in collage form.

A group of financiers agreed to finance our initiative and The Look Again Foundation was born. We presented the Look Again Life Skills coaching initiative to the candidates sent by the JEP. Over three years several hundred young people were empowered by our programme.

I enjoyed the process of empowering through coaching and began to refine my techniques. Amongst the many books that I read, these stand out: Peter Senge's *The Fifth Discipline*, Stephen Covey's *First Things First*, James Flaherty's *Coaching: Evoking Excellence in Others* and, later, *Co-active Coaching* by Laura Whitworth, Henry Kinsey-House and Phil Sandahl. The opportunity to do several coaching courses led me to the work which is my passion.

Soon afterwards, I was offered another exciting opportunity. Mike Boon and his Vulindlela Network were about to embark on a major intervention called *VUKA* (Zulu for 'awaken') for a financial services group. He was looking for experienced facilitators. I joined the team.

A significant part of the *VUKA* process is a two-day, 'immersion' stay in Soweto. Three senior executives and I were welcomed by a woman resident, owner of a typical Soweto four-roomed house. It was the coldest July night in years and, in spite of a power failure, we were offered a simple hot meal and two double mattresses on the floor. Our hostess told us not to worry about waking up in time to catch our 6am train the next morning.

Hyped by the discussion of the evening, we giggled and joked in the dark till late. We woke to the explosive sound of rocks falling on the roof, as if we were under attack. And then we heard our hostess laughing. 'Don't worry,' she said, 'that's my neighbour waking us up. She is my alarm clock.'

VUKA was, indeed, the opportunity of a lifetime. This initiative lasted five years and touched more than 30 000 people. As part of our duties, we coached the organisation's internal facilitators. Being part of this network led me to several extraordinary events. I joined initiatives and training programmes and worked on the cutting edge of Organisational Development work in South Africa ... and the magic continues.

As I review this story that began in the Grootwinterhoekberge in 1993 an important lesson rises to greet me.

Contemplation, being with one's unique and personal template, is essential to the quest for fulfilment, the realisation of personal dreams and visions and the process of inner transformation.

Giving myself the vision quest gift of contemplation, I was able to recognise and acknowledge the significant moments in my life.

I have experienced a life charmed by synchronicity and serendipity. The Granny's Cupboard season, the inspiration of Esalen, the quest for vision, the Vulindlela experience – all contributed to where I am now. As a facilitator and executive coach for transformation, I have found my niche and sense of purpose *letting the beauty of what I love be what I do.*

Closing Words

Marti Janse Van Rensburg

Our stories are as different as we are and are also told as differently as can be.

Helena starts by painting a beautiful image of pink tulips and takes her story from her daughters' questions back to her father and where the pink tulips came from, sharing three generations with us in a brief moment.

Ray begins his story with a vision quest at the age of sixty – a wonderful tale of starting a new life when most of us imagine it to be drawing to an end.

I tell mine, like a good scientist, in logical order. Maryse tells a feeling-motivated reflective story and Lloyd shares an interesting journey by telling us of the learning every step of the way and how it built up over time to where he is today.

Mike starts with the delightful question: 'Who are you when you are doing nothing?' And then he takes us through his constant quest to understand himself and other people. His business partner and co-author Tim tells a vivid story of dedication to a dream and goals, and I think a lot of us will relate to his varsity stories. Throughout his hard work there is a humbleness and gratitude for chances given.

In her story, Khatija shows her immense spirit of fighting injustice and how this influences all her decisions through a constant deep thought process.

The fascinating golden thread in all our stories is that all of us used our past, our entire history, whatever our different ages, to bring us to this place at this time.

PART TWO

Seven Interventions : Seven Stories

Introduction

Marti Janse Van Rensburg

We told our stories and got to know one another better. Then, in our Quiet Mountain retreat, after a few reflective minutes of preparation, we decided how to share with one another what we do and why, in a way that would not take more time than necessary but would be enough to intrigue and interest.

We shared our stories with you to introduce ourselves and allow you to get to know us, and now we will share with you seven different interventions, or seven stories of how we work. Not for you to choose, but rather to show that it all works in the right circumstances with the right group of people, and often we create an eighth or ninth or fifteenth story by mixing up these various interventions to fit another group and other circumstances.

Heraclitus said: 'You could not step twice into the same river; for other waters are ever flowing on to you.'[2]

---

[2] Heraclitus (540 BC-480 BC), *On the Universe*.

Input, Throughput, Output

Marti Janse Van Rensburg

Why should we be in such desperate haste to succeed, and in such desperate enterprises? If a man does not keep pace with his companions, perhaps it is because he hears a different drummer.

Henry David Thoreau

I believe very strongly that every human being and therefore every group is different; that if we can begin to understand where we are different, and therefore also where we are similar, it might be easier to work together in harmony. It might also be easier to *live* together in harmony, but then that is not what this book is about.

Furthermore, I subscribe to the work of Deborah Ancona[3] who maintains that a happy team is not necessarily a successful team. The premise of Ancona and Bresman's work is that happy teams, or teams that focus too much on creating a working unit, become too insular and protective of one another and do not always deliver. Their research has shown that teams having a very clear delivery focus, which also creates harmony and understanding within the team in parallel with this clear focus, often do the best work.

My aim with any team coaching contract is therefore to have the team be very clear about what they want to deliver as a team and what the contributions and roles of individual members of the team are within this delivery. Should the team have more than one deliverable then there should be clarity of the roles and contributions of each team member for every deliverable, as these might vary.

This brings me to the title of the chapter. It probably sounds a lot like an engineering process, but then one is always the sum of all one's parts and at heart and by nature I am a scientist who just switched

---

[3] Deborah Ancona and Henrik Bresman (2007): *X-Teams*. Harvard Business School Publishing Corporation.

from chemistry to human beings as a research and understanding focus. I will explain the three elements within the process and the tools I use, and I will then illustrate some of my thinking through examples of work I have done. In order to protect the identity of the teams and individuals involved the examples will not be specific, but will rather serve the purpose of illustrating technique.

Alan Mumford[4] discusses Reg Revans' action learning model in his work and then adds an initial and additional Q to Revans' equation of

P (Programmed Knowledge) + Q (Questioning) = L (Learning)

The equation then becomes

Q + P + Q = L

His argument is that it is useful to get some questions answered beforehand to determine the appropriate 'programmed knowledge' required. Some of the questions may be around objectives, etc. The second Q is questioning during the process to assist with the reflective part of the learning.

My *Input* (or starting process) would therefore be to meet with the team leader to determine what the purpose of the team coaching might be. What is it that the team needs to achieve from the viewpoint of the team leader? What are the company's requirements for the team? That would start to give some form to the *Output* required. What is the history of the team and why did the team decide to embark on this process at this point in time? Is it a new team being formed and they want to get it right from the get go (blank canvas and rather yummy), or is it a team with a history, and often in such a case a warring history (also yummy because if you can get it to work the change is phenomenal). I also collect any work the team has done to date. This could be personality assessments, other team work, interviews, etc. It is often useful at this stage to involve the HR practitioner if he/she is not already involved. Should the HR practitioner be closely involved with the unit or team, he/she often has valuable insights into the team

---

[4] Alan Mumford (1995): *Effective Learning*. London: Chartered Institute of Personnel and Development.

dynamic and functioning.

Should there be little to nothing available, I would recommend some individual personality assessments be undertaken and, if I have enough time, conduct individual interviews with the team members. These individual interviews are often a rare but wonderful opportunity to gain insight into the team.

The *Throughput* process can then be designed, taking into account what I have collected, could get (or not) and the time available. There are ideal scenarios, but then life happens and I believe in being as flexible as possible and working with what I have – within some very vague boundaries. One of these would be that a team process cannot happen in a flash – it takes time and therefore the process should ideally be done offsite with a two-day starting and foundation process and a few follow-ups over a six-month time frame. Within that there can be flexibility. The duration of the process is critical because any learning needs time, effort and practice to become entrenched. I have seen too often a team starting well but, after one follow-up session, deciding they do not have the time or do not need to continue. Invariably the *Output* is then less effective.

Within the design of the *Throughput* process, the golden thread is that the team needs to have a very good understanding of what the collective has to achieve and what each individual's role is within that collective. There are therefore two parallel streams running concurrently, one focusing on the team and the other on the individual. If need be the detailed *Output* required from the team can be created during the process. If it is there in some format it needs to be agreed and communicated – clearly. I find more often than not that there might be an understanding of the overall purpose of the team, but that this is seldom clearly defined. A brainstorming exercise which allows the team to play freely with what they want to achieve, and how, within a larger context is very useful.

The *Throughput* part is therefore open to change and interpretation. The only common theme would be to get the team members to understand one another: to understand how they are similar and how they are different; to understand that they do not have to be best friends but that they have to accept one another as they are.

Strengths and the nurturing thereof are a strong theme in my work. I agree with Jung that we need to nurture our preferences instead of trying to change them. Marcus Buckingham[5] used this theme in his work and took it further in a work context by defining 'strengths' not as that which you are good at, but rather that which gives you strength – or your preferences. I find that people are often guided to work on their weaknesses and to become experts at what these might be, becoming very mediocre in the execution of these weaknesses while their strengths or preferences are not nurtured and worked on. Surely you would not ask your country's best cricket batsman to start focusing on bowling, or a 100-metre Olympic track champion to start swimming?

I use several tools and processes for the purpose of identifying strengths and understanding of self and one another. Typically, I would begin gently: an example would be to ask the group to share stories about their childhood. These are often amusing and not known, setting an easy and comfortable tone. At intervals over the time period, I would then use tools such as the Myers-Briggs Type Indicator (MBTI), the David Kolb Learning Styles Inventory (LSI) or the Honey Mumford Learning Styles Questionnaire (LSQ). Any tools I use to examine personality or how we learn and think has to have as a premise that we are complex beings. I do not subscribe to tests that label and box people. I hate this being done to me and therefore do not do it to anyone else. The tests I like to use and/or discuss all assume that one has several layers and levels and that there are preferences as opposed to one-sided either/or choices. These tests and tools are described in more detail in subsequent chapters (pages 127-228).

I use at least one personality assessment. My preference is the MBTI. It has to be done in advance as the test can only be administered in South Africa by someone who has two degrees in psychology and is registered with the Psychology Association as a psychometrist. I do find, however, that this is one of the most widely used tests by companies and that the information is often readily available. I request permission of the entire group to use and discuss the information. During the session I show the group what their individual profiles look like when added together on a graph. I sometimes find that the individual team members have an understanding of what their profiles

[5] Marcus Buckingham and Donald O Clifton (2002): *Now, Discover your Strengths*. Simon & Schuster.

indicate, but also often find that they were given this information with no explanation as to what it means. In such a case, I spend more time on the history of the MBTI and what the various 'letters' they get in their profile mean.

I find the MBTI an invaluable tool. For example, the explanation that Extroverts (E) need to engage their vocal cords before their brain engages, and that Introverts (I) are usually two questions behind because they need to complete their thinking before they speak, or that extroverts get energy from people and that introverts lose energy to people, usually causes the proverbial lights to come on and is often the cause of bantering and laughter in the group. This process allows the group to understand that disagreements are frequently due to different preferences as opposed to 'you just do that to annoy me'. Friction usually falls away or becomes less important when individual team members realise what they have in common.

Should I find that the team has very similar MBTI profiles (this can happen, especially if they are a specialist group), I would suggest that they do the Enneagram as well. This is a very old system based on the work of Pythagoras and looks at nine elements that we all possess with certain ones preferred and others less preferred. This usually shows up some differences within the group. It is also a very useful tool to demonstrate how we might behave under stress and explains those moments when you feel an alien has taken over and you are behaving totally out of character. It is a lengthy explanation, though, and I do not always use it, especially if time availability might be a factor.

One personality test normally suffices for the first two-day session. I also use some smaller games and tools such as the I Ching cards as a fun, but profound exercise. This is explained in detail in a subsequent chapter (page 217). In short, it uses pictures as a metaphor for where we are and often shows up concerns in individuals. There are several games that are useful to lighten the mood and break the hard sitting, reflecting, thinking, discussing routine of much of this work. I would choose which ones to use according to the make-up of the team and will have a couple up my sleeve (or, to be more exact, in my suitcase) to use if I find an impasse in the proceedings or a drop in energy. Mike discusses the use of games as well as video clips in Part Three (page 224).

For the rest of the time we need to focus on the other parallel process – that of determining the purpose of the team, what they want to do, how they are going to do it, and who will be assigned which role. There are several ways of facilitating this brainstorming process. I often borrow from Edward de Bono's Six Hats process by asking the team first to list ideas without considering whether they are practical or possible. A typical question would be: 'What would the workplace (or work) have to be like in order for you to jump out of bed in the morning?' I do this in rounds with each person listing one item in turn until all ideas are exhausted. This way everyone gets to speak and one avoids the extroverts rushing off ten ideas with the introverts feeling left out. The process remains similar with the question differing, depending on the team and their requirements.

The ideas generated during this process are used to construct a framework with which the team can proceed. An example is the team of engineers who need to come up with ideas for the company but find that they are duplicating one another's work and that they are struggling to sell their ideas to the rest of the company; the process of coming up with ideal working conditions frees up their creative thinking without them competing with one another. Typically, I find that as the ideas go around the circle of the group, certain patterns begin to form. I ask the group to come up with some common themes out of this list and then break the big group into smaller groups to look at what can be done about these ideas. In the example mentioned above, I found that the team realised they needed to put smaller groups together to work on certain ideas and projects and that there would be some overlap in these groups. They also generated ways to communicate and keep one another in the loop. This example was a very powerful demonstration of how, when there is more understanding and a free flow of thoughts and ideas, the group come up with their own solutions. This is an ideal scenario as they have then so bought into their own solution that the momentum is generated for them to put in the hard work required to implement it when they get back to their offices.

Typically, at the end of the first two-day session I ask that each team member commit to one action item that is linked to the team and one individual action item. These are recorded and form the basis for the opening of the first follow-up about a month later.

At the follow-up session, I revert back to the individuals' growth and understanding by introducing a test that confirms and indicates how people learn or think. One of the most widely used tests is the Kolb Learning Styles Inventory (LSI). I also sometimes use a similar one called the Honey Mumford Learning Styles Questionnaire (LSQ). These two tests are similar and look at how we learn and our preferences in learning and how we should ideally learn. I also sometimes use Robert Sternberg's[6] work on how we think.

I find this useful in a second session. The group walked away from the first session with group and individual action plans, and the second session starts with feedback on what transpired between the two sessions. The feedback looks at progress made and is a good example of how we should learn. In terms of the work Kolb did (which was used as the basis for the work done by Honey and Mumford), we do something (the action plan), we reflect on what happened (often only done as part of the feedback process), we draw conclusions about what happened, and we plan what to do next, and so the cycle continues. As much as this process is circular, most of us are better at certain aspects of it than others. It is therefore the ideal time to introduce either of the tests. This then becomes the individual stream of the process and the use of the information to plan what to do next forms the other part of the parallel process.

Colin Rose said: 'An emotional content to learning is inevitable, because learning begins in that part of the brain.'[7] The link between our emotions and learning has become known as Emotional Intelligence and is regarded as a more accurate predictor of success than IQ. This theory is mostly attributed to John D Mayer and Peter Salovey, two US academics. The science journalist Daniel Goleman is, however, the most popular and prolific writer on the subject and he made it palatable to the man in the street. I used the example of a team of engineers above. These groups of highly intelligent specialists are often rather low on EQ and as much as they have brilliant minds and brilliant ideas, these are not always translated into success. Should this be the case, I would introduce elements of EQ into the process at this stage. As they understand the emotional content of their own learning, understanding can be generated for the learning of others who are different. This often helps with the selling and implementation of ideas

---

[6] Robert J Sternberg (1997): *Thinking Styles*. Cambridge University Press.
[7] Colin Rose and Brian Tracy (1995): *Accelerated Learning*. Simon & Schuster.

with which these groups struggle.

The purpose of the intervention is to get the team to where they want to be; all of the tools mentioned are purely a means to an end. The bulk of the work needs to be done by the team and has to focus on clarifying what they want to achieve, how they are going to do this and who will do what. I prefer that my direct involvement lessens over the time period and that the team takes over and does more and more of the work. This would then guarantee that the team has entrenched a different way of being and doing things and that as new team members join, or the team *Output* changes, they can do the work without intervention.

Just as coaching, like any other intervention or self-help book, is not the panacea to all the world's ills, a team coaching intervention will not sort out all problems either. If there are problems within the wider organisation then the team coaching intervention can assist the individual team members to a degree with understanding themselves and what they can influence. It cannot change what the team cannot influence.

I once undertook a team coaching intervention where there were insurmountable problems within the wider organisation. I quote the team leader: 'A difficult situation had developed in this team caused by the turnaround strategy for the unit, the infusion of new skills, the immaturity of individuals and the impact of personal agendas. The final outcome was disappointing as the team had to be split up and the envisaged end game could not be achieved. The team coaching intervention helped us get to the conclusion faster and demonstrated the inadequacies of leadership and team member behaviour quicker than would have been the case. It also demonstrated the wide chasms and the need for a fundamental change in the managerial approach and behaviour to avoid further degradation in the team's operating performance. While plans were implemented to achieve this, the impact of multiple private and hidden agendas did hurt the execution of this strategy.'

The team split up and the new units created were more in line with principles for that industry. The individual team members were better equipped to cope with their newly formed teams and to avoid some of the problems which had caused much of the original anguish and grief. As much as this was not an ideal end result, it did show that interventions have a better chance of being effective when done before there is too much bitter water under the bridge.

There is no better elixir, though, than a team that comes together with individuals understanding themselves better, their team mates better, and often their spouses and friends better too, while the team is delivering and having fun. I do love what I do!

Coaching Sporting Sceptics – against the clock!

Tim Goodenough

The principles of coaching are around today because they work. In an environment like team coaching for sports teams, some of the basic coaching principles need to be fine-tuned to support the outcome for the session. What is described below is the thinking that led to some of those adaptations.

I am a firm believer in creating a container, or rules of engagement, for any team coaching intervention. Where this becomes a challenge is working with sports teams, especially if you have had no prior connection or interaction with the team.

Typically, if you are called in to work with a team it would be for a short space of time – forty-five minutes to an hour, or up to two to three hours if you are lucky. As a generalisation, spending more than an hour with a team can be as much of a challenge as forty-five minutes, as you have to up the entertainment, engagement and collaboration aspects of the intervention.

Containers or, as we call them in Neuro Semantics and NLP, *'Frames'* for the intervention are created by asking the participants: *'How can we be together today, to ensure that we reach outcome X, knowing that Y may come up?'* where X is what is required for the session and Y is a foreshadowing of the direction of the session to get audience buy-in and build comfort. For example: *'How can we be supportive of each other when discussing what we learned from the early exit in the World Cup, knowing that emotions such as anger, disappointment and frustration may emerge?'*

The facilitator would have a menu list in his or her mind providing points of reference, but only once the audience has finished contributing would the facilitator suggest an important *frame* for the day, if the participants had failed to identify this particular aspect themselves. *Frames* often take the form of phrases or concepts such as, 'Respect for each other, honesty, hearing each other out, no personal attacks –

speaking about a person's behaviour and not their individual value, not being judgemental.'

This process might take ten to fifteen minutes, and may require some prompting and support from the senior players in the room. In a forty-five-minute session this is not practical. There is simply not enough time. You need to design your training around this limitation, by creating 'implicit and explicit' frames for the day. This can be done by carefully structuring questions to the audience, for example: *'Knowing that everyone tries their best to win, and wanted desperately to do well, what have you learned from the mistakes you experienced as a team?'* The implicit *frame* here is that individual mistakes are a team issue, and that no one purposely set out to fail, and so personal attacks are not encouraged. An explicit *frame* would be the facilitator asking the audience not to be judgemental and to hear each other out fully. When *frames* are generated by the facilitator without consultation with the participants, they can often be weaker than the preferred option, and so the facilitator has to be very vigilant to reinforce the frame if the participants start to ignore it. For example, *'Thank you, Peter, for your contribution. Can I just ask you to rephrase what you said without any judgements so that we can use this time to get maximum value from our learning.'*

In team interventions I am aiming for two things: engagement and contribution. These two factors support self-awareness and self-development. The paradox of sport is that you don't want to do much of your thinking during the game; your game should be about the doing. However, the quality of your doing is related to the quality of your thinking off the pitch, outside of game time. Players still have to think during competition, but that thinking is typically about making choices: what tactic should I use, A, B or C? Evaluate, make a choice and then *do*. This type of thinking can take place very quickly, allowing the player to focus on doing. In some sports, if players have to think about a thing for the first time during competition their performance can be affected. My primary aim for sports teams is to support them in becoming more engaged in their own high quality thinking. This can be complemented with deeper levels of education about how the mind works, which would give the team the option of making better choices on and off the field.

How this is structured depends on what the intention for the team is. Is it (a) to support the team in resolving a challenge, conflict or issue that is interfering with their ability to perform; or (b) is it to develop the team's overall performance capacity, maybe by as little as five per cent?

Option (a) is the traditional role of sports psychologists and they often excel in this domain, whereas option (b) lends itself more to the principles of coaching – taking what's good and making it better. Option (a) is much more dependent on time. Typically, you don't want to open up group issues and leave them unresolved, unless it is part of a planned and structured intervention. Normally you would need more time for this type of intervention.

So with that being said, is it ethical to accept an invitation to do team coaching with a sports team for forty-five minutes, given that you have not worked with them before? Can you add value?

My belief is that yes, you can add value. A forty-five-minute intervention would only be an option (b) intervention for me, an intervention with the aim of developing a team's performance capacity. Because of the time constraints, you would have to introduce a concept, model or theory around which the team would develop its self-awareness and hopefully self-development. The second intention of a forty-five-minute intervention would be to be invited back! Can you create enough trust in that time to support the learning process enough for stakeholders to want you to return?

If I waited for the 'perfect' amount of time, buy-in from players and management and other supportive environmental conditions for a team intervention with a team I hadn't worked with before, I may be waiting for some time. You have to be flexible and adaptable, and therefore the models that you work with need to be accurate and specific enough to be scalable. For example, in some one-on-one coaching methodologies, the first one-hour session or more would be designed to build trust, rapport and comfort with a client. If you have the opportunity to do that, it is a fantastic basis on which to create a high quality coaching intervention. Unfortunately that model would not be transferable to team coaching with sports teams.

A simple equation: rapport equals comfort plus trust. Rapport is critical to all coaching, so how do you generate comfort and trust?

I do as much pre-work as possible. I will interview the person who approached me to do the intervention, ask for access to coaches, captains and senior players and take what I can get. I read articles about the team, if appropriate, watch games, visit the stadium, grounds or training pitch to get a 'feel' for the culture, if possible. I will be trying to identify team norms; whether particular phrases, nicknames for players, and memorable moments in the history of the team or anything else that I can integrate into my intervention to build comfort and trust.

To further gain comfort and trust, I will ask a senior or respected member of the team to introduce me, asking them to emphasise that I am here to support a five per cent performance gain. I have often encountered resistance in teams about working with a 'mental guy', so how I am introduced is very important to help me avoid creating discomfort or mistrust. I say I am here to ask the question: 'How can you be at your best for longer, more often and in more contexts, like playing in finals or under pressure?' If there is any team history that I can integrate into my introduction, I will do so, with the caveat that I will not use team history that is at the expense of someone related to the team. For example, 'For many years you were a championship team, and it was fantastic to watch. My intention in being here today is to ask some questions that will remind you exactly why you were a championship team, and indeed still are one.'

I like to use music to create a mood when people enter the room – something upbeat with lyrics that are positive and supportive of the theme (if possible). I also like to use movie clips if I can find any that are related to the theme of the intervention, as this creates energy, engagement, and also creates something to talk about that can then ultimately be related back to the purpose of the session. It is often easier to talk about what happens in the movie clip first, before talking about what has happened on a team or individual basis.

When a sports team is gathered together an individual who plays the role of the joker (and sometimes even the saboteur role) may emerge, which often doesn't support the outcome of the intervention. I like to break up the room into groups as soon as I can, either groups of two using the Nancy Kline's Thinking Pairs structure, or groups of five or six or whatever is appropriate to the team size and outcome. These groups will be given a question to answer that is related to the outcome. Then, after they have spent some time in discussion, feedback will be generated from all the groups to stimulate further discussion as a large group.

In June 2007 Michael Cooper and I were invited by the Springbok sports psychologist, Dr Henning Gericke, to run a session with the Springbok team before the test match against Samoa at Ellis Park. Michael and I had met Henning while researching our book, *In the Zone with South Africa's Sports Heroes.* He found our work complementary to his ongoing work with the team, and asked us to run a session on one of the principles in the book. We had forty-five minutes.

The structure of the intervention was as follows.

Outline
- Start – Create Container/Norms/Boundaries
- Energisers/Engagement – Movie Clip
- Acknowledgements/Appreciation – Create Context
- Awareness/Change Model – Introduce Model

Henning introduced us to the group and we spoke briefly about what we do and what informed us; we shared a brief introduction to the research we had conducted, using a specially made PowerPoint presentation that included high tempo music and action shots of each one of the players.

Mike had found a great movie clip of an autistic basketball player called Jason McElwein who was his high school's kit manager for several years. Because of his autism he had never played a role in his team, until the coach asked him to suit up for the last game of the season, just to get a feel for what it was like. With four minutes to go, Coach Jim Johnston subbed Jason into the game. His first shot was a 20-footer from the right base line ... and he missed badly; his next shot was also a miss. During the remainder of the game he took six shots from beyond the 3 point line, and nailed every one of them, to the increasing delight and hysteria of the crowd. This is a great 'feel good' clip, but has the added bonus of being very complementary to the model we wanted to introduce – The Creating Dynamic Tension model.

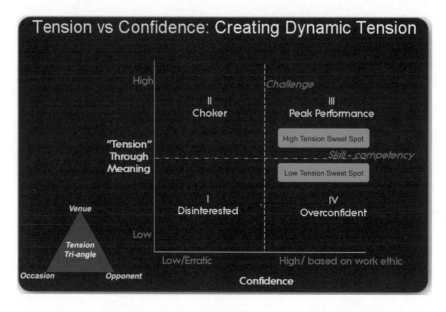

The model does several things. It provides awareness that athletes can be both confident and tense (anxious) – and asks the question for your next match: do you have the right level of confidence and tension for you? Secondly, it allows athletes to understand that everyone is indeed different, and having seriously intense players and relaxed joking players in a team is not always an indication of commitment or focus. A player's mood is usually related to their personal style which differs from player to player in order to be at their best. This creates dialogue about when am 'I' at my best? Do I have butterflies in my stomach? Do I feel like I am going to be sick, or am I relaxed and joking? Am I at my best when I have low or high tension? Where is my sweet spot? This creates more team understanding and unity.

The model also provides awareness of how the meaning of three key performance factors influences tension: the venue (where we are playing); the opposition (who we are playing and the occasion); how is this occasion significant (is it a final or a farewell match)? Some meanings will spike tension, and others will keep it at a very low level, eg playing a final versus playing against the worst team in the league.

After some discussion as a group we introduced the model and asked the group to break up into smaller groups to answer the following question: 'What meaning did I give to the game when I played my best, and what meaning did I give to the game when I played my worst?'

Once that discussion had concluded, we asked the players to rate their best and worst games on a scale of 1 to 10 for confidence and tension, to create self-awareness about when they are at their best. We also introduced the theory of how the venue, occasion or opponents are factors that influence dynamic tension, as well as the individual's strategy for creating confidence. Are you confident because of the quality of your training (which may be variable) or are you confident because of your commitment to work ethic (which is in your control and not variable)?

This created a useful context for some of the senior players to share their knowledge and experience, and after further discussion we summarised and wrapped up. We achieved our primary goal of raising self-awareness for some of the players while enjoying the challenge of creating a targeted and structured intervention.

Be prepared ... then prepare to let it all go!

Ray Sher

A Nobel laureate in physics was asked to whom or what he ascribed his success. Without hesitation he answered, 'My mother.' His answer was a surprise, because he is the son of East European Jewish immigrants who were simple people without any formal education, spoke very little English and weren't able to teach him much. He then went on to explain that when he was at high school, his mother would ask him on his return home, 'So tell me, my son, today ... did you ask a good question?'

The daily challenge one faces in teaching, coaching or facilitating is the shifting of the emphasis of activity from telling to asking. This is the legacy of ancient Greece's famous philosopher, Socrates. In order to have people think for themselves he engaged their learning capacity by asking questions. To some, this gift comes naturally; to others, it is a skill to be acquired.

Being authentic, not having to pretend to be the expert who knows everything, gets best results. Authenticity includes the humility and relief of admitting, 'I don't know.' This opens the door to curiosity, a characteristic that adds to trust-building. This is ongoing learning. For me, this reminder is part of internal preparation.

When preparing for a workshop or coaching event as teacher, coach or facilitator we have a part to play in creating the climate and conditions for people to get what they have come for and for the planned and desired outcome to be achieved.

I imagine we have all had those perfect moments when everything seems to be flowing, working to perfection, better even than we planned it, and the outcome exceeds our expectations. At those times it seems as though the world conspires with us for this to happen.

And then, there are those other times. How is it that unpredictable magic seems to happen without any apparent effort on our part on some occasions, yet on others, with the best will in the world, careful planning and preparation – well, it just doesn't work out that well.

What's the challenge in planning for an upcoming event? So much of what transpires in a workshop or coaching session is unpredictable. Do we attempt to provide for any or all eventualities, or is that a waste of time? Do we leave it to the gods or fate or chance and other magical and metaphysical entities, or is there something practical we can and should be doing?

Over the years, I have developed a ritual of preparation that seems to work. Some of the elements have been influenced by colleagues and friends and others come from personal experience and insight. There are many who have taught and inspired me to be aware of cultivating safety in the environment of the event.

Creating a safe container for everyone in the venue is a non-negotiable requirement and being conscious of radiating a spirit of welcome seems obvious. What isn't always obvious is the need to have a venue that is free from distraction, one that sends a message to participants that says 'You matter'.

Nancy Kline's book *Time to Think* identifies ten components as essential to creating an environment in which people can think well for themselves. One of these components is Place, the venue, where respect, comfort, safety and ease are evident. Also, having the list of participants' names before the event and sending a silent welcome adds subtly to the quality of safety and lays sound foundations for building the container.

Early arrival at the venue for setting up, having a checklist of requirements, checking equipment, having the seating configuration correct, lighting appropriate, all logistics in place and especially having time to sit quietly centring oneself is useful as part of preparation.

These quiet moments are a reminder that the best way to prepare for any moment in the future is to be fully conscious in the present. Walking the perimeter of the room, claiming the space the way animals in the wild define their territories also contributes to the container-building and assists in orientation.

There are venues that are challenging, unpleasant and not conducive to meeting the purpose and objectives of the event, that don't provide a climate for doing deep personal work. The implied message, although perhaps not intended, is 'You don't really matter'. This form of carelessness is evidence of the lack of awareness of the event organisers and venue hirers.

Another element of preparation is being mindful of Harrison Owen's 'Four Immutable Laws of the Spirit', which is always a good start:

1. whoever comes are the right people
2. whatever time it starts is the right time
3. whatever is handled is the only thing that could be handled
4. when it's over ... it's OVER

Thorough knowledge of the subject, taking nothing for granted, curiosity about what group dynamics emerge, seem obvious and all contribute to setting the internal compass. It's good, too, to remember that the job spec in coaching or facilitating is to enrol, not convict, convince or convert.

Cross-culturally, in many models, the context in which teachers work best is to be open to outcome and not attached. Experience has taught that one should be sure to prepare well, which includes being prepared to let it all go because the situation calls for something else.

I had a powerful opportunity to do that some years ago when I found myself working with a group of prisoners at Leeuwkop Prison, near Johannesburg. I had been asked to design and deliver a life skills programme for a group of prisoners due for parole.

There were forty-nine men, a number too large for one group to work effectively, so they were divided into two groups, each group having two days. It transpired that the first group were all literate, spoke English and had no difficulty understanding and responding to the designed two-day programme. The second group were mostly illiterate and had difficulty with English. This presented me with a daunting challenge. Nothing that I had prepared for the two days was appropriate.

The workshop venue was in the officers' mess complex, away from the prison cells. It was interesting to note that the prisoners and the warders wear the same colour overalls with their names printed on the right-hand pocket. The only way to tell the difference between the prisoners and the warders was that the warders had their numbers printed below their names.

After finding a translator amongst these men, I took the group on to the lawn outside the complex for some games activities. I had previously seen a group of ten-year-old boys playing a game that I thought was useful for demonstrating the power of visualising. They called it the two-string game and this is how it works. All that is required is two lengths of string, about one metre in length, and the ability to run and jump.

One length is placed to mark the starting point of the jump. Then one at a time the players take a long run, jumping from the string. Where they land, the second string marks the spot. The player then goes back to the first string, notes the position of the second string, where he landed and is challenged to jump further. He closes his eyes and visualises where he is going to land at the next attempt. He then forecasts his landing by placing the second string where he plans to land.

It is extraordinary how often this second attempt succeeds, however impossible the forecast appears to observers. The power of visioning is very clearly demonstrated in this exercise – they get it in their bones. This activity was relished by the prisoners and they had great fun, screaming noisily with each achievement, shouting encouragement to their buddies and laughing a lot.

After two hours of this it was time for their tea break. Now, I had a problem. What else to do with them! Two days to fill with activities that will provide life skills and my toolbox seemed depleted. On occasions like this when I don't know what to do, I close my eyes and say, 'Okay, God, what now ... send me a message.'

I did this and opened my eyes to see an attractive young woman approaching me. She was wearing a green suit and looked very stern and very corporate.

'I'm running a workshop inside and could not ignore all this noise and jollity happening here. What are you teaching the officers? What's going on?'

'Oh,' I said, ignoring her assumption, 'I've got this group of prisoners due for parole and we're preparing them to join society again.'

'Well,' said the young woman, 'there is only one thing I can tell you – unless they accept the Lord Jesus into their lives, they are doomed.'

This comment rocked me. I was about to counter with a reactive response like 'Hey, lady, that's a bitter pill for a Jew to swallow', but then thought, 'Wait a minute, I asked God for help and this is who he sent me. What's to discover here?'

And suddenly, I knew what to do. I gathered the men around in a circle for a chat. I knew that they all went to church on Sundays and that they were familiar with the Bible. I began the conversation by saying, 'Have you guys noticed how the Bible says that God spoke to men? He spoke to Adam and he spoke to Abraham and Isaac and Jacob and Moses and the prophets that followed, and he spoke to Jesus. And then, it seems, he stopped talking to men. Is that so? Do you think it's true?'

'Yes,' came the chorus.

'Why do you think that's so?'

'Well,' they all laughed. One of them said, 'The evidence is in front of you – we are all sinners, criminals, robbers, murderers!'

'No,' I said, 'I don't think so. When you hear rain on the roof … when you hear the wind blowing through the trees … when you hear the waves crashing on the beach … when you hear a newborn baby cry … when you hear the last gasp of a dying man … listen carefully – that is God talking to you. No, God hasn't stopped talking – we've stopped listening.'

'Listen,' I said, 'let's listen. Close your eyes and notice what you are hearing. Listen to the noises outside … the birds … the breeze … somebody's voice far away … the noise of an electric saw … the buzz of a motor car … listen to those outside noises. What else can you hear?'

I kept quiet for a while and then, in a much softer voice, I said, 'Now listen to what's happening inside your body. Listen to those sounds – can you hear your breathing, can you hear your heart beating, what else can you hear? Is there a buzz in your ears? Let's be very quiet now and notice what we can hear. I won't speak again for about ten minutes and then we can have a chat.'

When I asked them to open their eyes, the room was still and the atmosphere was one of peace and calm. And an extraordinary conversation happened. The men spoke of feeling peaceful, good and grateful. 'Why can't our life always be like that?' asked one of the men.

I had just read Deepak Chopra's *The Seven Spiritual Laws of Success* and introduced the idea of regular meditation, to which they agreed. The commanding officer of the prison gave permission for me to visit the prisoners to facilitate the seven-week programme with one chapter per week and the prisoners did well. The men from the first group joined us.

I took some time to simplify the language in the book and we continued having a translator from the group present. We had just completed the sixth chapter, the Law of Detachment, which states, *In detachment lies the wisdom of uncertainty . . . in the wisdom of uncertainty lies the freedom from our past, from the known, which is the prison of past conditioning.*

During the discussion period afterwards, one of the prisoners, speaking of an insight he had, commented, 'You know, I have realised that the warders are the ones who are really the prisoners here. I mean, in a few weeks we will be out of here and the warders will still be coming every day, doing this miserable job, being unhappy. You can see they are unhappy people which is why they are so horrible to us.'

Through some kind of spontaneous magic, we were being guided through a process of discovery of what possibilities life had to offer, in spite of the hardship of prison life. This practice was encouraging a sense of well-being in the prisoners that surprised me.

I knew that the book offers a life-altering perspective on succeeding, but having men who were living an institutionalised life constrained by the daily grind of prison discipline respond in this way, was unexpected.

Quoting from the book: 'Once we understand our true nature and learn to live in harmony with natural law, a sense of well-being, good health, fulfilling relationships, energy and enthusiasm for life and material abundance will spring forth easily and effortlessly.'

The response had exceeded expectations and they were moving into the possibility that the book predicts. I was aware of similar initiatives in other prisons overseas and thought I had a proposal that Correctional Services would want to introduce.

Shortly after completing the cycle I had a call from the commanding officer. 'I don't know what you've been doing with those men, but my warders are complaining,' he said with a smile in his voice.

'What's the problem?' I asked.

'They are saying the men are very quiet,' he said, 'not giving any trouble, obeying all the rules. They don't know what to make of it; the warders have hardly any work to do! But, seriously,' he continued, 'we can see a big change in the men. This meditating thing seems to work.'

Unfortunately, this story doesn't have the happy ending I had hoped for. Shortly after this chat, the commanding officer took his 'package', went on pension and went off to a new life. In his place, the new man who wanted to put his personal stamp on the running of the prison withdrew a variety of privileges from the prisoners who reacted badly, threatening to riot and demonstrate against this unfair move.

I never found out what happened to my group, because he also withdrew my permission to run these sessions for other prisoners, on the grounds that they couldn't guarantee my safety. However, I feel confident that at least some of those men took their seven-week journey in the realm of possibilities as a guiding beacon for re-entry into society and their new circumstances and were able to live fruitful, productive lives.

The models in which I have been educated, both as facilitator and coach, have as cornerstones the assumption that the client/student/participator is naturally creative, resourceful and whole. We all have lots of room for improvement and the interventions, programmes and coaching sessions are all invitations to the recipients to develop, learn and grow.

It took a while for me to realise what had transpired with the prisoners. By some stroke of luck, I had experienced a radical shift of attitude. Yes, I had begun with the judgement that they were illiterate, stupid, uneducated criminals. And then, after working with them for a while, somehow I had begun to accept them as creative, resourceful and whole.

When I had the inspiration to introduce the possibility that God could be talking to them, I had unwittingly sent a message that they were worthy of God's attention. Yes, they had been guilty of crimes and had done bad things. Most of them believed that they were bad through and through because of society's interactions with them, the problems they were, the criminals they were.

When I began to interact with them as worthy, creative and responsible, they responded. They began to show up in incredible ways. For some the shift was barely noticeable, but for most the transformation was dramatic.

The whole intervention, which included hard skills training in a variety of trades, and the small part I played, had given them tools and skills that they had not had at the beginning of their prison sentences.

But I believe that what really made the difference was the serendipitous moment I had after my interaction with the lady in green, the moment when I surrendered my plans, my intentions and preparations and, in effect, handed over to a power far greater than me.

That was a moment pregnant with possibility.

So, the Rules and Tools for Preparation are:
- Prepare yourself
- Prepare the venue
- Prepare to let it all go and trust your intuition

Meta-Coaching™

Michael Cooper

There are a number of processes from Meta-Coaching that I use and incorporate into my team coaching workshops. Meta-Coaching is the style of coaching I use in my personal coaching as I believe the methods and models it uses are the most advanced around today. It enables a coach to quickly and effectively get to the underlying beliefs and values which hold behaviours in place; it also offers the tools to effect change at these deep levels. To really effect change in an organisation we need to move away from superficial change which is often short lived. The coach needs tools to address the deep underlying concerns and attitudes of the teams he or she is working with. Meta-Coaching is based on the psychology of Neuro Semantics, developed by Dr Michael Hall and Michelle Duval, a master coach from Australia.

Work on self first

When I am preparing to work with a client I make sure that I am ready first. Most business clients are intelligent and mature and are often exposed to really good facilitators, so coaches who are unsure of themselves or insecure about their role or the direction of the day are going to be less than effective.

When working with clients I constantly refer to the need to operate from a highest intention. Our highest intentions are the true meanings and values that drive our behaviour. We can try to cover up our motives but if we are disinterested, scared or bored these intentions will come through to the group we are working with.

Take time the day before a coaching session to think about why you are doing this and how you feel about it. If I sense in myself the need to try and prove myself or the need to solve the team's problems I work hard to change it. When you have worked with lots of teams and you get really good at what you do, there is a danger that you may be tempted to start seeing yourself as this great team coach who, after one hour with a team, can diagnose all its problems and give it brilliant solutions to everything. This need to prove yourself and to have all the answers is a risk. The mindset a coach would like to develop is a curious, know-nothing state. Every single team is different, and you have to respect that. Every team has the ability to find the very best solution for themselves, and you have to believe that.

This realisation that the answers are there but need to be found by the members of the team themselves helps us see that patience is such a necessary quality. The temptation is to quickly give answers; but your answer will never be as effective as the one they find themselves. I find this a challenge at times when it is really obvious what the problem is, but the team doesn't seem to be able to see it. It requires all the coach's skill to elicit what is really happening in the environment. This can be very difficult because people often come to an event like a team intervention wearing their 'team faces' – the faces they are willing to let others see. This can lead to a false sense of accomplishment for the coach. Everyone says the right things during the session, they say how much they enjoyed it and got out of it, but then they go back to their offices and nothing changes. A coach recently described this to me as a mutual admiration society.

How do I make sure that what I am dealing with in the session is 'real'? I am really comfortable with making people uncomfortable. When they are challenged and pushed by the facilitator you will often get a more realistic view of what is really going on. The coach has to have the rapport with the team to ask the really difficult questions. I find that I set the tone for this right up front. I ask if they mind if I play the role of provocateur or devil's advocate. I ask if they want me to ask the really tough questions. This gives me the mandate to step in later and say: 'I am now stepping into my role as devil's advocate'.

The next tool in your toolbox is silence. After a tough question you will often be greeted with silence or a standard pat answer. Keep quiet. Let it get really uncomfortable. I find that breaking eye contact with the group at this point and just looking down at the floor prolongs the silence. At this stage someone usually gets uncomfortable with the silence and answers. Thank them and then ask, 'And what else?' This lets the team know you will not just accept the simple answers but are expecting to get to the real issues. I try to be sensitive to the politics that might be developing or that have walked into the room with the group. The team might have a dominant leader who is used to answering all the questions and providing direction.

I recently had a team session where every time I asked a question all twelve regional managers would turn and look at the national director. She would answer and then the rest would take their cue from her and give supportive answers. If there were any answers which she disagreed with; she would say so. There was no debate – only consensus. The other dynamic at play was that I had been hired by the national director to coach the team to take more responsibility for their own areas and be more independent. At this stage I could have found myself in a quandary. Should I challenge the very person who has hired me and contracted with me? Would she react well or would she be offended and how would this affect my future opportunities with this team?

I have always had a policy with individual clients and teams that if I don't ask or address the core issue I am not being truly professional and this is a very high value for me. At this point I stopped the process and gave feedback to them about what I was seeing. In Meta-Coaching good quality feedback is a really critical tool. What makes good quality feedback? I can only say what I have seen or heard or felt (hear/see/feel). There must be no judgement and I must be careful about putting my own personal opinions into my statement. After I have explained to the group what proper feedback is, it becomes a useful tool. You can stop the group during a process and ask someone to give feedback about what is happening. Because it is real time and because there is no judgement involved, I find it is easily accepted. In this case I told the group that every time I asked a question I *saw* them look to the director. I *heard* the director give an answer, and then I *heard* them give answers and comments that only supported her views. The next question is, 'If this is what I am seeing, what is going on?' The team cannot deny the feedback as it is based on what I saw and heard. If I had said 'You are only saying what the director wants to hear' this would have been a judgement on my part. It would likely have been followed by denial. The team acknowledged that they were feeling that they could not say what was really bothering them, and this led to a very frank and open discussion which boded well for the future.

Does this mean that coaches can never say what they feel? No. But make it very clear that it is just a *feeling*, an impression, rather than saying it as if it is fact. I call these 'tentative comments'. I make sure the team knows they are mine and that I am offering them as something to be discussed, rather than as a fact. I will sometimes say something like, 'I feel there is a bigger issue at play here which no one is talking about. Am I right and if I am, what is it?' This is a very direct way of addressing the 'elephant on the table, which no one is talking about'.

I use this hear/see/feel evidence in feedback in other ways too. One of the most useful is in trying to elicit outcomes or KPIs for the team. Often a team will tell you what they would like to have as an outcome but do so in language that is full of 'fluffy' words. This makes it very difficult to measure. A classic example would be a team that wants to improve its communication. 'Communication' in this context is a nominalisation. Nominalisation is the grammatical term for converting a verb into a noun. We take the verb 'to communicate' and turn it into a noun. We now make it seem as if communication is something we have or don't have. But you don't *have* communication, you *do* it. The hear/see/feel question cuts through this false logic. If you had great communication what would you see yourself doing? What would you hear yourself saying? And what would you be able to physically feel (eg a telephone list)? By making people be very specific about what it is they are trying to achieve and by being very specific about how they will know that, forces the mind to find the solution.

Benchmarking

Another use of the hear/see/feel question is in developing benchmarks for behaviours the team is trying to develop. Benchmarking is an advanced skill but it creates a very powerful tool which the team can use to measure the effect of the change. So much of what teams want to change seems intangible. Let's go back to the case I had recently with the twelve regional managers. Once they had come to the realisation that they were deferring to the national director, and she had seen how her behaviour had reinforced the very thing she was trying to change, they decided they would like to change their 'communication', specifically their meetings. They said they would like their meetings to be more open, robust and straightforward. Sounds good, doesn't it? Problem with an outcome like this is it is never measurable. It will always be subject to opinion and in a group of thirteen people there will be very different opinions on what 'robust' means. So we created a benchmark for their meetings. They could now sit and discuss how their meetings had progressed. They even chose one of them to keep score and then provide feedback for improvement at the end of each weekly meeting.

The benchmark measures the behaviour that they would all be able to see and measure against a scale. You have a level 0 behaviour if they did none of what they wanted and you would have a level 5 behaviour if they were perfect.

The levels are:

5   Mastery of the skill
4   High demonstration of the skill most of the time
3   Acceptable level of skill
2   More negative behaviour than positive behaviour
1   Very little demonstration of skill
0   No demonstration, only negative behaviour.

These numbers are meaningless in themselves, but they create a scale. When we link behaviour to the scale it provides an indication of where improvement can be made.

So I discussed with the team what the positive and negative behaviours were that could be demonstrated in meetings. They came up with interrupting, one person dominating, not expressing how they felt, no shared outcome as some of the negative behaviours, and full participation, respect, listening and questioning for clarity as some of the positive behaviours. We then asked what we would see if a person was listening at the different levels. At a level 1 there would be fidgeting, no eye contact, interrupting etc. A level 5 skill would be 100 per cent eye contact, nodding, note taking and asking of questions for clarification.

At the end of the exercise the team clearly had in mind what effective meetings were and had a scale that they could measure each meeting by. It also created a common language which could be used to give feedback if someone showed negative behaviour in a meeting.

The skill of building benchmarks is invaluable. As a coach one is often asked to discuss issues of team spirit, support and cooperation as examples. How could you create a shared understanding of what team spirit is if you didn't benchmark the behaviours that demonstrate team spirit?

The secret to building effective benchmarks is that each behaviour must be seen/heard/felt with no nominalisations. An outsider with a checklist could watch and count the behaviours so as to score the skill. It is also useful to clearly identify the skill you are benchmarking. In running meetings, for example, you might have three or four benchmarks, such as listening, speaking, supporting and chairing a meeting. The more specific the skill you are benchmarking the easier the tool becomes to create and use.

Five Fingers

Another useful tool I use in big team environments is called the Five Fingers. When evaluating many ideas and trying to build consensus you often have to put the idea to the group for consensus. A simple showing of hands in a yes/no type of setting is often too simple. It is more complicated than yes or no. Allowing each person to comment on how they feel is very time consuming and not always appropriate. So I set a stage by asking for a show of fingers as follows:

One finger	no way, do not agree
Two fingers	needs big change before I will support it
Three fingers	halfway there, with a few changes will buy in
Four fingers	will buy in even though I don't agree 100 per cent
Five fingers	love it

This simple device allows me to quickly poll the room about an idea or suggestion.

Axes of Change

For me one of the most powerful tools in Meta-Coaching is the Axes of Change. It is a model of change that breaks from all others currently in use in that it is not therapy-based but rather generative. It gives us a model for understanding the process of change in individuals and teams and helps a facilitator understand where in the change cycle we are and what the next step is. I keep it in mind as the structure I use in all my coaching sessions.

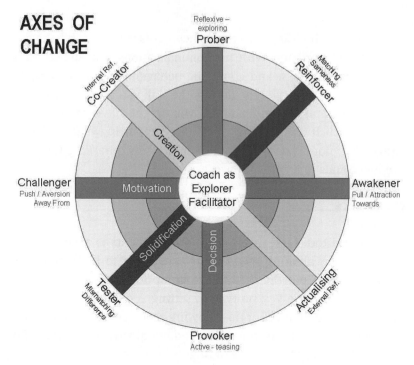

Source: Hall, L M & Duval, M (2004): *Meta-Coaching. Volume I Coaching Change,* Neuro-Semantics Publications, Clifton, CO, USA, p221

Here is a model that ties the change mechanisms and variables together and provides an understanding of how they relate to one another. Considering the need to see the interrelationships between the eight change variables, we find that we can classify them into four change processes or stages.

(1) The Energy (Motivation) Stage: 'Creating sufficient emotional energy, motivation, and creative tension to feel both the need and the desire for the change. This gives us propulsion for change: away from the aversions and pains and toward the attractions and pleasures.'[8]

Here the facilitator will step into the role of Challenger and expose the pain of the current reality. Why is there a need for change? What will happen if they do not change?

On the opposite side of this axis the facilitator would ask questions

---

[8] Adapted from Hall, L M & Duval, M (2004): *Meta-Coaching. Volume I Coaching Change;* Neuro-Semantics Publications, Clifton, CO, USA, p209.

to awaken and energise the team with the possibilities. If you don't want this, then what do you want? What would the ideal situation be? What is the very best solution?

These questions make sure there is willingness to change and create the energy for it.

(2) The Decision Stage: Creating sufficient understanding and knowledge about what to change, why it doesn't work, and generating enough decision power to create a readiness for change. This gives us the prod to say 'no' to the current way of thinking, feeling, and acting and 'yes' to the possibilities of a generative change.[9]

Here is the actual decision to change. The facilitator would ask reflective questions to see what is the thinking and the frames that are holding the current situation in place. Which of these need to change? The provoker is the role of edging the group to the point where they say 'enough', 'things can't go on', 'we will change'. I ask questions like: 'So do you really want this? Why don't you just leave it the way it is?'

(3) The Creation Stage: Creating a specific action plan that describes the change, giving us a step-by-step plan that we can then begin acting on and experimenting with. This gives us the plan to implement and actualise in real life.[10]

Here the facilitator realises there are two components in this creation. A new internal mindset or thinking and new behaviour changes. I explore both to make sure it is not just a focus on new behaviour without a supporting mindset.

(4) The Solidifying Stage: 'Creating specific rewards and support for the new actions that we celebrate and champion all the while testing, monitoring, and using feedback to make richer, fuller, and more integrated into our new habit and way of responding. This gives us a way to keep solidifying the change so that it becomes part of who we are and so that it fits ecologically into our life style and organisation.'[11]

---

[9] Adapted from Hall, L M & Duval, M (2004): *Meta-Coaching. Volume I Coaching Change;* Neuro-Semantics Publications, Clifton, CO, USA, p209.

[10] Adapted from Hall, L M & Duval, M (2004): *Meta-Coaching. Volume I Coaching Change;* Neuro-Semantics Publications, Clifton, CO, USA, p210.

[11] Adapted from Hall, L M & Duval, M (2004): *Meta-Coaching. Volume I Coaching Change;* Neuro-Semantics Publications, Clifton, CO, USA, p211.

I play the role of tester here. I ask questions to check for relevance and durability. I might ask: 'What will you do to make sure you follow through on this? What will you do if you find this doesn't work?'

I also reinforce them by congratulating them on a solution and asking what they could do to reward themselves for following through on their plan.

Let's look at the model in a very simple example of a single coaching client who wants to lose some weight.

In step one you check if there is some energy and motivation in really making the change. You might highlight the negative side such as how they look or feel and also their health. You would then build energy by comparing how good it might be if they did achieve their goal. Once you are convinced they really want this you move on to …

Step two, which is where they make the decision. Part of it is probing to find what are the beliefs and attitudes that are supporting the person at the moment in their current eating plan. What do they believe about themselves, their weight, their health etc? You also provoke to make the decision: 'Are you sure you are willing to let go of that?'

Step three. You now can't leave them hanging as if having awareness and wanting something is enough. What will they do differently? There are two parts: internal changes in thinking and attitude; and external changes in behaviour. Building new frames for action will help them complete the cycle and move away from endless reflection and not enough action.

Finally it is good to check what the person will do to reinforce the behaviour. Test them to see if they have really thought through all the issues. What if after a month of trying they have not lost as much weight as they thought they would? Will they give up? What is their strategy if they fail and binge once? Finally, what will they do to reward themselves for sticking to the plan?

The same steps are used in a group session except you have to work a lot harder to link all the different viewpoints into a combined decision and strategy. This model is very powerful as it gives me an idea of where the group is on their change process and what role I want to stand in to maximise the energy at any given moment.

This model is developed by Hall and Duval and you can find out more at www.meta-coaching.org.

Follow-up

Like any coaching intervention good follow-up with the client is critical to sustain change. I have found that follow-up sessions a month later are very powerful to reinforce the change and provide the coaching necessary where modifications are needed. I am careful to make sure the client does not become dependent on me. I want the client to become independent and able to facilitate these changes themselves next time. If this happens then I know I have had a successful intervention.

Transforming Team Meetings

Helena Dolny

We all spend so much time in meetings, and their quality of discussion and decision-making is hugely variable, as is our participation and satisfaction. Transforming Meetings is an application of Nancy Kline's Thinking Environment™ work. There are more than seventy accredited consultants in the USA, UK and South Africa – see the website www. timetothink.com.

Anyone can decide to undertake this training but I prefer to teach the process to people who work together, either as an intact team, or an executive team which meets regularly, or people who are associated through a community of practice. Otherwise if you are the only person in the room who wants to run a meeting differently you are likely to have a hard time. The benefit of undertaking the training together, or at least a critical mass of you, is that you all have the same reference points and can hold each other accountable. In April 2008 I was asked to spend a day with a group of eighteen people, community workers whose work intersected in various ways. This is an account of the day.

I knew only one of the eighteen people in the room, the person who had made the request. I needed an opening round to create a climate of ease. I needed questions that were non-threatening, that would allow the person to share a sense of themselves with others, but first of all I gave a short introduction to the day and an outline of how it would unfold.

Background to the Thinking Environment™

Thinking Environment™ work can be said to have its origins with a group of people, including Nancy Kline, who ran a school that started in the 1970s in the USA. The founders were interested in creating an environment in which the pupils would think well for themselves and therefore learn well. They observed carefully, and discovered that what mattered most was the way in which pupils were being treated; this superseded the factors of IQ, experience and background.

Today's format will be as follows

- An opening round of introductions
- Introducing some of the ten components which are foundational to running meetings successfully
- Liberating and limiting assumptions, which are powerful enablers or disablers in both our professional and personal lives
- Listening practice through working in pairs
- Dialogue (attentive versus competitive)
- The meeting process
- The council process
- Selection of three meeting topics and a council topic
- A coached meeting practice with rotating chairpersons
- Closing rounds

Round One questions: 'What is your name, the meaning of your name? What is your work, and a value that you seek to express through your work? Tell us something surprising about yourself.' This round took forty minutes. People were succinct, sincere and humorous. You can trust that people will always find their own boundary with what they are willing to share. It was simply a delightful beginning that set the tone for the day. The personal stories created a shared respect of others in the room. You need a 'pioneer', a person who will be willing to start, and ask them to indicate whether the round will progress to their left or right; in this way everyone relaxes and is ready for their turn to speak. 'Popcorn' style, which is more spontaneous, can be tense.

Of the components I chose to speak briefly on Attention, Ease, Equality, Diversity, Place and Appreciation. Of course if participants can be encouraged to read the book beforehand that would be best! The component of Place had been attended to with care by the workshop organisers; there was comfort, natural light, and so on. Ease is required because ease creates, whereas urgency destroys. It is hard to think well in a state of agitation. Homogeneity breeds homogeneity; creativity is more likely to birth if Diversity is present. Equality of capability and opportunity to apply our minds and speak our minds needs to supersede hierarchy. My being the boss of a team does not mean I'm doing the best thinking – indeed, others may have the time and opportunity for more focused thinking on an issue than a too-busy boss. A process that harvests the thinking of all, and that enables participation by overcoming personality dispositions towards being shy and introverted is an imperative. Evidence on the power of the component of Appreciation is the subject of current scientific research. Yes, the mind at work is enabled in the presence of appreciation versus fear and/or criticism. However, the Heart Institute's work on heart maths with regard to what happens to our physiology and the change in blood supply to the creative part of the brain, as well as Emoto's work on the physical effect of emotions on the shape of water crystals (and our bodies are more than 90 per cent water) have increased my respect for the component of Appreciation. If the group is smaller, and therefore the rounds take less time then, time permitting, I insert the video clip of 'What the Bleep?' on the effect of intentions on water crystals, and do an additional round: 'Share an appreciation that you have received recently, and how did receiving it make you feel?'

Round Two, Liberating Assumptions, required a different level of disclosure from participants. I knew I would not in one day be able to teach Kline's Thinking Partnership® process of how to pursue one's thinking to arrive at the component of the Incisive Question™ – that is, the question which, once crafted and asked, generates the answer that cuts through the limiting assumptions and dispels them. But I wanted participants to engage with the concept of limiting and liberating assumptions because they are so very powerful in our lives, and also relevant to a team pursuing a vision. The question for the second round was, 'Think of a challenge you faced in your life, which you succeeded in facing. What was the liberating assumption you made about yourself that enabled you to face the challenge?' Again the round was magnificent for its richness, and people were spellbound as they listened to one another, and saw one another with new eyes.

The practice of listening in pairs appears simpler than it is. You could simply divide people up, and tell them that they each have a turn to talk without stopping on a subject of their choice for so many minutes. But in order for it to be an experience which is consciously different to their normal listening practice, the setting up of the listening in pairs requires that the following points are covered: (a) types of listening: drawing people's attention to what they witness in their lives: be it *distracted listening* (just finishing my text messaging while you speak); (b) *competitive listening* (not really hearing what you are saying because I'm thinking of how to arrange my words for what I will say as soon as you pause, or I might even interrupt you, because what I have to say has to be said urgently, and after all, it might improve your thinking on the matter, so why would I respect your right to finish your sentence?); (c) *attentive listening*: catalytic listening with palpable respect and attention. Think of a time when the attention of another resulted in your pursuing a line of thinking out loud and arriving at a stream of thoughts that you had not arrived at before. Albert Einstein is quoted as having said, 'How do I know what I think until I hear myself say it?'

You also want participants to begin to be more aware of the kind of questions they ask. Since doing this work, I have become aware of Oscar award level performances in my workplace with regard to the practice of 'leading questions'. So getting workshop delegates to be more aware of closed versus open questions, and leading questions, and getting them to do a practice and notice the length and content of response is useful. *Closed question*: 'Do you want to go to the movies after work on Friday?' *Leading question:* 'What do you think of the idea of relaxing by going to the movies on Friday evening?' *Open question*: 'I'd like to do something to relax on Friday evening; what would you be happy to do?'

The last part is to get the participants to think of their self-presentation, and the fact that they are not in rooms with mirrors. We can't see ourselves as we are listening! Kline speaks of the need to pay attention to our facial expression, and that it needs to convey the message 'I'm interested'. There are three facial expressions she speaks of needing to avoid: the face of fear, the face of worry and the face of the cynic. Any of those actively expressed in response to what the thinker is saying will impact on the thinker, and they will react to your expression and be distracted from the pursuit of their own line of thinking; in fact you're hijacking their thought process, not through active interruption, but because of what your face is saying to the person.

Prior experience. At this point in a Transforming Meetings® workshop, I want people to reflect on their experience of meetings to date. In doing so, I draw on Kolb's work on the adult learning cycle. We all have our (a) *concrete experience* of something; we sometimes think about that experience (b) *reflective observation*. We might consider how we would like things to happen differently (c) *abstract conceptualisation*, and work out a new way that we want to try doing something (d) *active experimentation*.

The first Thinking Pair therefore asks the questions: 'Think of meetings that you have enjoyed, that have gone well for you, what was it that went well; what are your thoughts on good meetings?' The person has four minutes to speak their thoughts. Should they reach a point of silence, the Thinking Partner asks the following question, 'What more do you think or feel or want to say?' Asking questions is in and of itself generative, so this question can be comfortably repeated until the person has completely explored and expressed their thoughts. You will need a timer. This is a hot topic. It is very easy for people not to have finished expressing their thoughts in the given time – and the topic generates a high level of engagement. After switching turns, the team sits together again, and a round harvests the thinking. Each person is asked to convey what most struck them about the other person's thinking. In this way, people's ideas about what constitutes good meeting practice are shared – and if the group wanted to they could use this to draw up a checklist of 'good practice' for themselves. A second Thinking Pair listening practice asks people their thoughts on what is happening for them when they are at a meeting that is frustrating. I don't do a harvest because of time constraints. This time round I might ask the people to undertake dialogue, so that they notice the difference between the dialogues and what happens with uninterrupted speaking time.

I'm now ready to introduce Kline's Meeting Process. I go through the five principles and actions. I have an A3 double-sided sheet which summarises everything (see pages 95 to 98). I go through the meeting pre-work, and the process to be followed in the meeting. We spend time on the role of the chairperson in running a meeting in this way, and what it is that they are especially paying attention to.

There is also a Kline process called 'council' which a person can request to be used within a meeting when they want to make a presentation on a topic they are working on, and they want to receive the experience, ideas and wisdom of others.

If it is a smaller group and we have spent less time in rounds, then I would insert a reading of Nancy Kline's story, 'No one could stop

Dan'.[12] It tells the story of an angry person at a meeting at which he was listened to and the surprising outcome. I did not do this because the group was large and we were pressed for time.

We next spent our time generating topics that we could use to run a practice meeting. An important principle is that, 'The mind works best in the presence of a question'. So in listing items that need to be on a meeting agenda, it's important to identify what the question is that we are trying to address. This focuses the mind, and if the agenda is sent out in advance, with the topics and the associated questions, this can be an important time saver in terms of people's thinking already being activated and harnessed with a certain focus.

This group generated the following topics and questions: What are we going to do in response to (1) What is happening in Zimbabwe post-elections? (2) Women in Leadership: What is it that we could do differently to increase participation in women's leadership development? (3) The ESKOM energy crisis. What growth opportunities does this crisis allow us to consider and pursue? It was decided that the second topic would be led as a council topic, as the person proposing the topic was willing to do an introduction and would welcome the thinking of others. We settled on who would be willing to chair the different topics.

We had agreed on a late lunch of forty minutes, agreeing to reconvene at 14:15. We needed two hours to run the meeting, say thirty minutes per topic as this would be a normal allocation of time for an agenda item, and contracted that I would interrupt to coach on an as-needed basis.

Thinking Environment[TM] meetings always begin with a positive round, something that is going well for us as a team, something going well for each of us in our work or personal lives. Whoever is chairing the meeting is responsible for formulating the question. It's important because it frames the mindset. It could be that we are about to discuss a difficult topic about which there are heated opinions and intense feelings. The practice of a positive opening round increases the potential of a creative problem-solving discussion.

Similarly, the Kline process advises that meetings close with a threefold

[12] Nancy Kline (2001): *Time to Think: Listening to ignite the human mind.* Cassell Illustrated, pp24-27.

ending (a) a round requesting that any burning issues that have arisen and not been dealt with be stated and flagged for attention as soon as possible, (b) a round which requests, 'what went well for you?'; it does not matter how unpleasant the subject matter was, each person is requested to tap into the most positive aspect that happened for them; this can be important to shift mood and create respect and leave a residual goodwill which is a good foundation for the next possibly difficult meeting, (c) each person is requested to appreciate a quality they have admired in the team member who has been sitting next to them.

What emerged in the practice meeting in the workshop was the power of having the questions as the reference point. When a particular team member uses their turn to begin to vent their frustration and anger, simply sounding off, the chair was able to intervene and ask the speaker to address the question. Similarly, rather than the ESKOM energy discussion being one of ranting and venting anger, the presence of the question kept the attention present on the desired outcome.

In closure to this workshop I asked the question, 'What was your most valuable learning for yourself from today?' as well as requesting an appreciation of the person to their left. The round generated a surprising diversity of response. For some the value was the listening practice, for others the witnessing of the energy and depth of drilling down that can be so easily and quickly generated through the Thinking Pairs process. Two persons noted the generative effect of listening in rounds, as opposed to 'waiting in line'; they noted that they were influenced by the speakers before them, they carried on thinking and what they thought they might have said as the round began, changed as the round actually happened, and they gave their freshest thinking when their turn came. Three others mentioned the concept of liberating assumptions as revelatory. They had previously explored positive and negative thinking and assumed assumptions always to be limiting; the power of exploring and arriving at a liberating assumption which can then be used to formulate an Incisive Question™ to cut through the issue at hand was what they intend to further develop their skills.

The pages that follow are printed on a folded sheet of A3 paper and serve as a takeaway handout that people can use as a reference tool for future meetings.

PAGE 1 of Handout

'The quality of everything we do depends on the quality of the thinking we do first.'

Nancy Kline – author of *Time to Think*

1. **ATTENTION**
   Listening with palpable respect and without interruption
2. **EASE**
   Offering freedom from internal rush or urgency
3. **EQUALITY**
   Treating each other as thinking peers
   Giving equal turns and attention
4. **APPRECIATION**
   Practising a 5:1 ratio of appreciation to criticism
5. **ENCOURAGEMENT**
   Moving beyond internal competition
6. **INFORMATION**
   Supplying the facts
   Managing denial
7. **DIVERSITY**
   Welcoming divergent thinking and diverse group identities
8. **INCISIVE QUESTIONS™**
   Removing assumptions that limit ideas
9. **FEELINGS**
   Allowing sufficient emotional release to restore thinking
10. **PLACE**
    Creating a physical environment that says back to people, 'You matter'

PAGE 2 of Handout

THE THINKING ENVIRONMENT™: LEADERS TRANSFORMING MEETINGS

THE PROCESS

PRE-MEETING: Agenda circulated and topic questions formulated.

OPENING ROUND: The meeting opens with a round answering a positively focused question.

RECORDING: Decide on who and how the meeting discussion and decisions will be recorded.

MINUTES: Do this as succinctly as possible. If discussion is required, make it an agenda item.

MATTERS ARISING: Item with its question.

PROCESS TO BE FOLLOWED ON EACH AGENDA ITEM

STEP 1. PRESENTATION

If there is a presentation, there is agreement to hold questions and comments until it's finished. The presenter says what questions the presentation is answering and restates the question the discussants must address in the first round.

STEP 2. CLARIFICATION ROUND

Going systematically around the team, the chair asks if there are questions of clarification. All the questions are harvested, the presenter provides clarification.

The chair ensures that this Q&A does not become a discussion.

STEP 3. ROUND 1

The chair asks each and every participant for their contribution on the agenda question. The mind continues to think as they listen to others so the question is, 'What is your freshest thinking now?'

STEP 4. OPEN DISCUSSION

The chair ensures that people are not interrupted when they are speaking.

STEP 5. ROUND-DISCUSSION-ROUND-DISCUSSION-ROUND until the agenda item is dealt with.

SUPPORTING PROCESSES

THINKING PARTNERSHIP If appropriate, the chair asks the team to break into pairs for each person, for three minutes, to speak their thoughts to a listener without interruption. The chair then uses a round to elicit key ideas.

DIALOGUE Thinking Environment™ (TE) dialogue is more challenging than thinking in pairs because your own thoughts are likely to interfere with your ability to give generative attention, TE dialogue differs from free-flow conversation in that each person respectfully takes a turn, which is not timed, while the other creates the thinking environment and listens without interrupting.

REMOVING ASSUMPTIONS These questions can provide insight and breakthrough. What might we be assuming that could be limiting our thinking on this issue? If we could credibly assume something more liberating, what might our ideas be?

DECISION & ACTION The chair needs to make clear the process by which decisions and action items will be recorded.

DRAWING THE MEETING TO CLOSURE

BURNING ISSUES ROUND Timeously, towards the end of the meeting, the chair asks each person if they have a burning issue to flag that should be addressed another time. The flagging of unresolved issues is the prelude to a wholly positive closure.

CLOSURE ROUND What went well for you in the meeting?

APPRECIATION What one quality have you observed in your neighbouring colleague?

PAGE 3 of Handout

CHAIRING TRANSFORMED MEETINGS – YOUR ROLE AS COACH

1. **Is the meeting necessary?** Review whether the meeting is necessary, that it really requires people's thinking – if not, think of another way of achieving the purpose.
2. **Craft the agenda and questions** – Craft the question that needs to be answered against every agenda item. Do this by asking: What are the essential items that we need to address at the meeting? What outcome(s) do we want from each item? What question(s) would focus our thinking towards that outcome?
3. **Include the questions in the reading pack if there is one** – If a meeting pack is sent out ahead of the meeting, try to include the question that is to be answered. This will focus the thinking of the reader ahead of the meeting
4. **Restate, as appropriate, the ten components** – At the beginning of a meeting contract with the participants around the shared creation of a Thinking Environment™. Periodically review the five PRINCIPLES & ACTION (page 10 of work-book).
5. **Maintain focus** – Cellphones and text messages disrupt the thinking environment; they break focus and slow things down. Contract with people to disengage from their electronics.
6. **Contract regular breaks** – Every 80-100 minutes.
7. **Try to minimise clarification and discussion while a round is taking place** – If information is needed after someone's contribution to a round, provide it as efficiently as possible so that it does not interrupt the flow of the round substantially. Completed rounds that flow have a particular and valuable effect on the team.
8. **Eyes on eyes** – During rounds or discussion when you are not speaking remember to keep your eyes on the eyes of the person speaking.
9. **No side commentaries** – During rounds when it is not your turn, do not comment on what people say in their turns.
10. **A climate of ease** – Notice your body language. If you are agitated, generate ease through your focus of attention and interest.
11. **Using electronic visuals** – Learn to use power points etc in such a way that you can simultaneously sustain a strong, supple and personal connection. This is a challenge.
12. **Using flip charts** – When scribing wait until the speaker has finished. Get them to condense their contribution into a succinct phrase. Then write and use only their words.
13. **Judgement-free** – When chairing, take care not to comment after contributions in a way that may be perceived as judgemental.
14. **Appreciation:** succinct, sincere, specific. Do not begin with caveats, 'I don't know …' or use the occasion for self-deprecation, such as, 'I only wish I had …'
15. **Thank you.** When receiving appreciation, keep your eyes on the person giving it. Do not demean the giver by shrugging it off with a comment, simply accept it graciously.

PAGE 4 of Handout

MEETINGS IN A THINKING ENVIRONMENT™
FIVE PRINCIPLES AND ACTIONS

PRINCIPLE	ACTION
1. Everyone matters	Give everyone a turn to speak. Go round the room systematically at the beginning of the meeting, on each agenda item, and at the end of the meeting.
2. An accurate view of reality includes what is going well	Begin and end the meeting with a positive assessment of the group's work.
3. Knowing you won't be interrupted allows you to truly think for yourself	Allow each person to finish their thought, even fierce debate.
4. Exploring one's own ideas in depth can liberate the thinking of the group.	Give people time to think for themselves in un-interrupted turns of up to five minutes each.
5. Unexamined assumptions can limit thinking	Occasionally ask: - What might we be assuming that could be limiting our thinking on this issue? - If we were to assume something more liberating, what new ideas would occur to us?

Copyright acknowledgement
The above is derived from the work of Nancy Kline, taken from the Training Manual 'Transforming Meetings', 2007. Copyright © Nancy Kline. 63 Preston Crowmarsh, Wallingford, OXON, OX10 6SL UK
www.timetothink.com

Team Coaching with the Integral-Experiential Coaching Model

Lloyd Chapman

The Integrated-Experiential Coaching Model presented here is about facilitating integrated experiential learning in individuals and teams in order to facilitate personal growth, development and improved performance. I researched and developed this model for my doctoral thesis. I originally applied the model to one-on-one executive coaching and subsequently adapted it for team coaching.

Years of research and working with large-scale complex corporate interventions and strategy made me aware of the lack of an integrated theory that could help explain the complexities. Coaching individuals enhanced my awareness of these disparate issues and disconnections while becoming convinced of the potential of coaching as a very powerful medium through which this kind of mental integration can take place. I believed that if individuals could see the complexities in an integrated manner this would enable them to manage that complexity more effectively.

However, my search for an appropriate integrated framework to suit my needs was in vain. There were pockets of theoretical excellence, but nothing that created a comprehensive integration – useful for me and others working in this arena. My hypothesis is that because an integrated and systemic approach is often lacking, people tend to experience organisational interventions as disparate, incremental, possibly faddish, and possibly not having enough of a lasting impact. The cliché 'Necessity is the mother of invention' kicked into play for me.

Part One of this contribution deals with the theoretical underpinnings; Part Two recounts a case study of its application to team coaching.

PART ONE

A highly simplified version of the coaching theoretical framework/ philosophy model I developed is presented here. A more detailed description of this model will soon be published by Karnac Books in London under the title, *Integrated Experiential Coaching. A scientist-practitioner journey towards becoming an executive coach.* Two Meta theories or models underpin the theoretical framework. The first is Ken Wilber's Integral Philosophy (1995) and the second is David Kolb's Experiential Learning Model (1984).

Wilber's Integral Philosophy

Wilber's integral philosophy is grounded in developmental psychology and evolutionary thinking, as well as integrating Eastern and Western Spirituality with Western Psychology. According to Wilber's integral model an individual can only be studied and understood within the communal or collective context within which they find themselves. At the same time the individual and the communal has an exterior and interior domain. Wilber's model can best be explained in terms of his four-quadrant model presented in Figure 1.

Interior	Exterior	
Individual Experience & Consciousness	Body & Behaviour	
•Thoughts/ambitions	•Neuro – muscular system	Individual
•Feelings	•Genetics	
•Mood	•Body sensations	
•Sensory input	•Behaviour	
•Images	•Actions	
Group Membership	Social System	
•Language	•Natural & Human made Systems	Communal
•Social World		
•Rituals / History	•Technology	or
•Customs	•Processes & Structures	
•Culture – organisation/ family	•Physical laws	Collective
	•Objects	

Figure 1. Wilber's Integrative Model
Source: Adapted from Wilber (1996: 71)

The exterior domains or right-hand quadrants are the domains of empirical science. Everything in these quadrants has a footprint, which means that it can be seen and measured. Making use of a CAT scanner, for example, a depressed patient's neurological patterns can be seen.

To manage the depression, Prozac can be prescribed. This is a perfectly legitimate scientific way of dealing with the problem. If, however, I want to understand why the patient is depressed I have no option but to enter into dialogue with the patient; by doing that, I enter into the interior domains in the left hand quadrants. This is the domain of phenomenology and hermeneutic sciences. Figure 1 lists some of the typical areas covered in the various quadrants.

Wilber points out that the danger in Western Science lies in its trying to collapse all human experience into the right-hand quadrants, and in so doing denying the existence of the left-hand quadrants. The East on the other hand, has emphasised the left-hand quadrants at the expense of the right-hand quadrants. Wilber's model demands that we recognise the legitimacy of all four quadrants. If we want to study an individual holistically we have to study the individual within the context of the communal or collective, making sure we cover the interior and exterior domains of both. Not only do we have to take cognisance of the quadrants, we have to be aware of the various levels of consciousness that exist both in the individual and within society. Both individuals and society develop through various levels of consciousness and both can be at different levels of consciousness. Wilber points out that there are different world views associated with the different levels of consciousness. A simplified version of the evolution of consciousness is represented in Figure 2.

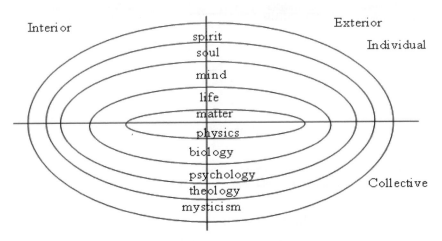

Figure 2. Evolution of Consciousness
Source: Adapted from Wilber (2000: 6)

Wilber's model provides the framework for integrative growth and development. It is a holistic developmental model. The question that Wilber does not address adequately, however, is how to help an individual develop in an integrated way. He points to a number of disciplines that the individual can practise to facilitate their growth; the problem, however, is that these disciplines are content and context dependent.

Kolb's Experiential Learning Model

The second Meta model is David Kolb's Experiential Learning Model. Kolb's model is likewise grounded in developmental psychology. Whereas Wilber's model provides the framework for integrated growth and development, Kolb's model provides a practical experiential way to learn and grow in an integrated way. Kolb's model is represented in Figure 3.

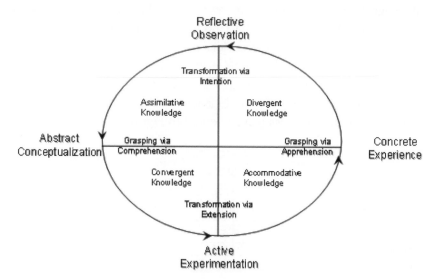

Figure 3. Kolb's Experiential Learning Model
Source: Adapted from Kolb (1984: 42)

According to Kolb, effective learning consists of four abilities:
- *Concrete Experience.* We involve ourselves fully, openly, and without bias in new experiences.

- *Reflective Observation.* We reflect on and observe the experiences from many perspectives.
- *Abstract Conceptualisation.* We create concepts and integrate our observations into logically sound theories.
- *Active Experimentation.* We use these theories to make decisions and solve problems.

This is a never-ending process and it does not always follow the above consecutive route. It is important that a person has all four abilities. The other important thing to note is the coexisting contrasts in the model, ie we grasp knowledge by apprehension (concrete experience) and by comprehension (abstract conceptualisation). The other contrasting symbiosis is that we grow via intention (reflective observation) or the journey inwards, and via extension (active experimentation) or the journey outwards. To grow we need both. Kolb's research shows that individuals tend to opt for a preferred learning style. Although we are able to perform all four abilities, we tend to settle for a *preferred learning style*, which is usually a combination of two of the four abilities:

- The *convergent* learning style relies on abstract conceptualisation and active experimentation.
- The *divergent* learning style relies on concrete experience and reflective observation.
- The *assimilation* learning style relies on abstract conceptualisation and reflective observation.
- The *accommodative* learning style relies on concrete experience and active experimentation.

By settling and over-depending on our preferred style we can actually limit our ability to learn and grow. The aim is to learn to access all four abilities in a more optimal way.

Integrating Wilber and Kolb into the Integrated-Experiential Coaching Model

Wilber's integral model caters for more developmental stages and covers more depth and breadth than Kolb thus providing a more comprehensive framework for integrated growth and development. It is argued that Wilber's model is more holistic and hence should be *the one* that should be used as *the* Meta theory for human growth and development in an integrated coaching model. Wilber's model, however, is weak in terms of the praxis for human development and it is here that Kolb's Experiential Learning Model is strong and robust.

My decision was to amalgamate both models, capitalising on the strength each offered, thus creating an Integral-Experiential Coaching Model as represented in Figure 4.

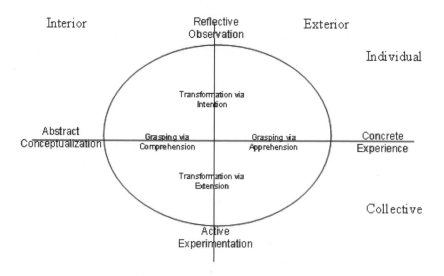

Figure 4. Integrated-Experiential Coaching Model
Source: Adapted from Wilber (1996: 71); Kolb (1984:42)

Wilber's (1995) model provides the Meta framework for integrated growth and development; while Kolb's (1984) model provides a practical experiential way to learn and grow in an integrated way. Figure 4 is an oversimplified presentation of two very complex models, yet it provides an accessible framework to explain the synthesis of the two models.

Thus the Integrated-Experiential Coaching Model proposes that coaching is about facilitating integrated-experiential learning in individuals in order to facilitate personal growth and development. It is integrated in that it caters for Wilber's Integral Model which caters for personal development through various levels of consciousness, especially in the personal and transpersonal levels. It is experiential in that it uses Kolb's Experiential Learning model as the developmental tool.

An individual will generally experience something concrete in the context of the collective, unless the individual lives in complete isolation. To make sense of that experience the individual needs to make use of the intention dimension, move inwards and reflect on the experience. Having reflected on it, the individual starts to develop some theory or concept about the experience. Abstract conceptualisation, however, is not something that belongs purely to the individual; it is influenced by the culture or system in which the individual finds him or herself. Kolb conceptualises experiential learning as a developmental process that is the product of both personal and social knowledge. The individual's state of development flows from the transaction of the individual's personal experience and the particular system of social knowledge with which they interact. Here Kolb disagrees with Piaget who sees it purely as an individual issue.

Having developed a theory, the individual then needs to engage the extension dimension and actively experiment within the collective environment. The beauty of Kolb's model is that it is context and content independent. The same methodology can be used to facilitate the learning of meditation, personal fitness training, designing organisational processes and structures or how to manage people. Done correctly and in a disciplined way, experiential learning will automatically move the individual through all four quadrants and develop all four learning capabilities that are a prerequisite for human growth and development. And the more developed the person becomes, the more integrative the experiential learning experience becomes, thereby facilitating personal growth, development and the transformation of consciousness.

My research findings generated the following hypothesis. The Integrated-Experiential Coaching Model facilitated both the prehension and transformational dimensions of Experiential Learning in individuals. The coachees understood and owned some significant behavioural dynamics inside of themselves, as well as between themselves and other significant colleagues. This underlines the possibilities of coaching as a staff development intervention to facilitate self-authorisation by working through one's own unconscious and dynamic behavioural issues. It is hypothesised that coaching presented from this model empowers individual employees to work towards their own cognitive insight, the experience of emotional meaningfulness and taking of responsibility for their own growth and career development.

PART TWO

The Integrated-Experiential Coaching Model applied in the team context

A client challenged me to apply the Integrated-Experiential Coaching Model to team coaching. The reason for this was that they wanted more people to experience the benefits and improved performance that individuals being coached by me had experienced. The second reason was purely economical; individual coaching is expensive and they wanted economies of scale.

Given that the Integrated-Experiential Coaching Model is about facilitating experiential learning in individuals it soon became apparent that the model could be adapted to teams with the greatest of ease. My hypothesis is that Kolb's genius is that he mapped out a very natural unconscious process. All that is needed to facilitate this learning is to make it conscious and give it some structure.

The entire coaching process is therefore about facilitating experiential learning. The first part of the process is highly structured to allow the members of the team to get to know one another better and to familiarise them with the experiential learning process. The four stages – concrete experience, reflective observation, abstract conceptualisation and active experimentation – are foundational to the team coaching design of activity.

The first day usually starts with a check-in and an expectations exercise. Then we start the process with where the team is at, that is, their concrete experience.

Concrete Experience
The tool that I use to facilitate this part of the process, to honour the team's personal experience, is Robert Rehm's (1997) Six Criteria for productive workplaces. Rehm believes that there are six basic human

needs that must be present for human beings to be productive; in fact
he sees them as the foundation for designing effective organisations. In
an unaligned organisation these six criteria will be adversely affected,
or they will not be optimised, which leads to lower productivity. The
six criteria for productive work (see the detailed write-up on these by
Helena Dolny in Part Three of the book, pages 180-185) are:

- Elbow room for decision making
- Opportunity to learn on the job and keep on learning
- Variety
- Mutual support and respect
- Meaningfulness
- A desirable future

Each individual is asked to rate how they are currently experiencing
their job according to the following scales. The rating scale for the first
three questions is: -5, -4, -3, -2, -1, 0, +1, +2, +3, +4, +5, where -5 =
too little, 0= just right, +5 = too much. The rating scale for the last
three questions is: 0, 1, 2, 3, 4, 5, 6, 7, 8, 9, 10, where 0 = none and
10 = good. After they have rated themselves they get together in the
big group and share their scores. Team members are encouraged to just
listen to their colleagues and they are not allowed to respond. They are
allowed to ask clarifying questions but that is all. The one rule that is
applied is that nobody apologises for their experience. The rest of the
team are encouraged to honour that experience.

Reflective Observation
Having done that exercise, the team is split into smaller groups where
they are asked to reflect on what they have just experienced and answer
the question: 'What did you learn from the previous exercise?' Having
explored the question in smaller groups, the big group reconvenes to
discuss their learnings.

The one big learning that usually arises from this exercise is the
phenomenological nature of experiential learning, that two people can
experience exactly the same situation of phenomena yet experience
it completely differently. It is not uncommon for structural, process,
procedural and role problems to be identified.

Abstract Conceptualisation

At this point I usually introduce the theory of the Integrated-Experiential Coaching Model and how the Experiential Learning process works, as well as using Buckingham and Clifton's Strengthsfinder™. The team is asked to identify their individual preferred learning style using Kolb's Learning Styles Inventory (LSI). Based on research and clinical observation of the LSI scores, Kolb developed descriptions of the characteristics of the four learning styles. The four descriptions are:

• *The convergent learning style.* Here an individual prefers to employ abstract conceptualisation and active experimentation. This learning style is strong at decision making, the practical application of ideas and problem solving. It solves problems through hypothetical-deductive reasoning. People who prefer this style of learning prefer to deal with technical tasks and problems. Social and interpersonal issues tend to be avoided.

• *The divergent learning style.* The individual prefers to utilise concrete experience and reflective observation. These people tend to like working with people, are more feeling-orientated and tend to be imaginative. They love to look at things from many perspectives and tend towards observation rather than action. They are good at brain-storming because of their ability to generate alternative ideas and to think of their implications.

• *The assimilation learning style.* This style draws on abstract conceptualisation and reflective observation. Individuals who prefer this style tend to have an ability to create theoretical models, synthesising disparate observations into meaningful explanations and they use inductive reasoning. The interest is more on ideas and abstract concepts than on people. Theories are valued more for their precision and logic than for their practical value.

• *The accommodative learning style.* Here concrete experience and active experimentation are employed as the preferred learning style. It is action-orientated and excels at getting things done, completing tasks and getting involved with new experiences. This style is accommodative because it is best suited for those situations where an individual must adapt to the changing circumstances. These individuals will tend to discard plans or theories when they do not suit the facts. Problems are solved in an intuitive trial-and-error manner. They tend to rely more on other people for information than their own analytical ability. Although they are comfortable with people, they can be seen as pushy and impatient.

Again, it must be emphasised that these are preferred learning styles. The ideal is for an individual to move through all four learning styles to optimise learning and growth. The problem, as was mentioned previously, is that individuals tend to get stuck or concentrate on one of the four learning abilities and in so doing limit their own learning, development and performance.

Having identified the individual learning styles, the individuals share their preferred learning styles with one another and map out the team's profile. The team then goes into a discussion about what the implications of the individual styles and team profile are for the performance of the team as a whole.

It is interesting to note that Buckingham and Clifton (2002) point out that strength is a combination of an individual's preferred learning style and their natural talent. They point out that a strength needs experiential and factual knowledge (Kolb's concrete experience versus abstract conceptualisation) and a skill, which is a series of steps carried out to do something. Those steps can be things you do (active experimentation) or think (reflective observation). And, lastly, you need a talent which is a naturally recurring pattern of behaviour, feelings or thoughts. Prior to the coaching intervention, each individual would have been asked to identify their natural talents using the Clifton Strengthsfinder™.

The next step of the process involves each individual team member sharing their natural talents with the team. At the same time the rest of the team is asked to validate or question the talents based on their personal experience and interaction with the individual. At the end of the two exercises the team will have a reasonable picture of the inherent natural strengths of the team.

It is my belief that, given the fast nature of change and the complexity that large organisations operate in, it is vitally important for the coach and the team to identify their natural strengths and learn to put those strengths to work as a team. The Integrated-Experiential Coaching Model puts the emphasis on learning and performance, not pathology. Philosophically, it is on a par with Buckingham and Clifton (2002) in putting the emphasis on optimising strengths and containing weaknesses.

This usually brings the first day to an end. The day is summarised, showing the team that they have completed most of the experiential learning cycle, namely: concrete experience, reflective observation and abstract conceptualisation. The day ends with a check-out process when the team is informed that they will engage in another concrete experience after supper.

Storytelling

After supper the team reassembles for a session of storytelling. ('Narratives' is the term more used by the academics and scientifically inclined.) I discovered the power of storytelling while I was doing my doctoral research. Storytelling was never originally intended to be a formal part of the Integrated-Experiential Coaching Model but I needed something to ground people in their own concrete experience. So I asked them to tell me their life stories and I shared mine so that we could get to know each other better before we started the coaching journey together. To my absolute surprise the research revealed that people experienced storytelling in a non-judgemental environment as very meaningful. We live in a world where we are continually judged and assessed by psychologists who diagnostically inform us who we are or what we should be or what is wrong with us. I have found that people find it very meaningful to tell their own subjective stories because it honours their uniqueness.

Storytelling to me is what Jan Smuts referred to as the discipline of 'personology'. Several of my South African colleagues are uncomfortable with my finding anything of merit in the work of Jan Smuts, given his deleterious contribution to South African history. However, his work on 'personology' stands for me; I have not found a better text on the subject.

Jan Smuts (1973) believed that the world needed a new discipline to study the pinnacle of evolution. He called this discipline 'Personology' since in his view personality is the supreme whole of evolution. It is a structure that has built on the previous structures of matter, life and mind. There is therefore a *creative Holism in Personality*. Even though my body and mental structure may have some resemblance to those of my parents and ancestors, my personality is indisputably mine. The personality is not inherited; it is a creative novelty in every human being that makes every person a unique individual. The discipline of Personology would therefore have to take into account this creative

Holism and incorporate all the levels of evolutionary development as well as the inner and outer aspects of the personality. It would incorporate the findings of empirical science but go beyond it. Smuts (1973) argues that psychology does not 'materially assist' in the study of personality, since psychology deals with the average or generalised individual and in so doing it ignores the individual uniqueness of the personality. At the same time, psychology limits itself even further by dealing only with the mental point of view which is only one aspect of personality. His proposed way of studying and developing this discipline was very interesting. He suggested that Personology should be studied by analysing the biographies of personalities as a whole. This study should be done synthetically and not analytically as in the case of psychology. This would enable the researcher to discover the materials that can help formulate the laws of personal evolution. Smuts (1973) called this the science of 'Biography' and he believed that it would form the basis of a 'new Ethic and Metaphysic' which would have a truer spiritual outlook on personality.

So I just get people to share their chronological life stories with each other. This is not T groups[13] so people share what they feel comfortable to share. In my experience as an individual and group coach, storytelling is one of the most powerful and awe-inspiring tools I have ever encountered. Personally, I am always left with a sense of awe and it has given me an appreciation for the uniqueness of every individual. Teams normally find that in this session they learn so much about their fellow team members. Assumptions are challenged and prejudices are shattered. We all think we know people when in reality we know so little about one another. We love to label and put each other in boxes. Storytelling in my experience tears open all those neat psychological boxes, leaves them in tatters and exposes a unique human being, a mystery that will never be fully known or classified. It gives us the freedom to explore our own unique journey.

Active Experimentation
On the second day I usually contract with the team about an issue they want to explore in coaching. Once the contracting has been done we get to work exploring the issue using the experiential learning

---

[13] A group of people undergoing therapy or training in which they observe and seek to improve their own interpersonal relationships or communication skills.

process. What is the issue we want to work on? (concrete experience). Why is it an issue? Why is it manifesting? (reflective observation). What are our options? What are the different scenarios? (abstract conceptualisation). This is where we formulate our own theory of the problem and how we are going to fix it. At the same time the team is reminded of what they had learned and experienced about each other on the previous day. So part of the option is how are we best going to use one another's strengths as a team to deal with the issue at hand. Who is the best person to do what? How do we compensate for any glaring weaknesses that are inherent in the team around the issue at hand? Lastly, we come up with an action plan for the way forward, the next steps with roles and responsibilities and timelines attached (active experimentation).

The second day is concluded by contracting a follow-up coaching session and date (or to conclude the coaching intervention). The final part is a check-out.

Follow-up coaching interventions

Any follow-up intervention will start with a review of how the plan (active experimentation) actually materialised (concrete experience) and a review of where the team is at (reflective observation). The process will then start all over again by contracting the issue at hand to be explored. It is a process of ongoing experiential learning.

Conclusion

In conclusion, then, the Integrated-Experiential Coaching Model is about facilitating experiential learning within the context that the team finds itself. Its major assumptions are that we are all unique with inherent strengths and weaknesses and that we can all learn effectively. Experiential learning is a natural process that we all identify with once it has been made explicit. Combined with our natural talents it yields our strengths that should be harnessed with the greatest of ease to improve team performance. And it does so by consciously making a choice to identify strengths and to use them. It is about harnessing the natural potential of individuals and teams rather than focusing on what is wrong.

References

Buckingham, M & Clifton, D O (2002). *Now discover your strengths. How to develop your talent and those people you manage.* London, Simon & Schuster.

Chapman, L A (2005). An integrated experiential coaching approach to executive coaching. Paper presented at 1st Annual Consulting Psychology Conference, Pretoria. November.

Chapman, L A (2006). 'An exploration of executive coaching as an experiential learning process within the context of the Integrated Experiential Coaching Model', unpublished doctoral thesis, Middlesex University.

Kolb, D A (1984). *Experiential Learning. Experience as the source of learning and development.* Englewood Cliffs: Prentice-Hall.

Rehm, R (1997). Participative Design. Unpublished paper.

Smuts, J C (1973). *Holism and Evolution.* Westport: Greenwood Press.

Wilber, K (1993). *The spectrum of consciousness.* Wheaton: Quest Books.

Wilber, K (1995). *Sex, Ecology, Spirituality. The Spirit of Evolution.* Boston: Shambhala.

Wilber, K (1996). *A brief history of everything.* Boston: Shambhala.

Wilber, K (1996). *The Atma Project. A Transpersonal View of Human Development.* Wheaton: Quest Books.

Wilber, K (1996). *Up from Eden. A Transpersonal View of Human Evolution.* Wheaton: Quest Books.

Wilber, K (1998). *The Eye of Spirit. An integral vision for a world gone slightly mad.* Boston: Shambhala.

Wilber, K (1998). *The marriage of Sense and Soul. Integrating Science and Religion.* New York: Random House.

Wilber, K (2000). *Integral Psychology. Consciousness, Spirit, Psychology, Therapy.* Boston: Shambhala.

Wilber, K (2000). *One Taste. Daily reflections on integral spirituality.* Boston: Shambhala.

Wilber, K (2001). *No Boundary. Eastern and Western Approaches to Personal Growth.* Boston: Shambhala.

Facilitating Reconciliation

Maryse Barak as told to Helena Dolny

People often say, *'I just can't trust that person ever again, so how can I be reconciled? It is not necessary to trust someone to take steps towards reconciliation. It is only necessary to take a risk, however small, and then move one step at a time.'*

Ron Kraybill, Track Two, November 1992

Background

The company featured in this story has two major processing plants, close to different cities, some few hundred kilometres apart. One plant, the smaller one, but which is closer to the major city, also houses the 'head office' from which the executives work and exercise jurisdiction over the 'junior' plant. The 'junior' plant people feel that they are at the real coalface, operationally responsible for the greater part of the company profits, and yet their power is relatively weak; they feel that they are on the receiving end of head office edicts.

The story of working with this company begins with a crisis which prompted first the suspension of a senior executive and then his subsequent dismissal. Expenditure outside budget parameters was one reason for the dismissal but the executive also left a trail of mayhem and relationship injury in his wake. One of the substantive causes of injury had been the executive's inconsistent hiring practices and the consequences this generated.

'I am a qualified, experienced human resources practitioner. That person B was hired after me, does not have the same qualifications or experience and earns double the amount that I do.' Employee A speaking of Employee B.

'I got a job offer stating the terms and conditions. I accepted. I started the job. I couldn't understand why people were so hostile to me, from the very beginning. What had I done unknowingly that had offended them so badly?' Employee B

These were the truths that would eventually be spoken out loud.

Two facilitators, Maryse Barak and Judy Bekker, who have a reputation for conflict resolution facilitation work were contacted, briefed on the history, and the design of a process to initiate healing began to take shape. It was within the company's human capital department that the damage was most tangible. This department of almost forty people has two teams which are split between the two production plants. It was decided to hold three workshops, the first of which would be done by each group separately. A third workshop would bring both groups together for two days.

The invitation

The invitation to the first workshop, drafted by Change Management within the Human Resources Department and sent with only two days' notice of the event, read as follows:
The facilitators wondered what the attendance rate would be to an invitation issued with only two days' notice!

This is to invite you to a day of productive conversation to explore what brought us to this point and to begin to create together an inclusive and enabling way forward.

Please bring your whole self to co-create new ways of being and doing.

They were amazed.
Everybody came.
And so the work of reconciliation took its first step.

The start-up

Maryse recounts, 'We began by sharing our way of being and the values that we, the facilitators, hold, and our recognition that stories form and get stuck in certain chapters.'

We established the historical, the reason for being together, and asked questions for an opening round. We asked people to tell us their names, to speak briefly of something currently working well for them, and last, but not least, the team members were asked, *'How do you feel about being here today?'*

The question that asks participants about what's going well for them is rooted in ground-breaking work on 'heartmaths'. This research has tracked changes in the rate of the heartbeat and associated blood supply to the brain and how this changes depending on the emotional state of the person. When a person is at ease and in a positive frame of mind the blood flow to the brain is increased in general, and thus also the blood supply to the frontal cortex. This is the area of the brain that is involved in creative thinking. Read more about this in Lloyd Chapman's chapter on Heartmaths in Part Three (page 186).

Guidelines were put forward and discussed as to how the group would work to secure an inclusive process. A process which secures an even participation also requires discipline for pace and timekeeping considerations.

Judy had cut out cards of cloud formations which she distributed with chunky felt-tipped pens, with the request that each person write out their desired outcomes for the day. These weren't signed so they were somewhat anonymous in an age of emails where so little handwriting passes between colleagues. The facilitators collected them and stuck them all on a wall for a 'gallery' viewing.

Listening

After a break, the facilitators set up Thinking Pairs. Each person had ten minutes to explore their thinking out loud on the following set of questions:

Q1. What is the issue?
Q2. What are your feelings?
Q3. Who do you think is responsible for which part of the problem?
Q4. What needs to happen now?

After twenty minutes, the team reassembled in plenary and the facilitators asked if anyone had gained any insights that they wished to offer for the consideration of the whole team.

The facilitators asked for some people to tell the story from the perspective of the team in the head office, and their perspective on the events that had led up to this point. People were free to contribute additional inputs to the story in order to make sure that the whole picture emerged for everyone.

This signalled the end of the first part of the design for the day. The context of what had happened now had shared ownership, as well as the recognition of the enormous amount of injury that needed to be healed.

The intention of the second part of the design was to get participants to consider the cycle of reconciliation; as a team it would be useful to take stock of the status quo. The team divided into two groups to discuss the following questions:

- Where am I in this cycle?
- Where are we as a department?
- What is useful?
- What needs to happen to move us on to the next part of the cycle?

The facilitators thought that they would then rejoin the two groups into plenary.

But that's not what happened.

In the moment, the facilitators realised that doing the exercise kinaesthetically, creating the visual reality of where each person stood in relation to the positions on the cycle of reconciliation, would be of impact for the group at this stage of the process. They speedily wrote the different names of the parts of the Cycle of Reconciliation on pieces of card and these were placed on the floor to replicate the Cycle. Participants chose the card/space that most described where they found themselves in this moment.

Ron Kraybill wrote about the Cycle of Reconciliation in South Africa in 1992, a time when reconciliation and forgiveness were high on the agenda to ensure the possibility of a peaceful negotiated transfer of power and transition to a non-racial democracy: 'Reconciliation is thought to be an event which magically erases the past. In fact it is a process, accomplished only through hard work that unfolds in stages over time.'

The readiness to offer apology and the readiness to accept apology may not coincide in their timing. The injured party needs to be in a state of readiness to be able and willing to acknowledge acceptance and forgiveness. There is sometimes undue pressure on the injured party to accept an apology.

'Time heals' is an adage which is often true, but often not true. As Maryse said in the introduction to the workshop, 'Sometimes we get stuck in our stories.' That's when the assistance of a skilled outsider can often be so useful, to help undo the stuck-ness and allow movement to the next stage.

Kraybill describes a seven stage process of reconciliation:

Kraybill's Cycle of Reconciliation

1. **Relationship risk** is the foundation of any positive relationship. Each party takes risks – sharing information about self, making and accepting promises, sharing resources. Out of mutual risk-taking grows trust. Initially trust may be low, so risks that are taken are low too. But as trust grows, bigger risks are taken, leading to increased risk and so on.

2. **Injury.** At some point expectations are not met. One party insults, exploits, betrays the other or is perceived as having done so. Risk has been rewarded, not with good outcomes and greater trust, but injury.

3. **Withdrawal.** Withdrawal follows injury. Sometimes people withdraw physically. Individuals may turn their back or leave the room, etc. Even when withdrawal is not physical, emotional withdrawal always takes place. People pull back into themselves to escape and assess. Withdrawal may last a second or a century. But it is a necessary and healthy response to injury. What happens next is pivotal if genuine healing is to occur. Sooner or later people start thinking about reconciliation. If they understand that reconciliation is a process involving several phases, chances are good that with time and commitment they can completely overcome the past.

4. **Reclaiming identity**. The first casualty of painful conflict is identity: self-esteem for individuals and confidence in its identity for the group. Thus reclaiming identity is a fundamental step towards genuine reconciliation. After all, people who feel like rats often behave like rats! Reclaiming identity is a twofold process of self-awareness and self-affirmation.

5. **Internal commitment to reconciliation.** The turning point in moving beyond withdrawal and reclaiming identity is an intellectual event. The steps that follow are risky and may not succeed at first try. There needs to be a conscious commitment to seek reconciliation, and to undertake the risks inevitably entailed.

6. Restoration of risk. Having suffered in the past, injured parties are understandably wary of risking further loss. Until there is restoration of risk, there can be no restoration of trust.

7. Negotiation to meet present needs. Whenever there has been injury, negotiation needs to follow in order to address current needs arising from old injuries. Sometimes the needs are emotional or symbolic; to hear admission of error and apology. Other times they are political or material and require redress at this level. Negotiation, if genuinely undertaken, frees both sides to return to a normal relationship.

Reconciliation is both a cycle and a process. Pain is engaged with, not avoided, in order to secure the transformation of the relationship.

The facilitators asked everyone to walk around the circle and choose the step in the cycle that most resonated with where they thought they were.

A couple of people placed themselves in the middle because they couldn't yet quite decide where they were.

Maryse invited those who were happy to speak to share their thoughts, to speak from their places on the cycle, to describe what it was like for them in this place, what their feelings were. The invitation was carefully optional, not compulsory. But as people began to share, ie *why I chose the place of WITHDRAWAL*, everyone listened with fascination. And as people listened to more people, some people started moving their positions. Some moved from *'injury'* to *'withdrawal'*. Others moved themselves to the very last step in the cycle, *'negotiation to meet present needs'*.

The contract was: no judgement, just to be present. People were invited to accept where their colleagues placed themselves, without judgement.

There was no deep therapeutic analysis. People simply spoke from the heart about their choice and what they needed in order to recommit.

When people had completed recognising their current 'still', that is, the collective photograph that they created through their choices, they were asked if they were in a place of readiness to do some more work to move forward. This required that they generate a high level vision for themselves.

In small groups, participants crafted the questions that needed to be answered in order to create the desired result.

Groups were tasked to take one or two questions that they would commit to working on in order to create a strategy to move forward.

This was going to be as far as the process could go on this first day. As a closure process, the design the facilitators had chosen was to bring a large selection of rocks, feathers, cloths, baskets. Each person was asked to make a choice of one artefact that most resonated with what had happened for them on that day. The choices were placed together in the middle of the room, thus creating a symbolic structure. People spoke about the artefact they had chosen and why.

This was not the planned ending, but the workshop had its own life and this was the right place to end for this day.

There were two creative co-facilitators working together in mutual support, in absolutely constant communication, checking how their design was in tune with the moment, and able to make adjustments. For example, the facilitators had the intention of introducing and practising more tools. The one they most wanted to introduce was the 'clean communication' tool wherein the group would identify what needed to be said to the CEO and the line managers, and having identified what needed to be said they would practise saying it.

This then seemed inappropriate. It was more appropriate to hold the situation, create the opportunity for quiet solo time, in which people could record their insights for the day. If there had been more time, the facilitators would have introduced a questions exercise to create the practical shift to implement the decisions: who, when, how?

But this is the art of facilitation of a team event. The design is an architectural sketch, and then in implementing the design, the reality of human interaction occurs and flexible responses are required.

The workshop was an unequivocal success. There was 'relief'. Even though there were still distances between people within the group, and there were some tears at the end, there was relief because the cycle of reconciliation had so firmly begun and people had been able to tell the truth.

This workshop was repeated for the team in the other city. Although the format was the same, the team's input was unique to them.

The third occasion brought both groups together. But they began the day separately; each group creating its own circle. The facilitators wanted them first to remember what had gone before; what had created the fracture? They reminded them of the Cycle of Reconciliation. They began with individuals checking in through answering the following questions with regard to the two distinct teams:

- What do we expect of ourselves?
- What do we expect of the others?
- What might they expect of us?
- What would we be willing to do?

The next activity was Thinking Pairs, but this time people paired up with partners from the other city. The outcome of their conversation was put on flip charts and a gallery was created.

Questions were crafted as a result. The questions below formed the basis of the World Café work.

- How do we increase alignment within the Human Resources division to achieve consistently high performance?
- How to develop our cooperation and be seen as credible by our internal clients?
- What is it that we are being called to leave behind from the past?
- What do we need to keep?
- What do we need to hold?
- What do we need to reinterpret?
- What is new that we are called to embrace?
- Who are we? What are our unique authentic qualities? What are we passionate about?

The facilitators gave a brief input on Angeles Arrien's work on the Four-Fold Way™, with the intention that people would be more alert to their dominant typology, the strength side of it and also the shadow side that they bring to bear.

The rest of the day was spent in 'World Café'. See www.theworldcafe. com

The room was divided into six discussion tables. Each table represented one issue/question. People chose tables according to the topic they were interested in. Each table had an appointed convener. People switched tables every forty minutes. The closure at the end of the working day was to get each member of the café group to offer an appreciation to each of the other five members at that discussion table, as well as present their work and thinking in the plenary session.

The next morning the new company CEO arrived. He had an opportunity to speak about himself and his leadership style and his intentions for learning and moving forward. The conveners of each 'world café' question group presented the summarised outcome of the day's discussion. From each presentation the combined group had to identify one key action.

The CEO was highly satisfied. There was movement forward, there were identified outcomes and associated actions for the work to begin. It was the first time the groups had ever been together and the world café presentations allowed the CEO to understand the thinking of the team and also provided an excellent opportunity for the team members to know one another and to work within the environment of respect which they collectively generated.

Closing Words

Marti Janse Van Rensburg

We started in Part One with our personal stories and then in this, Part Two, we have shared our interventions. As always, we have different ways of doing this, indicating our different personalities, views and philosophies, but arriving at the same place of learning and growth. Some of the stories, such as mine, describe an entire process and how it fits together, dances with the music of the moment and aims to deliver desired results. Ray looks at preparation of self, and also preparation to create safety for the participants – the upfront work, anguish and questions participants are often blissfully unaware of, especially if the facilitator or team coach makes it look so effortless. He shares a similar 'dancing' view as he also talks of letting it all go when necessary and shares a beautiful story in illustration.

Some of the others look at specific philosophies used in designing a process or elements of a team process. Tim addresses the fear most of us have that we will be so pressurised for time that we feel it will be impossible to deliver and he makes it work – within context, though. I do hope that this does not give executives the idea that team coaching can be done in forty-five minutes!

Mike uses the example of one of his team coaching interventions very effectively to demonstrate that the role of the coach is often to 'name the elephant'[14] (point out the problem or issue that everyone is pretending to ignore) and ask difficult questions in order to create sustainable change. He underpins this with his training and coaching methodology. And talking about naming elephants, Maryse recounts reconciliation and navigating conflict while being aware that forgiveness happens in different time spaces for different people.

How many of us have been utterly frustrated with the time wasted in meetings, the ineffectualness of some of them, and have also dealt

---

[14] See book review on page 267.

with clients who feel that they cannot manage their workloads because of frequent and ineffective meetings. Helena takes us through a superb process that can and does transform meetings into events that elicit our best creative thinking and are, therefore, effective. And Lloyd focuses on personal growth and learning and shares with us his model that integrates two theories, as well as the application thereof in a team setting.

The purpose of these shared interventions is to show that there are many effective ways of arriving at the same goal and, hopefully, to leave you empowered to find your own best way.

PART THREE

A Repertoire of Tools

Introduction: Tools to create self-awareness, reflection, energy, and conversations

Helena Dolny

Part Two presented seven stories of team coaching interventions, undertaken by seven different coaches.

What emerges is that each person crafts their design according to their learned skills, their dipping into their knowledge of appropriate tools, and their accumulated experience of what has worked for them on other occasions.

The choices are hugely situational. It is the team leader who will often define the outcome, discuss this with the coach, and the coach then comes up with the design that best corresponds to the situation described and the desired outcome.

The desired outcome is likely to fall into one of the following categories:

Optimising team performance

Whether it is a business team or a sports team, optimising performance is likely to be high on the agenda of the team leader.

Many coaches are trained to work with an individual to optimise the individual's performance, to ensure that the person's energy and talent is aligned with the life choices that they are making. Their work is to enable the individual to recognise more clearly their unique talents and how they can leverage these to be more effective; they may also work with an individual to contain their areas of weakness in order to diminish the possibility of their detracting from success.

Optimising team performance, however, requires a modified approach. The team is a team because there is a common purpose that it has to fulfil, and the optimal team performance is not necessarily the sum of each individual's optimal performance. Indeed, the proposition of Ancona and Bresman's X teams book (see review, page 264) is that the 'happiest' teams are not necessarily the best performing teams, the reason being that the optimally performing team deploys its skill according to the shared purpose and not necessarily catering fully to the preferences of individuals.

Clarification of strategic intent and team roles

Defining strategy, and aligning team roles and team interrelationships to best work towards achieving the strategy is also often high on the business leader's agenda. In fact companies would appear to continuously restructure themselves as they redefine or refine strategy and redetermine the organisational structure and composite team thereof that they think will create the optimal fit of different teams working towards a common goal.

It is not unusual for a team coach who is coaching in a large company to begin a team coaching intervention and in the course of the process have to embrace a change of team leadership and a change of the place of the team within the company organogram.

Conflict resolution

Teams are a composite of diverse human beings who work together, laugh together, and rub each other up the wrong way together. Maryse's team coaching case study, using the Cycle of Reconciliation is possibly a more acute story of conflict (see page 114). But it is a not uncommon situation that, in briefing the coach, a team leader reveals that certain members of the team are at odds with one another, they are mismatched in style and communication, they have crossed boundaries in terms of role definition; the team leader wants the team coaching to create a process that is a salve, that will begin to heal the conflict and set in place the foundation for an improved working relationship.

Different tools for different purposes

We have chosen a range of tools that we have used among all of us. It's a selection rather than a comprehensive catalogue. Our idea is to create the understanding of possibility for the coach as artist.

The first three sets of tools are about creating shared clarity of the purpose of the work, how you would know that you are making progress, and having a sensibility of what coaching choices will be appropriate according to the overall character of the group that you are working with.

The second focus is on what needs to happen in order to create greater safety, a climate of sufficient ease in which the group and the coach can begin their work. The process described in Maryse Barak's 'Building the Container' is something that she sees as foundational to the work that follows.

The Learning Styles Inventory, the Myers-Briggs Type Indicator®, Enneagram and Archetypes all allow for the possibility of individuals understanding more about their similarities and differences. The tools quickly take the individuals beyond the pure visuals of race and gender towards identifying the ways their brains are wired differently, or their mental default preferences towards introversion or extroversion. The process often provokes a curiosity and greater understanding about how their similarities and differences impact on the chemistry of their interactions.

There's a selection of tools that is more revealing about the team and their dynamics. Many of the tools are playful. They are about self and team discovery, but also bring a different kind of activity, movement and music. Michael Cooper and Tim Goodenough are masters at bringing music and video clips into their process as mechanisms for sparking humour and energy shifts. Ray Sher often punctuates his interventions with poetry, especially the poetry of David Whyte. Marti Janse Van Rensburg's I-Ching cards create another kind of empathetic group energy, and the Barnga card game can be riotously funny and revealing.

There are tools to build skills and reflective practice. The definition of stupidity is the doing of something the same way over and over again and expecting different results. There needs to be reflection, a decision to do something differently; an acquisition of skills enable that intention. This is essential. Otherwise the danger is that the team coaching intervention will have been an event rather than creating the basis for a sustainable difference. Team coaching aspires to initiate a conscious practice of continuous and embedded learning. Robert Rehm's work, discussed in Part Four, offers a tried and tested teamwork guide of what can be put in place to support sustainability.

So where to? The need for shared vision to map a way forward

Helena Dolny

The Cat only grinned when it saw Alice. It looked good-natured, she thought: still it had very long claws and a great many teeth, so she felt that it ought to be treated with respect.

'Cheshire puss,' she began, rather timidly, as she did not know at all whether it would like the name; however, it only grinned a little wider. 'Come, it's pleased so far,' thought Alice, and she went on. 'Would you tell me, please, which way I ought to go from here?'

'That depends a good deal on where you want to get to,' said the Cat.

'I don't much care where –' said Alice.

'Then it doesn't matter which way you go,' said the Cat.

' – so long as I get somewhere,' Alice added as an explanation.

'Oh, you're sure to do that,' said the Cat, 'if only you walk long enough.'

Alice's Adventures in Wonderland
Lewis Carroll 1865

Team leaders sometimes request that an outcome they desire from the team coaching intervention is that there be team alignment. Alignment assumes that there is a common understanding of how to align in relation to what – because if there is no clarity on what the common purpose is then alignment is arbitrary and/or meaningless.

The team coaching intervention may therefore require a process of creating a shared vision, or checking out to what extent there exists a shared understanding of what the vision is. It could be that the vision is crystal clear to the leadership but that it has not been sufficiently well communicated to the team, or it may indeed have been well communicated but for whatever reason there is not yet team buy-in.

Coaches commonly use three tools as access points to a vision discussion:

- • painting
- • journalling the future and/or
- • creating a Vision Board collage

Painting

Painting requires judgement on the part of the coach that the group will not feel intimidated or inhibited by the exercise. And it requires enough space, enough paints for everyone to choose to work in the colours they want, and a venue that permits messiness and allows the sticking up of pictures on the meeting room walls. Acrylic paints, finger paints and glitter dust are fun to work with.

A team coach might use this as a check-in exercise. You want to check where each individual within the team is, and how much commonality there is between people, and how much separates them.

It's a good thing to do as an early afternoon activity. People need about thirty to forty-five minutes to create their image on paper that is the size of a flip chart. The team then gathers and one by one each person displays their artwork and speaks to what informed their thinking in relation to their created imagery. Sometimes the paintings may express fears as well as hopes, and the fear imagery creates a platform for the discussion to begin.

Journalling the future

Describing the future is an exercise that coaches often use. Individuals are asked to write about a perfect day in their future several years hence. They're then asked to identify some steps that would allow them to make the transition between the now and the then, and also to identify some immediate step to be taken, however small, to create energy in the direction of the desired future.

Another tool to get individuals to identify desired change for an envisioned future is to ask that they write an obituary as if they had died the day before. The coach then asks them to write the obituary that they would like to be written about themselves as if they were to die five years hence. The identified difference in the obituaries creates the basis for discussion about what next steps might be taken to create progress to the desired change in description about the person's life and their achievements.

It can be more difficult to do this with a team than in a one-on-one intervention. Maryse Barak does it by getting the team to craft questions about their desired future and then to discuss what would need to happen in order to get there. Marti Janse van Rensburg asks teams to imagine that they enjoy their work so much that they are eager to get up in the morning and go to work. She then asks them to describe what the workplace would have to be like in order for this to happen.

Vision Boards

Vision Boards sometimes elicit more 'blue sky' thinking than words or painting. Maybe there is something about sitting with a pile of magazines and scissors and glue and a cardboard sheet on which to create a collage which allows a freer, more childlike, imaginative, exploration of possibility and associations.

Martha Beck, renowned coach and author, has for many years fostered the practice of creating team or individual Vision Boards. She observes two things. Firstly, once people begin to identify their vision, the very act of identification contributes to the energy of both intentionality and synchronicity. Secondly, she describes how sometimes she has been drawn to an image or created a set of words in the collage, while not being absolutely sure why she is being drawn to make that particular selection. And then the unexpected happens and years later a Vision Board can make even more sense than it did at the time of making it. She specifically cites the example of a Vision Board she made more than a decade ago in which there are words about Africa in the middle of the board. At the time, she did not anticipate that life would change and that she would find herself working in Africa so frequently. The suggestion is to allow the precognitive to register a life, rather than editing it out because it doesn't seem to fit or seems unlikely.

When a team creates a team Vision Board the power of the process is its contribution to the exchange of ideas and debates that contribute to the emerging of a common vision. I've seen this work with people sitting, sifting, cutting and then going around the table giving time to each person to talk about what's informing their selection. After discussion, the group begin to paste images and words that correspond to the discussion.

The final part of the process is again to ask to the question: 'If this is the vision, what are first steps that can be identified to make progress towards the vision?'

GOALS: Options, Testing, Rating Progress, Accountability and Celebration

Helena Dolny

Goals are more likely to be achieved if there is more to their setting than a statement of self-motivated desire to achieve. I wonder what the success rate is of New Year's resolutions: the setting of goals with good intention? Without doing a research survey, I expect that we would all, on the basis of our own experience, and observation of those around us, consider New Year's resolutions to have a fairly low success rate.

Many coaches, given the opportunity, might take one down the pathway of exploration as to what it is that's stopping us from achieving a desired goal. Is there a block, a limiting assumption, long embedded in the past of our personal history?

Let's assume that we don't necessarily have access to a coaching conversation to explore the hypothesis of limiting assumptions, to seek the cause of impediment, or identify the antecedents of a behaviour so practised that to reverse it would require us to de-programme our cellular muscle memory which generates our auto-response.

What can we do for ourselves as laypersons to increase the possibilities of success in achieving goals that we set for ourselves? People have come up with acronyms that represent models to test our goals at start-up time, to help us review and ascertain the conditions of possible success. These include SMART and SIMPLE and WFO. The SMART goal test asks us if a goal is

S   = Specific
M   = Measurable
A   = Attainable, Accurate
R   = Realistic, Relevant
T   = Timely

Another acronym is SIMPLE:

S   = Solutions, not problems
I   = In between action is Interaction
M = Make use of what is there
P   = Possibilities
L   = Language
E   = Every case is different

And there's yet another more complex check against something called the Well Formed Outcome (WFO). It's a great tool that makes me and you look at the consequences of our choices, beyond ourselves, what will be the impact on the lives of others. There are usually trade-offs to be considered in achieving any goal. An option to study has consequences for time available for relationships. A decision to write a book may have the consequence of not only less leisure time but an income decision to take days off to write. There is an excellent and accessible description of the 'Well Formed' outcomes checklist in Bavister and Vickers' *Teach Yourself NLP*:[30] '... it's considered essential that outcomes be "well-formed", that is, they meet a series of rigorous criteria or "conditions" designed to increase the likelihood of their success.'

The following list of questions and criteria is therefore designed as a checklist for you to do yourself.

- *If you had it, would you really want it?* You are asked to check if the outcome is 'ecologically sound'. This is a bit like the saying, 'Be careful what you wish for'. Be sure.

- *In terms of cost and time, is it worth it?* For example, that MBA qualification that the company won't pay for, but you really want to do it. It's expensive and there's evening and weekend study.

- *Be specific and state the outcome in positive terms.* Accentuate the positive NOT the negative. 'I don't want to be seen as having only an undergraduate degree' is less self-motivating than 'I want to be able to count myself as one of those people who have a postgraduate qualification that I enjoyed doing, stretched my mind, opened my horizons!'

---

[30] Bavister, S & Vickers, A (2004): *Teach Yourself NLP*. McGraw Hill.

- *Is the outcome within your control?* If the bursary is not forthcoming, do you have access to funds to be able to self-finance? A promotion, for example, is less under one's own control; it's contingent on the decision making powers of others. Another question is what control do you have during the process of achieving an outcome? Once you've initiated it, can you maintain it?
- *Identify a sensory-based evidence procedure.* When you achieve this outcome, what will you see? (visual = a certificate); what will you hear? (applause); how will you feel? Check all your senses: visual, auditory, kinaesthetic, olfactory, and gustatory. (I can imagine the taste of the champagne!)
- *Consider the context.* Where, when and with whom do you want to do this?
- *Access to resources.* Identify and apply the resources you need.
- *Ensure outcomes preserve existing benefits.* This may be challenged. So be sure the trade-offs are manageable and desirable. An outcome that requires so much time that it destroys your relationship may not be worth it. Can the consequences be contained?
- *Sense of self.* Does the outcome fit with the sense of who you are?
- *Review all of the above.*
- *Define the first step.* There's a process called 'chunking' which is useful to apply, especially if the outcome seems too big and almost overwhelming. But getting started on the first step can be a great energiser to create impetus.

There's an 'outcome sequitur'. After you attain the outcome, what will you do next? This may or may not be a useful question at this point of decision making, because so often conditions are ever-changing, and the environment in which one accomplishes a goal may be dramatically different to the one in which one started.

None of these would be my choice as a stand-alone. Instead, I'm suggesting a set of process steps which take one through (1) exploration, goal setting, (2) testing the ecological soundness of goals, (3) actually doing and reviewing progress steps, (4) holding yourself accountable by 'feeding forward', and (5) building into the process that you recognise and reward yourselves in celebration of steps towards achievement. That is a long mouthful of a process. In acronym terms it can be stated as GO TO SCALE AFF & R&R.

1. GO = Goal Options

This is the exploratory start-up, the identification of the possible goal to be pursued. The important thing here is to give the time that's needed for reflection to consider whether the identification of the goal is indeed the right one, and that it matters enough to you to want to seriously dedicate some effort into achieving it. The observation is that Western cultures so emphasise the doing, that there is a propulsion to deciding quickly what's to be done without sufficient exploration of alternatives and consequences. Eastern cultures, with more reflective practice, are more likely take more time before reaching decisions. Some such goal setting has serious societal consequences; subjective, emotionally influenced goal setting around fighting the war against terrorism by Western powers led to a precipitous decision to send troops to Iraq.

So do you really want to respond to the head hunter who is flattering your ego with overtures; would you really want that job, in that institution? Where does it fit into your life plan, and your recent decision to be serious about work-life balance?

2. TO = Test the Option

This is where the goal checking models kick in.

SMART		SIMPLE		P/IP/S		WFO	
S		S		P			
M		I		IP			
A		M		S			
R		P					
T		L					
		E					

SMART is possibly the one that most readily responds to a goal requiring task accomplishment; asking exactly *what, by when, with what resources* questions. SIMPLE is more nuanced and asks us to consider incremental steps, and to begin to work with what is already working. PIPS is a simple check-in that I particularly like to consider as a checking tool in goal setting. What is the likely impact of achieving the goal going to be, Personally, Interpersonally and Systemically? A senior executive, in pursuit of work-life balance decided to be home by 18h30 every evening, and achieved his goal almost immediately and with consistency. His wife, however, complained. His early evening arrival agitated the children and upset her previous routine of supper, bathing and winding down. In setting his own goals he had failed to consider the systemic impact.

WFO is the most complex of the 'checking goals models' that I've come across, but with the complexity comes a thoroughness which you may decide is well worth the effort.

3. AFF = Accountability and Feedforward.
It can be very useful to share goals with other people. There are two possible benefits. Firstly, you choose the persons who can be supportive of your intent, and secondly, you can ask them to hold you accountable so that they enquire about your progress and give you feedback when you behave in a manner that will detract from achieving your objective. Marshall Goldsmith[31] builds this process of 'feedforward' into his coaching model (see also page 215). He says that what he and his clients are trying to achieve so often depends on others, and if those identified others can be brought into the picture and involved, the chances of a successful outcome are dramatically increased.

4. Reward and Recognition = Celebration
Many people and teams are very good about celebrating big events such as births, marriages, graduations, or the winning of a business award. What is done less well is the creation and reward of recognisable milestones along the way.

The team coach may therefore play a role in facilitating a team discussion that:
- unpacks the steps of progress towards a goal,
- requests that the team identify how they will recognise that they have achieved each step, and
- identifies what would be an appropriate celebration to be enjoyed

---

[31] Marshall Goldsmith, Leader to Leader Institute, 2002.

Martha Beck, coach and author of the best-selling book, *The Joy Diet* (surely an oxymoron of a title!), outlines this process in relation to the objective of sustained weight loss which has become a more and more common goal in a world where the nature of work frequently requires less and less physical exertion and body fitness.

Beck adds one more factor into her approach, and that is the intentional creation of 'habit'. Creating new habits addresses the sustainability factor, that whatever is needed as a new practice to succeed in making progress towards the step goal is repeated with sufficient frequency that it becomes a habit. The process could look like this, say, in relation to weight loss. First there is the identification of steps. This could be to lose 500 grams per week over a period of 10 weeks. So what will I do differently? I'll stop taking sugar in coffee, and drink alcohol only at the weekends. What rewards will I put in place? I'll put fifty cents into a cookie jar every time I have a cup of coffee without sugar. Then there's a self-bargaining process which goes something like: If I manage to do this consistently, then at the end of three hundred cups of coffee I will have saved R150 and I will go shopping and purchase a CD to enjoy. Designing the appropriate material reward therefore plays a significant part in the process that Beck advocates.

A team I know has at times succeeded well in following this process in the business stepping. They have identified the bigger goal; they have identified the incremental steps towards that goal which are time bound. And on the Friday of the week of the deadline to achieve that step goal, they reserve time in their diaries and at 10am they have a break and share a chocolate cake decorated with colourful Smarties. The chocolate Smartie-covered cake has become synonymous with the ritual of team celebration!

The challenge is to create the habit of breaking work goals down into recognisable and celebratory steps!

Mental Development for Coaching

Tim Goodenough

In the coaching profession we work with many different types of clients with different needs. It is important to be able to ascertain quickly the individual mental development level of your client or the median level of the group that you are working with. This enables you to adapt your coaching style and techniques and focus accordingly, and it is especially important if you do not have the opportunity to screen clients.

Meta-Level is the Neuro Semantic label for the deepening levels of meaning one holds in mind about an idea, context or situation. (Meta-Levels are layers of reflexive thinking.) When someone gets to the 'heart of the matter' in coaching, it is often when deeper Meta-Levels are explored. For example, a person's first Meta-Level meaning about flying an aeroplane might be anxiety, and at a deeper Meta-Level it may emerge that the anxiety has been shaped by fear, frustration and despair. This means a client will only present anxiety at a surface level emotion; however, if you do not manage the deeper levels of fear, frustration and despair, the client will still experience the same disempowering emotions about flying.

Early in my career, I believed that you would find some clients who, whatever you did, would not shift their mental development levels to a deeper level. I would arrive in a room full of resistant minds (a company had 'told' their staff they were going on this training, whether they liked it or not!) and I would try to deliver the content or coach the group as per the requirement without first dealing with what created the resistance, what created the block. This approach just led to frustration all round, and it was not very effective at all.

I now know that my job as a facilitator is to move the group to the 'coached mind' space to allow the greatest possible outcomes to emerge for that group. I do this by creating rapport and deepening trust, and always understanding what phase the group is in, as this can sometimes change when the content changes. For example, a group may have a 'developed mind' about working on their vision, but a 'starter mind' on examining their weaknesses. Some groups will struggle to evolve their mental development level, and once I understand where they are stuck, questions about that 'stuckness' are often very valuable in shifting the group to higher levels of performance. 'So how is it that we can speak for fifteen minutes non-stop as a group, exploring all sorts of interesting aspects of the team vision, yet when I ask you about team weaknesses no one has anything to say?'

For me, working with a group is managing their flow of collective energy. The more challenging the topic, the stronger the container and the more positive energy is required to give the challenge context and positive relevance. I keep this model in the back of my head as I get to know groups, and begin to understand a bit about where they are.

I will give a brief explanation of the various mental levels that are shown in the model; each one may apply to an individual, an individual in a group, or the median (average) of the group you are working with. Each level is a symptom of the current rapport the facilitator has with the client(s).

Resistant Mind. The client either doesn't want to be there (being coached) or doesn't believe in coaching, or both. The focus point with a client of this type is just to allow the client to be heard, to pace them and build rapport by mirroring back the conversation. 'So tell me more about what pisses you off about being here with me?'

Starter Mind. There is some trust and buy-in, in that the client will not be actively trying to disengage. By eliciting and fine-tuning goals and positively reframing what is happening for the client in terms of their agenda you will be able to engage the client. Worksheets and questionnaires are often very important in this approach. 'Well, you are here now, looks like for the whole day, if we were to move beyond being annoyed about it, what would be the most valuable thing we could focus on for you?'

Primary Mind. The client is unwilling or unable to go Meta (deeper). However, you can reveal frames and create awareness and coach through the unconscious, either in the form of games/exercises or Neuro Semantic Patterns. This is often the level that team coaches work at, to elicit group frames and norms. An effective method with this type of client is to coach their body. 'When you think about how you interacted with your team in that team activity, is it similar or different to how you interact with them at the workplace, and if so, what does that tell you?'

Apprentice Mind. The client can explore one or two Meta-Levels, but cannot go beyond that. At this level some very meaningful coaching can occur in a short space of time. 'Now that you are aware of how controlling you are when you feel intense pressure, what are your thoughts about what you want to do about it?'

Developed Mind. At this level clients often have richly complex Meta-Levels that can be accessed through coaching; however, they do not have a specific outcome or need for their coaching, other than some vague generalisation or theme. The coach needs to spend significant time drilling down/Meta modelling (the precision questioning model of NLP to find out exactly the what, when, where and how, and how will I know when I have this? of a client's outcome) to ensure that the client's genuine needs are being met, rather than their symptoms. 'So out of all the things you mentioned, is this the one thing that will be most valuable to you and will have the biggest impact, and how will you know when you get it?'

Coached Mind. The client has access to all their Meta-Levels and arrives at a session confident and ready to pursue a predetermined outcome that has been self-developed – often over a period of time. 'After I asked my question I just noticed you looking up and to the right, and a frown developed across your face. What are you now aware of, and how does that relate to your coaching outcome?'

Until I understood what was going on, I used to fear resistance, either individually or one-on-one, but now I know that resistance is the built-up energy of an important breakthrough. My job is to be as supportive of that as possible without getting in the way or making it personal (about me or my ability, or them or their ability). It is what it is, and sometimes things won't be resolved immediately in the time that you have available. My responsibility is to give that person or group my best effort; it is their responsibility to do with it what they please.

Building the Container

Maryse Barak

During my many years of facilitating teams, when I enquire of people attending my workshops, what their best outcomes would be, highest and most frequently on the list are:
- To get to know my team members better
- To increase trust between us
- To create relationship

To create relationship. It seems to make no difference as to whether the team has been together for a long time or is a newly hatched one – relationship is top of the list. This is true whatever the team's task. Whether it is to create a new strategy or deal with difficult decision making, relationship somehow still tops the list of outcomes.

I believe that all our outcomes are a product of, and dependent on, the quality of the team's interaction among its members. A major responsibility of a team is the ability to think well together; to be able to think creatively, intelligently and innovatively so that the outputs it delivers on are of the highest possible standard.

Conversely, in situations where team relationships are minimal or tenuous, where respect and trust are unsecured, the resultant thinking will be cautious and limited.

Try this as an experiment: Bring to mind someone with whom you do not get on and imagine that you and this person have to design a project together and then take it through to implementation. What would be the quality of your thinking together? You will likely find that your thinking becomes more restricted; you become cautious, avoiding the risk of testing new ideas or going to the edge of unknown thoughts and alternatives.

In relationships that are not based on trust and respect, we feel judged and vulnerable and so naturally become cautious, self-protective and defended. In such a situation our capacity to think well is immediately inhibited. We then do the best we can within those constraints.

It is very powerful to understand that the quality of our relationships impacts the quality of our thinking! *What is needed, then, is to create the context that will enable the most productive and vibrant relationship.*

So, if *quality of relationship* is sought by team members in a team coaching intervention, but people are afraid to risk their best thinking in the environment that currently exists, how can the team coach enable the team to deliver high quality outcomes?

What is it that is needed to enable team members to interact with openness and trust so that relationships are forged which will generate high quality thinking, trust and fun? My belief, as a team coach, is that none of the above can happen unless there is the presence of what has been called a Container.

What is a 'container' in this context? *A container is an object that has the capacity to hold. In the work that I do it means the quality of atmosphere – mostly invisible yet very palpable.*

This idea of 'container' implies something spacious and empty but with definite boundaries. In team coaching, setting up a container gives people a sense of ease and safety. When the coach or process leader understands the importance of making this container space it becomes the underpinning for the whole structure and design of the team coaching process. This safe container allows each person to accept the risk of the feelings of discomfort that may come with learning, reflection, feedback and challenge. Each of us is familiar with a bodily sensing of discomfort when we enter a room that has an atmosphere of danger and judgement – where we experience or feel that we are not accepted for who we are. One of the foundational elements of a safe container is the atmosphere of respectful acceptance.

How is this 'space' or container created/generated?

The very beginning of this creation is in the facilitator himself or herself. How do you prepare yourself for the work that is ahead? What is the nature of your internal environment? Do you know a place of inner stillness and spaciousness from which creativity and action can flow? Whatever discipline you use, that primary internal experience is the start of creating the container. Having done any necessary exploratory work with the team, having designed whatever process would most serve their outcomes, etc, I take some time to prepare myself. As I breathe, slowly and deeply, I consider the people that I am going to welcome into this process. I generate my own personal outcome for the event. I articulate it simply and clearly to myself. Sometimes I write it down. I breathe into the positive and creative outcome of what will be. I welcome the unknown and the unexpected and I visualise the success of the designed process. This is not a mysterious process; it is just a keen awareness of the importance of the atmosphere in order to create a safe place for people to work.

How is this container built?

It is created both invisibly and visibly, internally and externally.

Firstly, it is created by the care the team coach takes with the preparation of the meeting room itself. This seems a small and obvious thing but is so often overlooked. What is the structure? How should the seating be arranged to best provide for optimal participation and a sense of equality? Temperature? Light? Comfort? Does the space itself say: *Welcome. You are each important?* Music? A sense of stillness and ease? Is the team coach *internally* ready to welcome and greet participants?

At the outset the team coach is responsible for the creation of this atmosphere. Even with teams that meet quite frequently for coaching and for whom this ethos has become familiar, each person will still enter with some trepidation about the unknown that lies ahead. A consciously created container assists in encouraging each person to engage with what emerges from the collective learning and intention.

The next step in container building is more visible and is the start of the first team coaching session. I initiate the collective building of the atmosphere in the way I welcome people, set the context, introductions, guidelines or working principles, outcomes and objectives, icebreakers and so forth. These steps can be viewed as the 'ritual structure' that also enables the building of the container. The ways in which these 'start-up' aspects of the day are facilitated include hearing every voice, making the values explicit, and generating safety step by step. This foundation facilitates team members' engagement with the responsibility of doing their own part in both generating the container 'substance' and holding the container steady so that real and honest conversations can happen.

People generate safe containers through open hearts, open minds and the willingness to learn and participate. Part of the team coach's role is the eliciting of these factors from the start of the process.

It is a challenge to describe the building of something that is generally invisible yet carries impact and influence. I see part of my role as team coach in being as explicit as possible about what we are doing together beyond the content of the learning and interaction. I invite people to be aware and conscious of their part in sustaining the environment of safety and encouragement.

As I have said, the container is both spacious and empty but with definite boundaries. There is space here for diversity, opposing perspectives, strong feelings, experimentation, and learning through making mistakes. The boundaries that create safety are held by the principles of interaction – respect, listening, etc.

There is a huge difference between strong views expressed inside or outside a container. Outside the container the impact can be damaging, inside there is containment and possibility for creativity and increased understanding.

A colleague of mine often begins to build her team container through fun – physical games that invite participants to move and play, that generate laughter and lightness. The participants choose to include themselves in the process, so they give something. Once the choice is made and some level of participation is entered into, the container begins to grow larger than the facilitator and it becomes collectively created and owned.

The container is, after all, the space we create to enable the most productive work and learning to take place within an atmosphere of trust and no judgement. Once the work is done, closing the container is as important as its initial creation. Closure includes: acknowledgement, appreciation, review, roles and actions taken, commitments taken, expressed and witnessed.

Each time the team members come together there is a need to reactivate and generate the container. But it becomes easier to renew each time as the participants understand the process and how it enables their work together.

The work of team coaching is done within the container. It is powerful when the team develops an understanding of this 'atmosphere' and then begins to self-generate it in each situation; meetings, giving and receiving feedback, doing performance reviews and team reflections.

Friends from the Ashland Institute in the USA have developed this list of questions for container building:

- What do you do to establish the environment for change and transformation?
- What do you do that enables people to feel OK being in that space?
- How do you prepare yourself before a class/workshop/dialogue etc, any event which you facilitate/lead, which demands people's full and open participation?
- What do you think you are responsible for in creating the 'environment'?
- Do you think that there is such a thing as a collective 'container' – an area of reception, an environment that would encourage defencelessness?
- What do you think of the idea that there is an overarching group spirit?
- Is there a larger intention than your own that is showing up for the collective that is coming together? If so, can you describe your awareness of it? How does it get generated?

Reflecting on these and other questions that you may ask yourself will give you a map of how you can uniquely generate the quality of container that will invite the building of relationships that promote excellent quality thinking, action and results.

Learning Style Preferences: Honey and Mumford contrasted with Kolb

Marti Janse Van Rensburg

Honey and Mumford are of the opinion that one of the reasons why coaching has not caught on as widely and successfully as once anticipated is because the learning style of the individual is not taken into account. An *Activist* will not enjoy the coaching process if the particular coaching style is perceived as 'passive', that is, long-winded and analytical. The *Reflector* would enjoy the opportunity to watch someone or to review and reflect but would not like to 'perform' without preparation. The *Theorist* would typically respond well to prepared coaching situations and non-directive questioning but not to ad hoc sessions. The basis of the coaching would have to be intellectually respected as well. The *Pragmatist* would probably be highly responsive if the subject matter has clear relevance to his/her own current performance, and provided the coach is seen as an authority.

Where there is brainstorming involved – as there would be for most team coaching sessions – it is useful to note that the Activists will enjoy creating ideas but might find the evaluation of the ideas tedious; the Theorists will be inhibited by their preference for logic, the Pragmatists will struggle to suspend judgement of the ideas until later, and the Reflectors will find the pace far too fast. Typically the Activists will enjoy the generating of the ideas, the Theorists will participate in the evaluation of the ideas with a fair amount of logic; the Pragmatists will create an action plan and determine how and when the learning/ideas can be applied, and the Reflectors will arrive later with thoughts on what actually happened.

The Honey Mumford Learning Styles Questionnaire can be used either before or during a training programme. Using it beforehand as part of the 'input' process will assist in determining the learning needs of the group and therefore the design of the programme. Using it during the training programme has its benefits too as the participants get to do something, which is especially useful for the Activists in the room. Seeing the results and plotting it is usually fun for the group and the theory behind it is interesting for the Theorists. There is also a fair amount of reflection involved for the Reflectors. What to do with the information and how to apply or use it is where the Pragmatists come in. The latter is my preference, even though it means that if I find surprises in the group, I might have to change what I do and how I do it in the moment to accommodate the majority in the team.

Overall, if one assumes that there might be a representation of all styles as a preference in the group then the design of any programme should be:

- Practical enough for Pragmatists
- Soundly based for Theorists
- Novel for Activists
- Paced to suit the needs of the Reflectors with gaps between the sessions of at least a couple of weeks

David Kolb's work on preferred learning styles and his Learning Styles Inventory (LSI) were foundational to Honey and Mumford[15] who based their work on that of Kolb and acknowledge their debt to him as a major influence on their work. However, they became less comfortable over time with the content and results of the LSI as it is based on a response to 36 words that they felt did not sufficiently align to managerial activities. They also found in their research with managers that the descriptions of the four styles as *Converger, Diverger, Assimilator* and *Accommodator* were not always congruent.

As their focus was to find a way to improve the effectiveness of learning, they developed a similar four-stage process and four main styles of learning. Their process therefore has much in common with the work of David Kolb. There are two main differences. Firstly, the Learning Styles Questionnaire (LSQ) is based on a set of 80 questions that are statements around managerial behaviour. An example is: 'I am attracted more to novel, unusual ideas than to practical ones'; this requires a yes or no answer. The descriptions of the four types are consequently also different. Secondly, the answers are regarded as a

---

[15] Peter Honey and Alan Mumford: *The Manual of Learning Styles; Capitalizing on your Learning Style*, and Peter Honey: *Effective Learning*. These books are currently unavailable for purchase, but are available at some university libraries.

starting point, not a finishing point, and much work was done on how to develop the less dominant learning styles.

Kolb's LSI is nine sets of four words each which require a preference ranking to each set with a number (1 to 4). The results are plotted on two axes to indicate the scores of the four stages of learning: Concrete Experience, Reflective Observation, Abstract Conceptualisation and Active Experimentation. After a subtraction exercise there is a two by two matrix that indicates a preferred learning style as Accommodator, Diverger, Assimilator and Converger. See Lloyd's chapter in Part Two (page 99) for a more detailed description.

By contrast, the Honey Mumford LSQ is a set of 80 sentences where one would tick correct or incorrect (yes or no) for each statement. The yes answers are added up and plotted on two axes to indicate preferences against a norm as an Activist, Reflector, Theorist and Pragmatist. The diagram is shown below with the average norm for 1300 people across a wide range of professions.

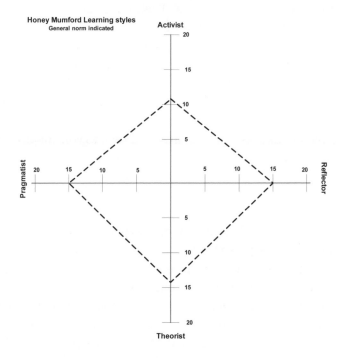

Figure 1: Honey Mumford Learning Styles indicating the norm
Adapted from the *Manual of Learning Styles*, Peter Honey and Alan Mumford (1992)

Some people consider making 80 yes or no choices simpler than preference ranking 9 groups of 4 words. I prefer the yes or no choice, even though there are 80 questions. Moreover, the descriptors are more accessible and easier to assimilate. I have, however, used both Kolb and Honey and Mumford to great effect, although obviously not together in order to avoid confusion.

The short descriptions that follow of each of the four types are taken verbatim, for accuracy, from *The Manual of Learning Styles*.

Activist

'Activists involve themselves fully and without bias in new experiences. They enjoy the here and now and are happy to be dominated by immediate experiences. They are open-minded, not sceptical, and this tends to make them enthusiastic about anything new. Their philosophy is "I'll try anything once". They dash in where angels fear to tread. They tend to throw caution to the wind. Their days are filled with activity. They revel in short term crisis fire fighting. They often tackle problems by brainstorming. As soon as the excitement from one activity has died down they are busy looking for the next. They tend to thrive on the challenge of new experiences but are bored with the implementation and longer term consolidation. They are gregarious people constantly involving themselves with others but in doing so they hog the limelight. They are the life and soul of the party and seek to control all activities around themselves.'

Reflector

'Reflectors like to stand back and ponder experiences and observe them from many different perspectives. They collect data, both first hand and from others, and prefer to chew it over thoroughly before coming to any conclusions. The thorough collection and analysis of data about experiences and events is what counts so they tend to postpone reaching definitive conclusions for as long as possible. Their philosophy is to be cautious, to leave no stone unturned. "Look before you leap"; "sleep on it". They are thoughtful people who like to consider all possible angles and implications before making a move. They prefer to take a back seat in meetings and discussions. They enjoy observing other people in action. They listen to others and get the drift of the discussions before making their own points. They tend to adopt a low profile and have a slightly distant, tolerant, unruffled air about them. When they act it is as part of a wide picture which includes the past as well as the present and others' observations as well as their own.'

Theorist

'Theorists adapt and integrate observations into complex but logically sound theories. They think problems through in a vertical, step by step logical way. They assimilate disparate facts into coherent theories. They tend to be perfectionists who won't rest easy until things are tidy and fit into their rational scheme. They like to analyse and synthesise. They are keen on basic assumptions, principles, theories, models and systems thinking. Their philosophy prizes rationality and logic. If it's logical, it's good. Questions they frequently ask are: "Does it make sense?" "How does this fit with that?" "What are the basic assumptions?" They tend to be detached, analytical and dedicated to rational objectivity rather than anything subjective or ambiguous. Their approach to problems is consistently logical. This is their "mental set" and they rigidly reject anything that doesn't fit with it. They prefer to maximize certainty and feel uncomfortable with subjective judgements, lateral thinking and anything flippant.'

Pragmatist

'Pragmatists are keen on trying out ideas, theories and techniques to see if they work in practice. They positively search out new ideas and take the first opportunity to experiment with applications. They are the sort of people who return from management courses brimming with new ideas that they want to try out in practice. They like to get on with things and act quickly and confidently on ideas that attract them. They don't like "beating around the bush" and tend to be impatient with ruminating and open-ended discussions. They are essentially practical, down to earth people who like making practical decisions and solving problems. They respond to problems and opportunities "as a challenge". Their philosophy is: "There is always a better way", and "If it works it's good".'

These learning styles are useful for both individuals and groups. In a group setting I often indicate on a flipchart everyone's 'diamond'. It becomes messy when it is a big group; the overall picture is very effective though. In any group of specialists – for example, engineers or accountants or marketers – the diagram often becomes much skewed to one side as there are often similarities in how they learn. In any group of people that 'govern', a typical managerial or executive committee, there are differences because one would typically have an accountant, a marketer, a human resources practitioner and an operations person. In this case the overall profile for the group often indicates more of a balance in preferred learning styles. This is good for the team; it also has its problems as there are many opportunities for disagreement and friction due to the differences in learning, and therefore thinking, styles.

Below is a typical profile of a group of ten, indicating the norm and the ten profiles. This group has a relatively balanced profile, which suits them because they are tasked with coming up with new ideas and implementing them. There are strong reflectors and theorists to come up with ideas and then enough pragmatists and activists to make things happen.

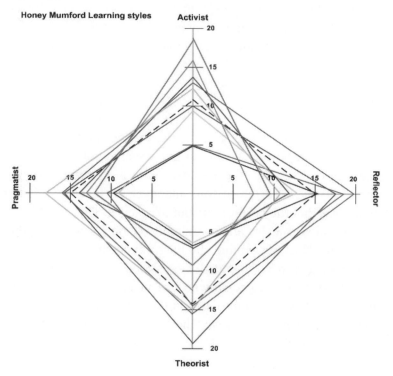

I frequently share with a team the tendency for certain groups to fall into certain areas. An example would be that scientists are often strong Theorists and Reflectors. I have had individuals come to me after a session indicating that they are qualified for a certain profession but fall strongly into another quadrant. More often than not, this question is a precursor to another question, such as: 'Is this why I am not comfortable in my profession and want to make a drastic career change?'

Below is a profile that indicates a couple of very strong reflectors/ theorists. This is typical of scientists.

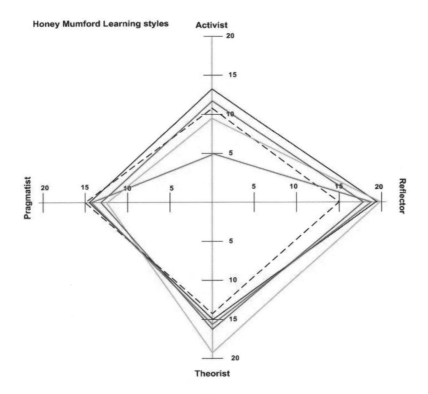

These different styles show up in different learning or training activities. Typically, Business Schools favour logic, systems and rational thinking. This makes the Theorist very happy. Should there be a requirement for analytical reflection, the Reflectors will be comfortable. The Activist and Pragmatist are uncomfortable, though. Should there be role play involved in the process, the Activist will enjoy it. Should the Activist(s) have a low Reflector score though, they will, in spite of enjoying the process, not learn much as they will often be uncomfortable observing others or reflecting on their own learning.

In conclusion, I would typically in any session use either the Honey and Mumford version of thinking styles or the David Kolb version. I find that it helps with the team dynamic, to create understanding and to determine who should play which role in the team. Since the Kolb version is better known, if the team has been exposed to it then I would use it rather than the Honey Mumford one to avoid confusion. If not, then I prefer to use the latter.

The Myers-Briggs Type Indicator® (MBTI)

Marti Janse Van Rensburg

The MBTI® is probably one of the most widely used and popular personality assessments available today. I have an affinity for it because from the first day a friend mentioned it to me, I realised that it is an assessment that doesn't label you, but rather indicates that you have different elements to your personality; that even though you might be more of an Introvert (I) than an Extrovert (E) you always have at least a smattering of both in you. The complexity and simplicity both appealed to me. The MBTI® has an interesting history and I will recount a condensed version of it. I will then give a brief explanation of the various streams of measurement and how I use it in a team setting.

Diversity and temperament or personality differences have a long history. We often confuse being equals – a theme of democracy – with being the same or alike. Psychologists and philosophers have discussed what drives us, or what motivates us, for a long time. Recent thinking (last century) had Freud believe that we are driven by Eros; Adler thought we all seek power, and the Existentialists such as Fromm had us looking for the self. Even though their work has immense value, all of them assumed that we have but one instinct. In the 1920s Carl Jung disagreed. He believed that we all have the same four instincts (or archetypes) driving us but that often one is dominant or more important than the others. Jung's work had a medical and psychological underpinning and was geared more towards wellness than illness. His view was that one should nurture these preferences, not try to change them. His was therefore probably the most holistic view of his time.

At about the same time, and independently of Jung, Katherine Briggs[16] started classifying people in terms of their lifestyle. She was not a psychologist. When she encountered the newly translated

---

[16] This is taken from Otto Kroeger and Janet M Thuesen (1988): *Type Talk: The 16 Personality Types that determine how we live, love and work*, Dell Publishing, and Isabel Briggs-Myers with Peter B Myers (1980, 1995): *Gifts Differing: Understanding Personality Type*, Davies-Black Publishing.

'Psychological Types' of Carl Jung she became a fan and then, together with her daughter, Isabel Briggs-Myers, she developed the Myers-Briggs Type Indicator® during the latter part of World War Two. Katherine Briggs' daughter was not a psychologist either, and for a long time the psychology profession shunned their work and disagreed with its validity. This is now rather ironic considering that in South Africa the test may not be administered unless you have two degrees in psychology and are registered with the Psychological Association of South Africa – even if you hold a foreign qualification to administer it. It was only in the late 1960s that the work started gaining the credibility it has currently. To date it has been translated into Japanese, Spanish, French and German and some other translations are in the process of being validated.

The 16 Types of the MBTI® are made up of a choice between two extremes on four different levels or streams.[17] *The first stream has to do with the source of your energy.* The two extremes are the Extrovert (E) and the Introvert (I). As an Extrovert you get your energy from other people or from outside of yourself. As an Introvert (I) you lose energy to other people or get it from inside yourself. It is important to note that no one is either one or the other but has a preference. It can be a strong preference but it can also be any variation in between the two extremes. Some people are borderline, in other words they show up as Extroverts some of the time and as Introverts at other times. An easy way to observe the difference in a group is that the Extroverts talk to think and the Introverts think to talk. In other words, the Extroverts need to talk in order to think and the Introverts need to think first and talk once thinking is done. The general population has roughly a three to one preference for E to I.

The second stream is about how you gather information. If you look for data, facts, figures and literal information then you have a preference to be a Sensing (S) type. Should you be more random and figurative in your approach then you are more likely an iNtuition (N) type. The Sensing type tends to look more reflectively back at history, what we know, and what has happened. 'What data do we have?' The iNtuitive types look forward. They are more inclined to take what they

---

[17] This explanation is taken from Otto Kroeger with Janet M Thuesen and Hile Rutledge (2002): *Type Talk at Work: How the 16 Personality Types determine your success on the job,* Dell Publishing.

have available and wonder what they can do with it. In children the S child will build the exact picture on the Lego box and the N child will be more inclined to throw the box away and build something different every time. The general population has roughly a three to one preference for S to N.

The third stream looks at your preferred way of making decisions. If your decision-making process is rational and objective then you are probably Thinking (T); but if your decisions are based more on feeling and are more subjective, then you have a preference for the Feeling (F) type. There is an equal split in the population between the T and F, although gender-wise there is a difference: the majority of women have an F preference and most men have a T preference.

The last stream involves your lifestyle. If you prefer your life to be decisive and planned, then your have a Judging (J) preference, and if your lifestyle or preference is to be more flexible and spontaneous then you have a Perceiving (P) preference. Modern society, and especially the corporate world, forces most people to be decisive and to plan meticulously. It is important to note that this test indicates a preference rather than how you might be forced to operate. An easy explanation would be that Js like to plan their holidays to the last detail and Ps like to have some flexibility as to what they do when. There is an equal split in the population on this preference, which probably indicates that there are a lot of people in a time conscious and structured business environment who are rather unhappy and uncomfortable.

These four preferences then add up to 16 different combinations or types. They are ESTJ, ISTJ, ESTP, ISTP, ESFJ, ISFJ, ESFP, ISFP, ENTJ, INTJ, ENTP, INTP, ENFJ, INFJ, ENFP and INFP. The books listed in this chapter give detailed descriptions of these types.

As a description and explanation, I like to use the Keirsey Bates[18] version. Where this differs from other sources is in the use of the original four temperaments. Apart from Jung, Adickes, Kretschmer, Adler and Spranger identified four themes in human values. These tended to be very similar to those identified by Hippocrates more than twenty centuries earlier as choleric, phlegmatic, melancholic and sanguine. Hippocrates' original four temperaments derive from the four

---

[18] David Keirsey and Marilyn Bates (1984): *Please Understand Me: Character and Temperament Types* (distributed by Prometheus Nemesis Book Company, Del Mar, California). There is a new edition available as well: *Please Understand Me II*.

bodily fluids and as such have limited reference. Mythology, or more specifically, four Greek gods, also represent the four temperaments very well and are a lot more palatable. I find these metaphors very useful and applicable in my work and, since I am an ardent fan of mythology and its power to teach, it really suits me well. The gods are Apollo, Dionysus, Prometheus and Epimetheus. Zeus commissioned them to make man more like the gods. Apollo embodied beauty, not only physical but also inner beauty and therefore a sense of meaning (similar to Fromm's sense of self). Dionysus invented wine, and therefore embodied a search for joy, mostly in physical activities such as playing an instrument or practising a skill. Prometheus stole fire from the gods and gave it to man in order to harness nature and gave man science. Epimetheus, his brother, gave man a sense of duty and tradition.

The temperaments determine behaviour in the sense that they indicate what we must have and what we long for. Epimetheans long for duty, Dionysians long for joy and freedom, Apollonians long for a sense of meaning and beauty, and Prometheans long for the power to harness nature or to fully understand and master all there is to know about it.

For the Dionysians (SPs or Sensing Perceiving Types) action does not have an end goal. Action is taken for the enjoyment thereof. Incidentally, Dionysians often made good warriors – in the days when a soldier fought without weapons of mass destruction. They love using tools, whether it is flying an aeroplane, wielding a scalpel or a paint brush. They are often found embodied in the great artists, whether performing or otherwise. They make great painters, dancers, sculptors, photographers and athletes, and also great gamblers. The action in which they participate is its own end. It has to be done and enjoyed for what it is. They are therefore often very impulsive. The Dionysian SP can often be seen to spend hours doing the same thing. This is not a discipline in mastering a skill, it is action by compulsion. Because of their need for freedom and abhorrence of limits, they thrive in a crisis situation. Because of their ability to live with flourish and be only temporarily defeated, the Dionysians have a lot of endurance. Where the other types suffer hardship, SPs are not moving towards a goal and therefore never question their ability to endure, they just continue. Although most people are fascinated by the SP's way of life, they also get frustrated with their impulsiveness, playfulness and perceived lack of depth and motivation. They typically make up about 38 per cent of the population.[19]

Epimetheus embodies the SJ (or Sensing Judging style) very well. They also make up roughly 38 per cent of the population.

It might be useful to tell a longer story about Epimetheus and one needs to bring Pandora into the story here. Pandora was the first human (or mortal) woman. To make her especially attractive to men, all the Olympian gods contributed something. For example, Aphrodite made her beautiful; Apollo made her musical; and Hermes made her seductive. Her name means 'all-gifted'. The gods then decided to give this perfect woman as a gift to Epimetheus. Prometheus (with foresight and some paranoia and distrust of the gods) told his brother not to accept the gift, but he did. How could he refuse the perfect woman? However, she came with a trick in the form of a jar or vase (not actually a box). The story of Zeus telling her not to open it is interesting as he knew well that this was what she would do. It allowed the gods to unleash all kinds of ills on the world but also allowed an interesting theme in humankind: blame. We do love to blame someone else for all our problems and ills, whether it be Pandora or even Eve. One should remember, though, that at the bottom of the vase was 'hope'.

Now back to Epimetheus. The strength in him (and the reason he was given Pandora) was loyalty and duty. Through all of the blaming, he stuck with her. Where the SP is compelled or driven to be free and independent, the SJ is compelled or driven to be bound and obligated. They live to serve and do duty. They are caretakers, not the ones being cared for. The SJ or Epimethean temperament has to belong to a group or society and they are often the custodians of tradition and rules and regulations. They have a need to be useful. There is also often a sense of pessimism in the SJs as opposed to the optimism of the SPs. It was probably an SJ who made up Murphy's Law of 'if anything can go wrong, it will'. They typically make very good administrators.

The Promethean temperament is the exact opposite of the Epimethean. Mythologically, they are the yin and yang, the two opposites that are needed to create balance. Prometheus stole fire from the gods

---

[19] The percentages quoted are based mostly on the USA as the origin of most of the research. There are however recent studies that incorporate averages for other countries and population groups.

to give to man. Fire symbolises light, energy, heat and the sun, and man therefore gains control over nature. The NTs are therefore driven to gain and possess power. They are rather infrequent, only about 12 per cent of the population – and just as well! We probably cannot have too many more of them running around inventing things, harnessing energy for new uses and being rebellious and anti-authority. The NTs like to understand, predict, explain and control nature. Since these are also the underpinnings of science, most scientists are NTs. This minority group – and this is more prominent for the Introverted NTs or INTs, of which there will be only about 3 per cent – often feel they do not fit in, that they are living with aliens. I have found that groups of engineers or scientists, where the majority of the group might be NTs, function very happily as a group but struggle in the bigger organisation, where they are by far the minority. The extreme Promethean can often be seen as addicted to acquiring intelligence and storing up wisdom and knowledge. They are the most self-critical of the four temperaments. For most of the time an NT feels that they are on the verge of failure, if not entirely a failure. Their communication style is rather compact and logical. They also live to work and struggle to play.

The Apollonian temperament, or the NFs, pursue an extraordinary goal that is difficult, even for Apollonians, to put into words. They are often seen as speaking in riddles. Found in only about 12 per cent of the population, they search for meaning. This search for self and for meaning often becomes circular: 'How can one achieve a goal, when the goal is to have a goal?' There is constant need for self-actualisation that often leads to a spiritual or even physical search. The impact of the Apollonians on society is profound, though, as most writers come from this group. Where technical and science writers are mostly NTs, the writers who wish to inspire are mostly NFs. They are also found in professions such as psychiatry and the ministry. It is interesting to note that Katherine Briggs, her daughter Isabel Briggs-Myers and Isabel's son Peter Briggs-Myers were all three NFs. It explains the endless search for meaning in the work they did, in spite of the criticism and scorn of the psychology profession. NFs have a rare ability to be what the other person wants to see and often find it amusing that people see them as different to what they know themselves to be.

It is significant that the archetypes as described by Keirsey and Bates do not follow Jung's archetypes strictly. Jung's intuition (N) either becomes the self-actualisation of Apollo or the harnessing of power and science in Prometheus. It is therefore either combined with the feeling (F) of Apollo or the thinking (T) of Prometheus. By contrast, the Sensing types (S) choose either the Dionysian freedom motive (P) or the judgement (J) in Jung's work to become duty bound in the Epimethean temperament.

Companies often use the Belbin® Test as a personality assessment. It is a spider graph that looks at the eight team roles identified by Meredith Belbin with an overlay of the Myers-Briggs profile as well. I use the MBTI® and not the Belbin® team role version. I would just take the MBTI® information from the spider graph if that is what is available.

As mentioned before, and as a word of caution, a registered professional needs to administer the test. I ask permission from all team members to discuss the information in a team setting and will indicate to the team how their profile looks when plotted on one graph. This often shows up specific themes. A team of engineers or scientists usually has a strong NT profile with more than the norm being Introverted and a mix of Js and Ps. This tends to indicate that the team is good at brainstorming, but not always that good at implementing: they keep on inventing. If there is a lost S or F in the room, they often feel alienated and frustrated because the NTs do not often look at data, do not like to repeat methods that worked in the past and do not take others' feelings into account.

I once worked with a team running a unit that needed to derive new ways of working and new ideas that was entirely made up of STJs, or administrators, with only one F in the room. It helped them to understand why they were so good at maintaining the status quo but were not coming up with new ideas.

Should the team be a balanced mix, it is a very useful tool to indicate where the differences, and therefore causes of conflict, are.

I find that the MBTI® helps individuals to better understand how they operate and why. In a team setting, it assists the team members in understanding one another as well as showing them how to harness individual preferences for the benefit of the team as a whole.

The Enneagram

Marti Janse Van Rensburg

'We are all driven by a deep inner restlessness ... What if there were a system that could enable us to have more insight into ourselves and others? What if it could help us discern our filters more clearly, and take them into proper account? What if this system could show us our core psychological issues as well as our interpersonal strengths and weaknesses? What if this system did not depend on the pronouncements of experts or gurus, or on our birth date, or our birth order, but on our personality patterns and our willingness to honestly explore ourselves? What if this system showed us not only our core issues, but also pointed out effective ways of dealing with them? ... Such a system exists, and it is called the Enneagram.'

The above quotation is taken from the preface to *The Wisdom of the Enneagram*[20] and is so eloquently put that I simply have to start with it.

The word 'Enneagram' is derived from the Greek words *ennea*, which means nine, and *gram*, which means model. It is a system of nine personality types with many levels and complexities, the same as us human beings. It is a very powerful tool to enhance and grow self-awareness. I recently had a client phone me after she was invited to speak to a big group of people. She was excited about the opportunity and yet very nervous and couldn't understand why as she had spoken at big events often before. We discussed her Enneagram type and how as a 3 she needs to be seen as successful and is concerned about what others think of her. She had been asked to speak about a topic that could be controversial and she knew that at least half the audience would probably not like what she was saying. Once she understood that the nature of the topic and the possible rejection from the audience tapped

---

[20] Don Richard Riso and Russ Hudson (1999): *The Wisdom of the Enneagram*. Bantam (pp 1 & 3).

into her basic fear, she relaxed, prepared well and gave a beautiful and thought-provoking talk.

As mentioned in my chapter on the process I use to design a team coaching intervention (page 58), I use the Enneagram with a group only when I feel it necessary to highlight subtle differences, especially when the MBTI and the Kolb or Honey and Mumford styles are similar. It is also not the easiest intervention to use in a big group, as it can be rather time consuming. An example of the effective use of the Enneagram in a team coaching environment would be a team where the Kolb Test showed that most of the team were strong on 'thinking' with some 'watching' and some 'doing' and therefore showing up as either assimilating or converging. (For more on this, see the relevant chapter, page 149.) On the MBTI they all showed up as Ts (or thinking) and were mostly NTs. The Enneagram showed a wider variety. There were Eights, Threes, a Five, a One, a Six and a Seven. This clarified a lot of the conflict and misunderstanding in the team and allowed the team to utilise these differences to their advantage. I also use the Enneagram quite often in my coaching with individual clients where there is more time to explore and understand the complexities of the system and to apply and use it effectively.

I will give here a brief history of the Enneagram and what it looks like. The best books on the subject are thick and I obviously cannot do it justice here. I have listed the resources and suggest that you explore further if you are interested. This is but an appetiser.

The Enneagram is a symbol that can be taken apart as a circle, a triangle and a hexagram. Nobody knows where it came from, much as we don't really know who invented the wheel. The geometry of the symbol and the mathematical derivation do seem to link to classical Greek thought and can be found in the theories of Pythagoras, Plato and the Neoplatonic philosophers. The person accredited with bringing the symbol in its current form to the modern world was George Ivanovich Gurdjieff,[21] a Greek-Armenian born around 1875.

---

[21] Don Richard Riso and Russ Hudson (1999): *The Wisdom of the Enneagram*, Bantam. They also wrote several other books, such as *Personality Types and Understanding the Enneagram*. Some of the material in this chapter is taken from my course notes in training with Don and Russ and the Teleconference Series with Don, Russ and James Flaherty of New Ventures West about coaching the nine types. Information can also be sourced at http://www.enneagraminstitute.com.

Gurdjieff believed that the ancients had developed a complete science for transforming the human psyche, but that the knowledge was subsequently lost. He formed a group with some friends, called the Seekers after Truth (SAT), which explored and shared their learnings on different teachings and philosophies. Their travels in search of wisdom took them to Egypt, Greece, Persia, Afghanistan, India and Tibet. Gurdjieff started teaching from this vast reservoir of learning in Russia just before the First World War. He explained that the three component parts of the Enneagram symbol represent three Divine laws, which govern all of existence. He did not teach, or write about, the Enneagram of personality types.

Enter Ichazo, a Bolivian also interested in rediscovering lost ancient wisdom. Oscar Ichazo is credited with finding a connection between the Enneagram symbol and the nine personality types after travels to the Middle East around the 1950s. The nine types were put together from the seven deadly sins (lust, gluttony, sloth, pride, greed, wrath and envy) with the additions of fear and deceit. The philosophy behind the seven deadly sins was that we all have all of them in us, but one often crops up more than the others and is the root of our imbalance and hence our biggest potential for growth. More about the 'sins' later.

Nearly two decades later, a student of Ichazo, Claudio Naranjo, a psychiatrist, started to connect Ichazo's teachings with psychological theories and psychiatric profiles. Don Riso later wrote the first Enneagram book in 1987 and, together with Russ Hudson, added the nine levels of development for each type and the explanation of levels of integration and disintegration.

The nine basic personality types of the Enneagram show us our very human nature and its complex interrelationships. Each of these nine types has its own way of relating to others, its own set of perceptions and preoccupations, its own values and approaches to life. We all have all nine types in us but, as mentioned before, one dominates and unhinges us the most. It also gives us an indication of where the answer might lie to the question: 'Who am I and why am I here?'

Typically, the One in all of us wants to change the world, often to what our view of perfection is. The Two in all of us wants to help and heal people but can also be very possessive. The Three in all of us wants to be seen to be successful and may blindly pursue success and status. The Four in all of us wants to be seen as an individual and may be very creative, but also often somewhat moody. The Five in all of us wants to invent and gather knowledge and may also be eccentric. The Six in all of us wants to belong, lives for commitment and may also become anxious. The Seven in all of us is the enthusiast and highly energetic, but may be impulsive and scattered. The Eight in all of us wants to challenge and be powerful and may control and intimidate others. The Nine in all of us wants peace in the world and, in the interest of conflict avoidance, could become very passive.

In a business environment we need all nine types. Let us use starting and establishing a successful new business as an example.[22] We need the technical expertise and innovative ideas of the Five; a well-designed product and a sensitivity to its emotional impact on individuals from the Four; the vision and confidence of the Eight and the promotional and communication skills of the Three. Then on the people side, we need the ability of the Nine to bring people together and to listen to them; the ethical standards and quality control of the One; the ability to serve people and anticipate their needs of the Two; the teamwork and self-regulating feedback of the Six; and the energy and optimism of the Seven. Thus, each type is a necessary component of the whole, and without it something important will be deficient or even entirely missing.

Don Riso and Russ Hudson indicate that it is preferable to use the numbers as opposed to the descriptions for each number as the descriptions vary. As much as there are tests to determine the dominant type, the best way to really decide what your dominant type is, is to study all nine types and then to be aware that the type where you feel the most uncomfortable with the shadow side is probably your type. That being said, I include on pages 172-173 a quick test called QUEST,[23] should you be interested in finding out what your preferred style might be. I indicate below the pictorial representation of the Enneagram, showing the symbol (as explained earlier) and the nine types. Please note that the numbers do not indicate a ranking system.

---

[22] This is taken from the website: http://www.enneagraminstitute.com
[23] Don Riso kindly gave his permission for the test to be included here. It is not however to be copied, changed or sold.

The Enneagram with Riso-Hudson Type Names

Further levels of complexity are described by separating the nine Enneagram types into three groups of three groups of three (not a misprint) or 'the Triads', the Hornevian groups and the Harmonic groups. There are a further nine developmental levels within each type of which the first three are Healthy, the second three Average and the last three Unhealthy. Added to this are the directions of growth and integration and the direction of disintegration. This might sound very complex, and it is. That is what makes it such a powerful tool for self-development and growth. I will endeavour to explain some of this briefly.

The Triads indicate our centres, these being an Instinctive Centre, a Feeling Centre and a Thinking Centre. As much as we all have instincts, feelings and thoughts, the 'Centre' indicates some function that became blocked. The personality is formed in an attempt to compensate for the distortion or blockage. It is not that people with a Thinking Centre are able to think better than the others, rather it is a function around which the ego has formed: 'it is the component of the psyche that is least able to function freely'.[24]

The Instinctive Centre (types Eight, Nine and One) has to do with body intelligence. These types have issues with independence, boundaries, being separate and seeking autonomy. 'They create ego boundaries specifically in an attempt to use their will to affect the world

---

[24] Don Richard Riso and Russ Hudson (1999): *The Wisdom of the Enneagram*, Bantam (p50).

without being affected by it.'[25] They do it in different ways, though: the Eights try to control their environment, the Nines try to hold back and the Ones want to remake their environment.

The Feeling Centre (types Two, Three and Four) formed personalities around distortions and blockages in feelings. These types are primarily concerned with the development of a self-image and seek attention and affirmation. The Twos try to please others in order to be liked, the Threes want to be seen as successful and be admired for that, and the Fours place huge value on their uniqueness.

The Thinking Centre types (Five, Six and Seven) have distortions in their thinking. They easily lose contact with their sense of inner knowing and become obsessed with looking for a strategy or finding the next move or plan. The ego is formed to create a sense of security, safety and support. The Fives try to figure everything out on their own, the Sixes look to authority figures for support and the Sevens try everything by a process of elimination.

'The Hornevian Groups indicate the social style of each type and also how each type tries to get its primary needs met'.[26] Karen Horney, a psychiatrist, developed some of Freud's work and identified three fundamental ways in which people attempt to solve inner conflicts and get what they want. There is an assertive style, a withdrawn style, and a compliant (or dutiful) style. All nine types fall into these three fundamental ways. The Threes, Sevens and Eights use an assertive style ('look at me, see me, value me'); the Ones, Twos and Sixes a compliant style ('how can I be of service and a responsible person') and the Fours, Fives and Nines a withdrawn style ('I don't fit in').

Riso and Hudson discovered a third significant way to group the nine types which they have named the Harmonic Groups. Where the Hornevian Groups look at how people get their needs met, the Harmonic Groups look at how each person deals with not getting what they want. It therefore reveals the fundamental way that we defend ourselves against loss and disappointment. The three groups are the Positive Outlook Group, the Competency Group and the Reactive Group. The Positive Outlook Group (Nines, Twos and Sevens) invented the Monty Python song 'The Bright Side of Life' and will often cope by

---

[25] Ibid.

[26] Ibid (p59).

saying 'I don't have a problem'. The Competency Group (Threes, Ones and Fives) use logic, rationality and objectivity to solve the problem and tend to put their feelings aside. The Reactive Group (Sixes, Fours and Eights) react emotionally to not having their needs met. You will know they have a problem.

Back to the seven deadly sins (+2). In the Enneagram these are indicated as the passions. We easily associate these very one-dimensionally with the literal meaning of the word as opposed to understanding that it is intended as a metaphor for a more generic or holistic picture. Let us use gluttony as example. Gluttony is the passion of type Seven and is easily associated with overeating, whereas the intent of gluttony as a passion is to indicate an insatiable desire for life and new experiences. The passions therefore indicate how we lose our centre and become unhinged. The Seven tries to fill an empty space with an endless stream of new adventures and experiences, very much like someone with Prader-Willi Syndrome (PWS) who cannot stop eating. Another example would be the Nine and the passion sloth. Sloth here is not about laziness, but rather about disengaging from life or being unaffected by it – very much like someone lying on the couch and being slothful (which is the metaphor) except that Nines can be very active – they just do it without fully engaging in life.

Then there are the directions of integration and disintegration. I will share an example that might help to explain some of this. The Fives are known as the Investigators. They are somewhat similar to the Myers-Briggs INTJ, although this is not always a clear indication or correlation. Fives easily withdraw into isolation and a knowledge ivory tower. The Five disintegrates at an average level to the average Seven. This shows up where your introspective 'I-like-to-be-left-alone-with-my-books' Five suddenly looks as though the aliens got hold of her and she starts partying up a storm. The same Five could also show up like an average Eight (direction of security) when she feels secure within her immediate environment and starts challenging people. Ideally the Five should learn from the healthy Eight (direction of integration) and be confident, not in her knowledge, but in her connection with the world.

David Helfgott, portrayed in the movie 'Shine', is probably a Five. He descends into the unhealthy levels and then shunts across to the Seven and becomes manic. He actually manages to spiral back up the levels and becomes more functional and confident, as mentioned in the previous paragraph. Howard Hughes was a typical Eight; he descended into the unhealthy levels and then disintegrated to the Five and became reclusive and isolated. He unfortunately remained there. Ophelia in Shakespeare's *Hamlet* is a good example of a Nine who spiralled into an unhealthy level and became disorientated, disassociated, confused and self-punishing. The mayor in the movie 'Chocolat' is a good example of a One who spirals down, becomes enraged, hypocritical, compulsive, obsessive (when he eats the chocolates and passes out in the window) and finally finds redemption.

This is such a powerful tool for development. Should you be interested in finding out more, you could go to the website mentioned in the second footnote. There is a quick test to assist with determining your type that is free as well as a longer version that is not. As mentioned earlier, a quick test, QUEST, is included here if you want to start playing immediately. Riso and Hudson suggest that the best way to determine your type is to study all nine and then decide which type description (especially the not-so-nice bits) makes you cringe the most. And remember that all of us have all nine types in us and that the type that you are the least is as important as the type that is dominant because it will indicate parts of you that you are ignoring. On courses and in personal experience with clients I have seen that the type that comes up with the highest score is not always the dominant type. An example would be a client who showed up as a Six, but actually on reflection and studying realised that he is a Nine. The usually rather complacent Nine can easily disintegrate to the anxious Six, and as the client was under severe stress at the time of the test he showed up as a Six.

QUEST: Quick Enneagram Sorting Test

GROUP I

Weight: _____

A. I have tended to be fairly independent and assertive: I've felt that life works best when you meet it head-on. I set my own goals, get involved, and want to make things happen. I don't like sitting around—I want to achieve something big and have an impact. I don't necessarily seek confrontations, but I don't let people push me around, either. Most of the time, I know what I want, and I go for it. I tend to work hard and to play hard.

Weight: _____

B. I have tended to be quiet and am used to being on my own. I usually don't draw much attention to myself socially, and it's generally unusual for me to assert myself all that forcefully. I don't feel comfortable taking the lead or being as competitive as others. Many would probably say that I'm something of a dreamer—a lot of my excitement goes on in my imagination. I can be quite content without feeling I have to be active all the time.

Weight: _____

C. I have tended to be extremely responsible and dedicated. I feel terrible if I don't keep my commitments and do what's expected of me. I want people to know that I'm there for them and that I'll do what I believe is best for them. I've often made great personal sacrifices for the sake of others, whether they know it or not. I often don't take adequate care of myself—I do the work that needs to be done and relax (and do what I want) if there's time left.

GROUP II

Weight: _____

X. I am a person who usually maintains a positive outlook and feels that things will work out for the best. I can usually find something to be enthusiastic about and different ways to occupy myself. I like being around people and helping others be happy—I enjoy sharing my own well-being with them. (I don't always feel great, but I generally try not to show it!) However, keeping a positive frame of mind has sometimes meant that I've put off dealing with my own problems for too long.

Weight: _____

Y. I am a person who has strong feelings about things—most people can tell when I'm upset about something. I can be guarded with people, but I'm more sensitive than I let on. I want to know where I stand with others and who and what I can count on—it's pretty clear to most people where they stand with me. When I'm upset about something, I want others to respond and to get as worked up as I am. I know the rules, but I don't want people telling me what to do. I want to decide for myself.

Weight: _____

Z. I am a person who is self-controlled and logical—I don't like revealing my feelings or getting bogged down in them. I am efficient—even perfectionistic—about my work, and prefer working on my own. If there are problems or personal conflicts, I try not to let my feelings influence my actions. Some say I'm too cool and detached, but I don't want my private reactions to distract me from what's really important. I'm glad that I usually don't show my reactions when others "get to me."

Instructions:

Rank the paragraphs in each Group from 3 to 1, "3" being *the one that best describes your actual behavior.*

Then add up your rankings for each combination of letters on the table below to identify the *three most probable personality types* for you. [One type will have the highest score of "6" when totaling both Groups. Two types will have "5".]

To determine the most likely one, read the three descriptions (over) and choose the one that most authentically captures you in a holistic way.

This test does not indicate your sub-type or relative importance of the other types in your personality.

Name

2-Digit Code	Add Weights	Type
AX		7
AY		8
AZ		3
BX		9
BY		4
BZ		5
CX		2
CY		6
CZ		1

The Nine Personality Types of the Enneagram

1. The Reformer. *The principled, idealistic type.* Ones are conscientious and ethical, with a strong sense of right and wrong. They are teachers, crusaders, and advocates for change: always striving to improve things, but afraid of making a mistake. Well-organized, orderly, and fastidious, they try to maintain high standards, but can slip into being critical and perfectionistic. They typically have problems with resentment and impatience. *At their Best:* wise, discerning, realistic, and noble. Can be morally heroic.

2. The Helper. *The caring, interpersonal type.* Twos are empathetic, sincere, and warm-hearted. They are friendly, generous, and self-sacrificing, but can also be sentimental, flattering, and people-pleasing. They are well-meaning and driven to be close to others, but can slip into doing things for others in order to be needed. They typically have problems with possessiveness and with acknowledging their own needs. *At their Best:* unselfish and altruistic, they have unconditional love for others.

3. The Achiever. *The adaptable, success-oriented type.* Threes are self-assured, attractive, and charming. Ambitious, competent, and energetic, they can also be status-conscious and highly driven for advancement. They are diplomatic and poised, but can also be overly concerned with their image and what others think of them. They typically have problems with workaholism and competitiveness. *At their Best:* self-accepting, authentic, everything they seem to be—role models who inspire others.

4. The Individualist. *The introspective, romantic type.* Fours are self-aware, sensitive, and reserved. They are emotionally honest, creative, and personal, but can also be moody and self-conscious. Withholding themselves from others due to feeling vulnerable and defective, they can also feel disdainful and exempt from ordinary ways of living. They typically have problems with melancholy, self-indulgence, and self-pity. *At their Best:* inspired and highly creative, they are able to renew themselves and transform their experiences.

5. The Investigator. *The perceptive, cerebral type.* Fives are alert, insightful, and curious. They are able to concentrate and focus on developing complex ideas and skills. Independent, innovative, and inventive, they can also become preoccupied with their thoughts and imaginary constructs. They become detached, yet high-strung and intense. They typically have problems with eccentricity, nihilism, and isolation. *At their Best:* visionary pioneers, often ahead of their time, and able to see the world in an entirely new way.

6. The Loyalist. *The committed, security-oriented type.* Sixes are reliable, hard-working, responsible, and trustworthy. Excellent "troubleshooters," they foresee problems and foster cooperation, but can also become defensive, evasive, and anxious—running on stress while complaining about it. They can be cautious and indecisive, but also reactive, defiant and rebellious. They typically have problems with self-doubt and suspicion. *At their Best:* internally stable and self-reliant, courageously championing themselves and others.

7. The Enthusiast. *The busy, productive type.* Sevens are extroverted, optimistic, versatile, and spontaneous. Playful, high-spirited, and practical, they can also misapply their many talents, becoming over-extended, scattered, and undisciplined. They constantly seek new and exciting experiences, but can become distracted and exhausted by staying on the go. They typically have problems with impatience and impulsiveness. *At their Best:* they focus their talents on worthwhile goals, becoming appreciative, joyous, and satisfied.

8. The Challenger. *The powerful, aggressive type.* Eights are self-confident, strong, and assertive. Protective, resourceful, straight-talking, and decisive, but can also be ego-centric and domineering. Eights feel they must control their environment, especially people, sometimes becoming confrontational and intimidating. Eights typically have problems with their tempers and with allowing themselves to be vulnerable. *At their Best:* self-mastering, they use their strength to improve others' lives, becoming heroic, magnanimous, and inspiring.

9. The Peacemaker. *The easy-going, self-effacing type.* Nines are accepting, trusting, and stable. They are usually creative, optimistic, and supportive, but can also be too willing to go along with others to keep the peace. They want everything to go smoothly and be without conflict, but they can also tend to be complacent, simplifying problems and minimizing anything upsetting. They typically have problems with inertia and stubbornness. *At their Best:* indomitable and all-embracing, they are able to bring people together and heal conflicts.

The Enneagram Institute
3355 Main St., Route 209 Stone Ridge, NY 12484
Tel: 845-687-9878   fax: 845-687-7486   info@EnneagramInstitute.com

What is the relevance of Archetypes in Team Coaching?

Ray Sher

In our daily interactions with people, we are conscious of our personal experience, which includes feedback, but there is another layer of reality that predates the present moment. Although for most of us this is an unconscious reality, we are nonetheless impacted by it. Becoming aware of and understanding these influences on our behaviour and how this contributes to the team dynamic is useful for both team leader and team members.

Unconscious influences impact on our relationships. Team relationships can improve when there is more awareness of the seen and the unseen. The Learning Styles work is one manifestation of what influences the way we behave and are seen by others. The Enneagram descriptors provide another perspective. A tool which accesses yet another source of insight into self and others is that of Archetypes.

There is an enormous amount of researched information, volumes having been written by many well-known authors on the subject of archetypes, this chapter doing no more than pointing to items of interest that might awaken the curiosity.

What are archetypes?

Archetypes are blueprints for human behaviour, which are present in the mythic structure of societies the world over. Carl Jung proposed that the entire human experience is stored in the 'collective unconscious' and manifests in our lives as archetypes, a type of 'hard-wiring'. He suggested that they are collectively inherited unconscious patterns of thought, ideas and images that exist in our individual psyches. Archetypes affect our actions, motives and behaviour.

While we each experience the archetypes in our own unique individual perspective, there are at least five different ways to explain them, depending on our world view. Some see them as *gods and goddesses* encoded in the collective unconscious and ignored at our peril. Scientists would call them *mind patterns* that control how we experience the world. Some would look at *history, mythology and folklore*. Others would emphasise *one God*, dismiss the idea of gods and goddesses and distinguish the spiritual truth of monotheism from the pluralistic psychological truth of archetypes. Many would see them *as guides on our life journey*, bringing tasks, lessons and ultimately gifts, teaching us how to live and experience the full human potential within all of us.

What should I know about archetypes?

Drawing on a limitless supply of myths and folktales from a variety of cultures around the world, many authors have identified hundreds of archetypal patterns that have a significant effect on our daily lives and relationships. Archetypes pattern the thoughts, feelings, source of energy and relationships of all people. Systems have been devised, using groups of four, eight or twelve archetypes. There are many programmes based on Jung's work; several use the following four archetypes:
- Sovereign
- Warrior
- Magician
- Lover

Many professional people, course designers, coaches, facilitators, psychologists and others in the field of human development actively discuss and continually revise this work, as knowledge of the inner, instinctual human world progresses.

Research has shown that cross-culturally, from indigenous to first-world communities, many people draw on the power of these four archetypes to live in harmony and balance with our environment and our own inner nature. Because each archetype draws on the deepest mystic roots of humanity, we too can tap into their wisdom.

When we understand that these expressions of energy are universal and available to all people, regardless of culture, belief system or practice, we are in a better position to experiment with them and discover the means by which we navigate our internal landscape.

In our society, we express our *Sovereign energy* by our mature leadership, wisdom and vision. *Warrior energy* is expressed by our demonstration of loyalty, conscious thought and decisive action, like the ability to say 'NO!' and mean it; *Lover energy* feels empathy, passion and gratitude, and *Magician energy* is expressed through our perspective, creativity, makes things happen, having dreams come true.

Sovereign	Warrior	Magician	Lover
Sees whole picture	Confronts reality	Curiosity	Supports
Wisdom	Boundaries	Openness	Empathises
Mature leadership	Honesty	Humour	Nurtures
Generosity	Courage	Perspective	Surrenders
Affirms, blesses	Tough edge	Intuition	Meditation
Serves the whole	Penetration	Clarity	Gratitude
Establishes purpose	Strength	Mirrors	Authenticity
Defines the realm	Ferocity	Strategy	Creativity
Assurance in being	Risks	Transforms	Connects with others
Creates vision	Tells the truth	Introspection	Flows

Adapted from numerous sources, including *King, Warrior, Magician, Lover* by Robert Moore and Douglas Gillette, and *Sacred Contracts* by Caroline Myss.

How can knowledge of the four archetypes augment my experience?

The hypothesis is that optimum health in an individual or a team is the equal expression of all four archetypes. For many people, this balance is far from reality. Most of us are dominant in one area, leaving the other three unclaimed and underdeveloped. We usually run into relationship difficulties when one or more of these immature archetypes show up.

Let's assume that your dominant style is warrior. Are you fully developed in this role or is there more to learn about being a warrior by adopting the leadership qualities and visionary skills of the sovereign? And how about the gifts of creativity of the magician and the empathy of the lover?

Four dimensions of consciousness and four archetypes

Archetype	Shadow archetype	Quality of character	Primary emotion	Key question	Element
Lover	Manipulator	Compassion	Sadness	What am I feeling?	Water
Warrior	Sadist	Loyalty	Anger	What am I doing?	Fire
Sovereign	Tyrant	Maturity	Joy	What am I expressing?	Earth
Magician	Witch	Intuition	Fear	What am I believing?	Air

Adapted from numerous sources, including *King, Warrior, Magician, Lover* by Robert Moore and Douglas Gillette; International Emissaries 2006

What is important to recognise is that, although our archetypal patterns are neutral, they do have both light and shadow aspects. The word 'shadow' suggests a dark, evil, questionable presence, lurking in the wings, waiting to instil fear and do harm to others as well as ourselves. *'Whether the shadow becomes our friend or enemy depends largely on ourselves,'* wrote Marie Louise von Franz, Jung's closest colleague and confidante.

'The shadow, although as yet unclaimed, is not necessarily always an opponent. In fact it is exactly like a human being with whom one has to get along, sometimes by giving in, sometimes by resisting, sometimes by giving love – whatever the situation requires. The shadow becomes hostile only when it is ignored or misunderstood.' These shadows may be seen as dragons to be slain, but as Marie Louise von Franz says they could be our allies.

On one of my team coaching assignments, a number of dragons appeared. The team had ignored an agreement to start on time and arrived late, were busy with an impromptu meeting of their own, some were chatting, others were on their cellphones.

I interrupted the impromptu meeting to draw their attention to two facts: one, they had broken an agreement by not continuing the session at the agreed time and, two, they had ignored a decision taken just that morning to improve communication.

A barrage of reaction erupted. Blame, anger and frustration were directed at me. I saw the transformation of magicians into witches, lovers into manipulators, sovereigns into tyrants and warriors into sadists. There was chaos. For a moment I was bewildered and then my dragon spat fire in a short outburst. Then, spontaneously, I started laughing. In seconds, everyone else was laughing. This was a classic case of shadow archetypes showing up.

Reviewing the event from the archetypal perspective, I noted the role of these invisible forces. As team coach, I was calling on Magician energy. When I was faced with mutiny my shadow Lover and Magician put in an appearance and I experienced feelings of fear and sadness: Magician and Lover energies. The team leader in his Sovereign energy reacted as the Tyrant when he was challenged. When I laughed, I was Magician back in fullness, which is irresistible. It is not unusual to slay dragons with humour and laughter.

Describing archetypes to a team, and getting team members to classify themselves, and move to the corner of the room designated as that predominant archetype is a simple and fun exercise that can evoke both curiosity and awareness of a different kind of diversity present in the team.

The most natural way for us to wake up is when the sun shines into our room. We all have shadow aspects to our being and the best way to free ourselves of our shadow's influence is to focus light on our inner potential. As we illuminate the natural ability of our archetypes they are enlivened, become active and enrich our lives. They are also our energy guides to our highest potential. Why would we not be curious about them?

The reading list below may satisfy some of our curiosity:

Carol S Pearson (1991): *Awakening the Heroes Within: Twelve archetypes to help us find ourselves and transform our world*. San Francisco: Harper.

Robert Moore & Douglas Gillette (1990): *King, Warrior, Magician, Lover*. San Francisco: Harper.

Carl G Jung & M-L Franz (1964): *Man and His Symbols*. New York: Doubleday.

Caroline Myss (2003): *Sacred Contracts: Awakening your divine potential.*

New York: Harmony Books.

Angeles Arrien (1993): *The Four-Fold Way*™. San Francisco: Harper.

Joseph Campbell (2004): *The Hero with a Thousand Faces*. Princeton University Press.

The 'Six Criteria' of Productive Work: Self Rating

Helena Dolny

Self Reflection: How do I rate myself on each of the criteria and how I do I feel and what are my reasons for selecting my score?

-5 ← The scoring is from -5 to +5 → +5			
Too little ZERO is the perfect score Too much			
CRITERIA	Sub criteria	RATING	What are my reasons for choosing this score?
1. Elbow room for decision making			
2. Opportunity to learn on the job and go on learning	Setting goals		
	Getting in time feedback		
3. Variety			
1 → 10			
The criteria are scored from 1-10 with 10 being the best			
4. Mutual support and respect	Giving		
	Receiving		
5. Meaningfulness	Socially useful		
	Seeing own part in bigger picture		
6. A desirable future			

Optimising team effectiveness: the six criteria of productive work

Introduction

How can people judge for themselves how they feel about their work, their relationships with other team members, and the quality and timing of the feedback that they get? Teams are made up of people with different styles and different needs; a shortcoming in terms of variety of activity for one person may be too much variety for another.

Robert Rehm drew on the work of Kurt Lewin, Fred and Merrelyn Emery and Eric Trist who, after the Second World War, were engaged in a project to identify what critical factors need to be addressed if we are to feel good about our work, do our best, and have good relationships with team members. This work was originally done to rethink the way work was organised in the British coal-mining industry. It does seem amazing that fifty years later it is still applicable.

So what are the conditions which need to be present for us to do our best work? The Emerys' work, applied and written up by Robert Rehm, was specifically developed within a conceptual framework of 'self-managing teams'. Rehm's book, *People in Charge*, includes a case study of how this was applied at the Land Bank of South Africa in 1998-99. The adaptation of their work as presented in this text, and currently being used by some team coaches, uses the 'Six Criteria of Productive Work' as a team learning exercise in which people learn about themselves in relation to others, and the team gets a view of itself as a whole. An added benefit is that sometimes the way people choose their scores identifies issues of concern which the team leader may not have been aware of. Team members discuss their reasons for the selection of their scores. This lays the foundations for their discussion about what needs to happen in order for the scores to shift to their optimum – and what behavioural change and skills learning would need to take place to support that shift.

Just as increased team awareness of one another's preferred learning styles can enhance team interaction, so too does shared understanding of how we each feel about our work and the challenges presented.

Productive Work: The Six Criteria[32]

Robert Rehm's text, abridged and adapted by Helena Dolny

Being productive is a basic human need. Kurt Lewin[33] said, 'People don't live to produce, they produce to live.' We have a psychological (and probably biological) need to be productive; it's a natural part of being human. Being productive means being creative, caring about the quality in whatever we are doing, and being useful.

Here's a thought from the American biologist Lewis Thomas:[34]

> One human trait, urging us on by our nature, is the drive to be useful, perhaps the most fundamental of all our biological necessities. We make mistakes with it, get it wrong, confuse it with self regard, even try to fake it, but it is there in our genes, needing only a better set of definitions for usefulness than we have yet agreed upon.

Fred Emery and Einar Thorsrud identified six human needs that should be satisfied for people to do productive work. They are called the 'six criteria for productive work'. An organisation, a team, or an individual will be most effective when work has been designed to satisfy these human needs.

1.   Elbow room for decision making

To be productive, we humans need enough freedom of movement in order to feel that we can control our own efforts. At the same time, we need enough direction to know what to do. Each person has his or

---

[32] This text is derived and adapted from Robert Rehm's book *People in Charge*, Hawthorn Press, Great Britain, 1999. Rehm has approved this adaptation of the text.

[33] Kurt Lewin was a social psychologist and a Jew who escaped Nazi Germany in the mid 1930s. His direct experience of the horror of autocracy led him to a lifelong study of the potential of democracy – in society, communities and workplaces. Lewin invented group dynamics, action research, and the field that we now call organisation development. Kurt Lewin and Fred Emery can be considered as the pioneers of workplace democracy.

[34] Thomas, Lewis (1992): *The Fragile Species*. Simon & Schuster.

her optimal level of elbow room. One person may thrive with lots of freedom, while another, doing the same job, prefers less involvement in decision making. Almost everyone, though, does not appreciate a boss hovering over them, breathing down their neck, telling them what to do. To some extent, people need to feel as if they are their own boss.

2. Ongoing learning

There's much discussion these days about the learning organisation and how to get one. The truth is that people are learning all the time. Being alive is a process of constant learning.

Learning, in this view, is the ability to set goals and get feedback. Research[35] shows that when feedback, formal and/or informal is provided, timeously and with a developmental intent, the employee's performance improves significantly.

People learn best when they set reasonably challenging goals for themselves, and then make sure they get timely, accurate feedback to see how they did. The combination of goal setting and feedback are essential to learning. I cannot improve my pronunciation of a new language unless I receive feedback. I am likely to continue making the same mistakes in my golf swing unless I am open to hearing and receiving the feedback of an observer.

Learning in the workplace is similar. Hopefully you are party to setting the goals, rather than their being imposed. Feedback may not always be easy to obtain timeously. Customer feedback may be distorted through several layers of messaging before you receive it. The most effective feedback potential is from the immediate environment, the people who work with you on a daily basis. Teams can, as far as they are able, set up their own production and service goals, as well as their skills development goals. They can set in place their own feedback processes, putting in place mechanisms, surveys and checkpoints all along the production or service delivery process.

---

[35] Corporate Leadership Council research, 'Driving Results through Employee Development', found that both formal and informal feedback provided regularly made a significant impact on employee performance and job satisfaction, resulting in higher retention levels, etc.

3.   Variety

Every person has their own need for variety. Getting the right level of variety is a balancing act between boredom on the one extreme and the fatigue of doing too many different things on the other. Being optimally productive means being able to vary your work tasks so you don't get too bored or too overstimulated. A well-designed workplace offers opportunities for everyone to optimise their needs for variety.

4.   Mutual support and respect

The golden rule is to treat people as you would have them treat you. It's natural for people to cooperate and help one another. Humans need to cooperate to work together towards a common goal. Getting the right amount of support and respect in the workplace knows no bounds. You can never have too much. Recent work on heart rate and mapping of blood flows to the brain indicates the positive physiological and psychological response to support and appreciation.

5.   Meaningfulness

We all know that what separates humans from other life forms is the need to find meaning in all that we do. In the workplace, people need to feel that they are having an impact because of the work that they do. They need to feel some connection between what they do all day and some higher benefit to their community or society at large.

6.   Desirable future

People thrive on hope for the future. They want things to be better tomorrow than they are today.

These six human needs are common across cultures and peoples throughout the world. How can the workplace be designed so that, as far as possible, each person can satisfy their human needs in the workplace?

By way of example, three of the authors who work together in the same work team decided to do the exercise to demonstrate to the others.

The exercise was really instructive for the three of them in drawing attention to issues that they were not aware of, especially of how strongly a particular person felt about a specific issue. Tim's request, for example, to divide his job into different roles, and score separately provided new insights. Helena's low score on 'socially useful' revealed her ambivalence about working in the financial services sector in contrast to more vocational work that has been a focus at other times of her life.

Tim, whose cherished dream is to become a full-time sports coach, scores himself as a 6 on the 'desirable future' in this workplace. Seven months after doing this exercise he did, indeed, leave to follow his dream.

Scoring

The first four topics have to be scored as too much or too little, ranging from +5 to -5. Therefore the most desirable score is 0.

The last topics are scored out of 10 with 10 being the optimum.

		Tim (rest of role)	Tim (mentoring manager role)	Khatija	Helena
1. Elbow room		+2	-2	0	+1
2. Learning					
	Setting goals	+1	-2	+1	0
	Getting feedback	-1	-1	+1	0
3. Variety		+2	-3	0	+2
4. Mutual support and respect					
	Receiving	8		10	10
	Giving	8		8	8
5. Meaningfulness					
	Socially useful	9		10	6
	Seeing the whole product	9		10	10
6. Desirable Future		6		10	10

Teams dealing with Stress: Heart Maths and the Thinking Environment™

Lloyd Chapman

In my experience as a coach I have found that despite having the potential to manage complexity, many executives and senior managers are still being overwhelmed by complexity. The natural question was why was this happening to people who had the potential and experience to manage complexity? Over time I became more and more convinced that stress was a major factor. As a result I started to research the impact of stress on cognition. At first I tried to find out what research had been done in this area. I soon found that a number of psychological research projects had been undertaken, but there was one major problem: most of the research had been done on rats. Needless to say it was a bit disappointing to find that the research was limited to rats. I work with people, not rats.

I then turned my efforts to the field of biofeedback to see if any work had been done on the impact of stress on cognition. It was then that I stumbled on the research that the Institute for Heartmath (2001) had been doing in this domain. Theirs is a very novel approach which is discussed superficially below.

They examined the way in which stress impacts on heart rate variability and how that, in turn, impacts on cognition. They found that negative emotions and stress lead to disorder in the heart's rhythm and the autonomic nervous system. Figure 1 is an example of an erratic and chaotic heart rate variability pattern produced by a negative emotion like anger and/or frustration. Under conditions of severe or prolonged stress an individual will have a similar heart rate variability pattern.

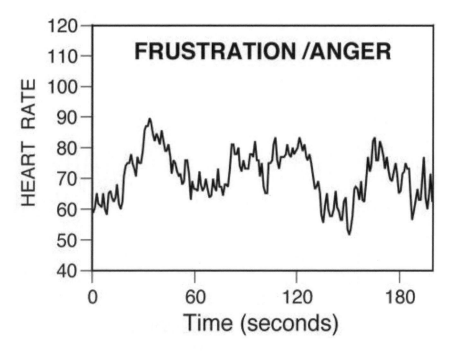

Figure 1. Heart rate variability pattern showing frustration or anger
Source: Adapted from the Institute of Heartmath (2001,18)

The research showed that a chaotic heart rate variability pattern had a
negative impact on cognition and as a result an individual is inclined
to experience:

- Less ability to think clearly
- Less efficiency in decision making
- Less ability to communicate effectively
- Reduced physical coordination
- Higher risk of heart disease
- Higher risk of blood pressure problems

On the other hand, positive emotions and better stress management
create harmony and coherence in the heart's rhythm and improve
balance in the nervous system as can be seen in Figure 2.

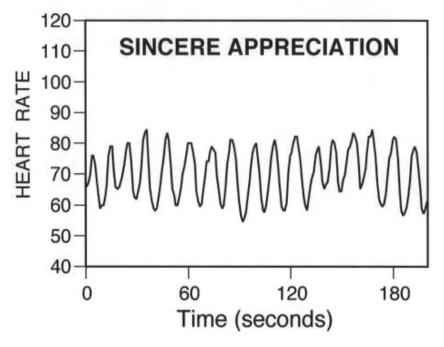

Figure 2. Heart rate variability pattern showing sincere appreciation
Source: Adapted from the Institute of Heartmath (2001,18)

This coherent pattern leads to:
- Improved mental performance and achievement
- More creativity and problem solving
- Better decision making
- More flexibility in the way we think
- Improved memory
- Improved immunity to disease

My experience has been that individuals who learn to get into a more coherent heart rate variability pattern through effective stress management are able to significantly improve their experiential learning process during coaching. The more relaxed an individual is, the more effectively he or she learns, which in turn increases their ability to handle managerial complexity.

Heart rate variability training is a very powerful tool to improve performance for individuals, but how do you apply it in the group or team coaching context? In the team context one does not often have the luxury or the time to train every individual. One of the areas that I am currently exploring and starting to play with in the team context, is the work of Nancy Kline (2003) – not so much her Thinking Partnership coaching methodology, but bringing in the Ten Components of a Thinking Environment™ as a way of being and working with one another. It is my working hypothesis (which still needs to be researched scientifically) that if a team coach can effectively create the right conditions for a Thinking Environment™ via the ten components, it is possible to create the same physiological state within an individual as represented in Figure 2. It is a discussion that I have started with Nancy and a possibility that intrigues both of us.

The Ten Components of a Thinking Environment™ are:

1. *Attention:* Listen with palpable respect, interest and without interruption
2. *Incisive Questions:* Removing assumptions that limit ideas
3. *Equality*: Treating one another as thinking peers: giving equal turns and attention. Keeping agreements and boundaries
4. *Appreciation:* Practising a five-to-one ratio of appreciation to criticism
5. *Ease*: Offering freedom from rush or urgency
6. *Encouragement:* Moving beyond internal competition
7. *Feelings:* Allowing sufficient emotional release to restore thinking
8. *Information:* Providing a full and accurate picture of reality
9. *Place:* Creating a physical environment that says to people, 'You matter'
10. *Diversity:* Adding quality because of the differences among us (Kline, 2003:35).

Another team application of the Thinking Environment™ and its ten components has been described in Part Two in Helena Dolny's case study of Transforming Team Meetings. She unpacks the process you would follow to begin to establish the operationality of the Thinking Environment™ components within a group. Based on the research of the Institute of Heartmath (2001), the only aspect I would add is positive feelings that allow for optimal thinking. Early indications are that people experience the Ten Components very positively, which possibly helps facilitate the experiential learning process. It is an area that is intriguing me more and more and it has become the focus of my research efforts.

References

Chapman, L A (2006). 'An exploration of executive coaching as an experiential learning process within the context of the Integrated Experiential Coaching Model.' Unpublished doctoral thesis. Middlesex University.

Heartmath Research Centre (2001). *Science of the heart. Exploring the role of the heart in human performance.* Boulder Creek: Heartmath Publishing.

Kilburg, R R (2000). *Executive coaching. Developing managerial wisdom in a world of chaos.* Washington DC: American Psychological Association.

Kline, N (2003). *Time to Think. Listening to ignite the human mind.* London: Cassell Illustrated.

Diversity: The Barnga Card Game

Marti Janse Van Rensburg

People are inherently different. We often talk about diversity and mostly we think that it has to do with race or gender or religion. There are, however, so many different ways in which people are different, yet also the same. These different ways are not always spoken, written about or clear, and often cause much havoc in relationships and therefore also in teams. The purpose of the Barnga Card Game is to show how all of us have unwritten or unspoken rules that affect our behaviour and perceptions of the behaviour of others.

The Barnga Card Game is based on the work done by Dr Sivasailam Thiagarajan, or Thiagi as he is affectionately known. Thiagi also is known as 'the Resident Mad Scientist' at The Thiagi Group,[28] an organisation whose mission is to help people to improve their performance effectively and enjoyably. Internationally recognised as an expert in multinational collaboration and active learning in organisations, Thiagi has lived in three different countries and consulted in twenty-one others.

In practice, a group of people – and ideally there should be more than sixteen – are divided into groups of four, with a table per group. Each table gets a set of playing cards and a set of instructions. The picture cards are taken out of each deck before they are given to each table. Therefore each table will have a set of cards consisting of the number cards (two to ten) and the Ace (A). There are four suits in each deck. The purpose of the game is to see who at the table can win the most rounds. After a mock round to allow everyone to get comfortable with the game and the rules, the instructions should surreptitiously be removed.

One critical rule of this game is that no talking is allowed while the game is being played. After an agreed time, typically about five minutes, the winner at each table moves up a table and the loser down a table. The facilitator can at random assign numbers to the tables.

---

[28] More information can be found at http://thiagi.com. There are also several books available with training games and information on how to design your own training games.

Therefore for the second round some tables will have two new players and the first and last table one new member each.

This is usually where the fun starts. The sets of instructions given to each table are very similar and look alike but there are small differences. As the playing starts for round two, havoc usually ensues. It is useful to observe players' behaviour carefully and to continuously remind people that they are not allowed to talk. Some will start looking for the instructions to verify the rules. They are not there any more. Those who wanted to check the rules will either decide that they are correct in their interpretation and the rest are wrong, or they will look somewhat perplexed as they wonder whether they got it wrong in the first place. Some just give up and go with the flow and others forcibly assign rounds to people.

In a group of sixteen, or possibly even twelve players, the game doesn't go much beyond the second round. Should the group be really big, twenty or more players, then one should ideally assign observers, who should be informed of what is happening and the game can then typically go to a third round.

The game is a fun and energising exercise especially after lunch, but the learning is really in the discussion afterwards. Typically there are statements like: 'He is not following the rules', 'He is cheating', or 'He is using different rules'. It is interesting to note that the winners usually have more confidence and are more inclined to want to force the situation, whereas the losers are reserved and seem to feel that they are losing because they are not getting the rules right.

The personalities in the room are also shown up, with the more assertive types forcing the game and the more reserved types being inclined to go with the flow. Often there is at least one person who quickly catches on to what is happening, observing for a while and then adapting to the new rules and quietly playing to win.

The post game discussion can be extended by having the group describe times in their lives when they realised that the rules were unexpectedly different. These rules can be as simple as differences in how we are brought up: do you walk into someone's house and sit down or wait to be asked to sit down? Do you interrupt people to greet them or is that considered rude?

There are no longer hard and fast rules for these things today. Cultures are becoming more and more integrated as people mix, travel and work in different countries. I often suggest to a group that they should ask, clarify, and then agree what rules would work for them.

And to remember that Anaïs Nin said: *'We don't see things as they are, we see them as we are.'*

Games for Team Building

Michael Cooper

As you read through this book one thing that should be abundantly clear is that we are all firm believers in experiential learning. Human beings learn most powerfully when they have experienced something with all of their senses. How better to bring the senses into the team facilitation than through games? Many team builders have had tremendous experiences in changing teams' behaviours just through the use of games. As coaches we do a lot more, of course, but we often use games and activities as one of our tools.

One of the things to keep in mind is space and size. Team builders often have access to large open areas and expensive equipment. Most coaches do their work in boardrooms and conference centres so space and size become an issue. I have had tremendous success with small and relatively cheap equipment. I would like to give some examples and explain how these can be used to best effect.

I am by no means a team builder and this is not a comprehensive list of games or activities but merely examples of some of the games I have found effective. Google 'team building activities' or go to the bookstore and purchase one of the many books available. Most of the equipment can be bought or made by someone with a little handyman experience.

Some points to keep in mind

- Practise the activities before you use them in a team environment. It could be very embarrassing if a team can't find the solution and then turns to you only to find that you don't know either.
- Keep it safe. Some activities require people to support or carry others. I don't use any like this, but if you do please keep in mind that you will be held responsible if anyone gets hurt.
- Don't just play games for games sake. Choose an activity because it is relevant to the group you are working with or the outcome

you are trying to achieve.

- The real value is not so much in the activity itself but in the debriefing afterwards. This is where the lessons learned are extracted, discussed and applied to the work environment. I have seen some facilitators rush from the activity with little time for debriefing. This is foolish as it is the most powerful component and the most valuable.
- Keep it light. Be vibrant and energetic. Games often push people out of their comfort zone. Your attitude and ability to get people involved is important. If you don't have the personality to pull it off don't do it.
- Don't embarrass people. Make it safe for people to get involved, even those who are more withdrawn. Don't emotionally bully people who don't want to participate but make it seem so much fun that they want to.

Sample Games

Mr Potato Head

Everyone knows Mr Potato Head from Toy Story and you can buy this toy from most toy stores or on the web. It is a shape like a potato and you put the ears, arms and face etc together to make up Mr Potato Head (see photo below). I don't tell the group that they are going to build Mr Potato Head but ask for four volunteers to come to the front to help with an activity.

I seat the four volunteers around a table and then blindfold them. At this point I take all the pieces you need to build Mr Potato Head out of a bag I have kept out of sight and dump them on the table in front of the four. I ask the audience, which is the rest of the team, to please keep quiet as many of them instantly recognise the pieces and might say something.

Mr Potato Head before surgery

I now tell the four volunteers that the components of an object are on the table in front of them and that I would like them to build whatever it is. Then I step back and watch.

Mr Potato Head well on his way to recovery

The value of the game is that it allows the spectators to analyse how effective the communication of the four blindfolded individuals is. Sometimes it is great, but mostly it is poor, with one person eventually taking over and doing everything themselves. I then discuss how most projects are like this. We are trying to build something that we are unsure of and each one of us usually has to carry out a part of the whole. How we communicate affects the quality of the end product. It is also useful to ask the question: Which is more important, the process or the product? It is very relevant to some teams where either the product or the process is pushed at the expense of the other.

This is a cheap, lightweight, portable game. It is fun and safe and only takes about ten minutes. And it has a number of applications in the business environment.

Nail Balance

This is a game that seems impossible at first. It is simple to construct. All you need are about twenty four-inch building nails from a hardware store and a solid block of wood. Nail one of the nails into the wood so that it is standing upright and you are ready to go. I give the group the block with the nail in it and the other nails and tell them that the object of the game is to balance as many of the loose nails as possible on the head of the upright nail. They may not use any other materials and the 'construction' must stand alone without any support from them.

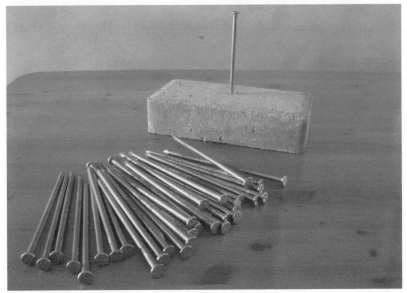

Their first attempts make it seem an impossible task because the nails keep falling off. I then tell them that the solution allows them to balance at least twenty nails on the head. That really gets them worked up!

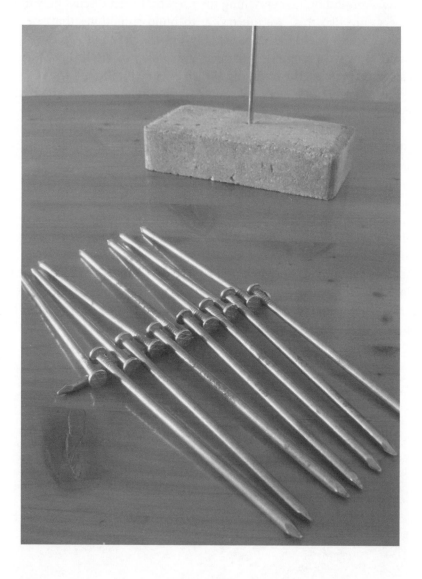

This is a great game for developing lateral thinking and also putting the team under a little stress. In today's hyper competitive workplace people don't like a problem they can't solve easily.

The solution is interesting. Look at the photos. It requires you to create the structure next to the nail first and then lift it into position.

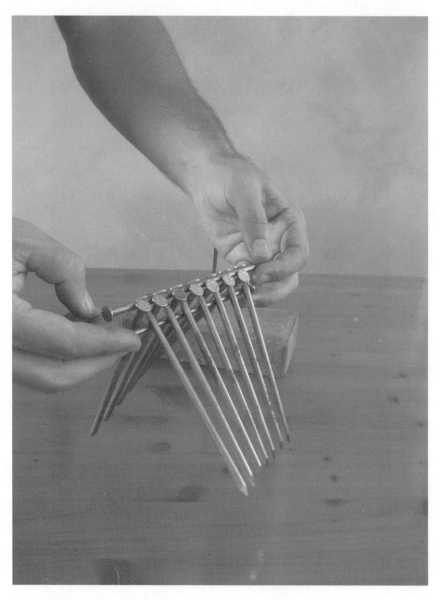

Lift carefully and place on nail

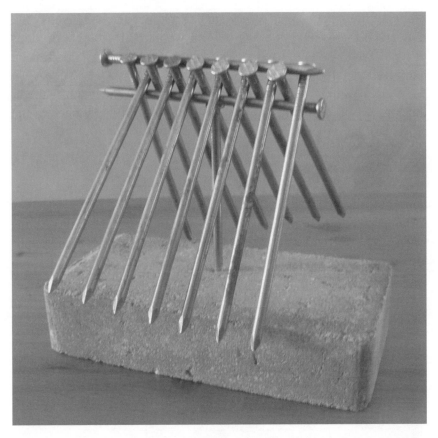

The finished article. I have my anchor nail in a brick instead of a wooden block

The learning opportunities are many. I like pointing out that trying to pile one nail on top of another (the most common method) normally ends in the nails coming crashing down. If you build the structure carefully you can balance a huge number. Our lives are like that – we try to cram in more and more and still remain balanced. It is amazing, though, how much you get done if you stand back and look in a structured way at what you are trying to accomplish. Balance is possible even if it doesn't seem so at first.

I also like the way this game creates conflict and how the group quickly sorts itself into the very proactive people who want to try and keep trying without really thinking first, and the very reflective ones who withdraw and sit and watch the others. It is useful afterwards to ask people which they felt themselves more inclined to do. You will probably find they act in a very similar manner in their teams. You may ask if this is always effective. Can we accommodate both kinds of style? I am also interested in seeing how quickly the group gives up and asks for the solution.

A great game that is cheap, mobile (you can put it in a briefcase), quick to set up and play, but has lots that you can apply back to the workplace.

The da Vinci Bridge

Leonardo da Vinci gave us so much. Did you know he designed a team building game too? No, it wasn't really him – but one of his drawings for a portable bridge made of logs has inspired one. He designed this bridge to be portable so an army on the move could cross rivers easily. We do not know if it was ever used in this way but I love building it in class as an activity.

You will need ten long dowel sticks with grooves cut in them as shown in the illustration below.

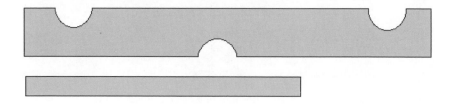

You then need five shorter dowels with no grooves. They should also be of a smaller diameter. Build the bridge at home and note how big a distance your bridge can span.

In the session I place two books on the floor or two desks this distance apart. Then I ask the team to build a bridge using only the sticks I have provided to bridge the gap.

The pieces

The learnings from this are very similar to the ones for the Nail Balance above. I really like it, though, because it is so visual. If there is a big team that needs to be involved the Nail Balance can become rather crowded, but this is not such a problem with the bridge because the scale is much larger.

Getting started

The solution

Awesome! I like to point out to teams that the best solutions are often simple and sublime.

Count to Six

Some activities are designed purely for fun. This is one and it can be used as an energiser or ice-breaker. It may look easy but it challenges us because it needs whole brain functioning and helps to awaken the whole brain. It was found in a book by Sam Sikes and John Irvin.

Get the team to stand so that they are all facing you. The view below is with the facilitator seen from behind. The facilitator shows the different *right hand* positions as he counts up to six.

Once the team has mastered this, show them the *left hand positions* as you count up to six.

Now the fun part starts. Make them count to six with *both hands.*

Start slowly and then speed up. I guarantee absolute pandemonium with everyone laughing and relaxed. Some take it very seriously and want to make it competitive. This usually makes it even funnier. This is one you really need to practise at home. Your husband or wife might think you are crazy, but rather that than stand in front your team and get it wrong!

I got some of these games from a book called *Team Building Puzzles* by Anderson, Cain, Cavert and Heck. Have a look around; there are many books and websites with great ideas. Try some. It will add an element of spark and fun to your team coaching sessions.

Building and Benchmarking Coaching Conversation Skills

Helena Dolny

One of the outcomes of team coaching that many coaches will want to achieve is to leave team members more aware of the skills they apply in their conversations with one another. In peer conversations between team members the need for problem solving, for exploring a way forward around an issue, is common. It is also probable that team members are line managers and have direct reports with whom they have performance coaching conversations.

Listening and questioning practice are often built into team coaching designs because of the need to build the coaching and relationship skills that will sustain the team into the future. Introducing people to a simple model for a coaching conversation has proved to be a constructive contribution. Introducing people to the idea of 'benchmarking' is helpful because they can begin to rate their progress as they pay more attention, practise and get better at certain skills and behaviours.

Listening

Listening is the foundational skill; the art of questioning is complementary. If someone is listening very well, the right question is likely to emerge, more so than if they are absorbed in their own thoughts wondering which clever question they might ask next.

The Transforming Team Meetings case study in Part Two (page 88) describes the setting up of Thinking Pairs around a specific topic. The simple exercise that precedes it of practising closed, leading, and open questions creates awareness. Team members can be introduced to the concept of Listening with TING which is the Chinese character for 'listening'. The calligraphy for 'listening' pre-modernisation and simplification was a composite of symbols that included the ear, the mind, the eyes, the heart and the symbol for I.

Ear   Listen with your ears
         To hear the word, the tone, the pitch

Mind   Listen with your mind
         To understand
         To analyse, and to broaden perspective

Eyes   Listen with your eyes
         To see the facial expression
         To read the body language, and
         look at the 'window of the soul'

Heart   Listen to your heart
         To feel the emotions
         To empathise
         To respond

Coaching conversation models: structured and purposeful

The coaching literature and coaching companies offer us a variety of coaching conversation models. The practice is to come up with a memorable acronym, which provides a guide through the suggested steps. John Whitmore's championship of Graham Alexander's GROW model has made it one of the most well known and widely used:

G	Goal
R	Reality
O	Options
W	Wrap Up

If you are coaching in a company, and there is a wish to create a common language, then you need to find out which is, if any, the preferred model. If no preference is indicated, then you need to think what may work best situationally. Identify the culture shift you are hoping to contribute to; which model will best serve that purpose?

	Original	Adaptations
C	Contracting	+ Commitment, Connectivity
L	Listening	+ Listen, and Listen some more
E	Exploring	+ Ease, Empathy, Encouragement
A	Action	+ Accountability
R	Review	+ Reflect, Record

For example, an organisation of action-orientated doers, with few reflective strengths, might find the CLEAR model serves them better in terms of culture shift, because it emphasises the listening and exploratory part of the conversation. Peter Hawkins developed this model in the early 1980s. You can see how acronyms lend themselves to adaptation – unless of course they're trademarked, copyrighted, etc.

Other models are CIGAR and FRAME. You can find even more: DEFIE by David Lane; OUTCOMES was created by Allan Mackintosh. Google 'coaching conversation models' you can lose yourself in thousands of references.

C	Context and Current reality
I	The Ideal is scoped out
G	Gaps between current reality and the ideal
A	Actions and Accountability
R	Review and Reinforcement

CIGAR is the model developed by the Full Potential Group in the UK. www.fullpotentialgroup.com

F	Focus each interaction
R	React non-judgementally
A	Ask thought-provoking questions
M	Monitor progress and learning
E	Encourage continued growth

The overwhelmingly positive attribute of the above models is that they make people think more purposefully about how they can navigate their way through a coaching conversation. They can make people think more carefully about the composite steps. Perhaps there will be more holding back, less of a hurry to offer unsolicited advice and resolve for others, and more willingness to listen. There are complementary tools that can powerfully assist the conversation further. A particularly strong tool to offer to team members is Argyris's Ladder of Inference, developed by Chris Argyris, which proposes that we become more explicitly aware of the assumptions we deduce from data, and the meaning that we derive in consequence of the assumptions we've made.

Coaching conversation skills

There are three sets of two-sided skills that it is useful to get people to pay particular attention to.
- Listening and Questioning
- Self Awareness and Awareness of Impact on Others
- Giving and Receiving Feedback

If possible, get the team to benchmark themselves and choose a focus area of improvement, and thereafter commit to journalling their experience of conversations in which they've been conscious of their need for these skills and to record their reflections on what went well, and what they may still feel they can improve upon. What is offered below is a work-in-progress benchmarking for the above skills. There is no reference for the following tables. They're made up, influenced by much reading, and contributions, and will be improved by their use and feedback.

	Listening
5	Catalytic listening. Coach talks 20 per cent or less of the time. Strong eye contact, listener never interrupts. The listening is catalytic and elicits insights as evidenced by an exclamation or 'aha' moment, as well as supportive voice and body language. Silence recognised as a powerful question. A good listener will hear the unsaid as well as what has been said, and may pose a question about the unsaid.

4	Attentive listening. Coach talks, at most, 20-30 per cent of the time. The direction of the conversation is more clearly in the hands of the coachee. The facial expression is one of interest in the thinking of the thinker. There is eye contact, head nodding, the body posture is appropriate. There is verbal acknowledgement in the wording of questions respecting the choice of words of the coachee. There is no interpretation or judgement in the framing of the questions.
3	Coach talks 30-40 per cent of the time so they are still actively contributing their thoughts. They are skilled at dialogue. They do not interrupt, their body language and eye contact is supportive.
2	Coach talks 40-60 per cent of the time, more attentive, but there is a lack of full concentration as evidenced by asking for information to be repeated, by paraphrasing what the person has said, substituting their own words for the words of the speaker.
1	Inattentive listening. Coach talks 70-90 per cent of the time. They are more absorbed in their own thinking on the issue than truly listening to the thoughts of the speaker. Interruption and finishing the sentences of others is not uncommon. Their ego is in the way of their listening.
0	Distracted listening: Moving around, doing other activities (packing a bag, typing, tapping in text messages on cellphone), lack of eye contact, irrelevant or disassociated questions that confuse the client.

	Questioning
5	Generative questioning. The ability to ask open questions, and appropriately repeat those questions in a manner that generates a drilling down to new insights and reflection in the coachee.
4	Open questions. Questions that truly request the thoughts of the coachee, and may assist exploration of the subject matter.
3	Contextual questions. Questions that the coach asks in order to get more information about context – not necessarily useful to the coachee, who is already the expert of their own context.
2	Closed questions which may simply result in monosyllabic yes or no answers.
1	Leading questions: a more nuanced version of telling. The questions contain the answer in the formulation of the question. Quite often can be a directive statement with a 'don't you think?' tagged on to the end.
0	Telling – no attempt to question, the coach goes straight into advisory mode.

	Self-awareness
5	Ability to understand your emotions; to bring emotions to conscious awareness. Ability to shift to more empowering emotions through choice. There is a sensitive awareness and ability to choose to shift to the emotional expression that will best serve you in the situation.
4	Ability to get a broader perspective of what emotions are affecting self, with a greater acknowledgement and awareness of the interpersonal and systemic impact on self.
3	Ability to identify and understand emotions and the contributing factors to the generation of that state of emotion.
2	Some thinking about self beginning to happen: an emerging ability to identify the emotion being experienced.
1	Experience the event with an absorption as to how it affects self, with almost no awareness of how own behaviour attracts and/or generates a response from others. For example, 'He was rude to me', with no self-questioning as to what one might have contributed to elicit the rudeness.
0	Experience an event as is – with no awareness of how one's own mental state impacts on one's own behaviour. And a total lack of self-consciousness about how one's way of being or doing impacts on the lives of others. (Artists are sometimes accused of being so self-absorbed that they fall into this category!)

	Awareness of Impact on Others
5	Self-awareness of positional power and ability to create ease. Aware of the interaction within broader life context, thoughtful, the other person leaves the interaction feeling validated. Welcomes feedback from the other.
4	Can identify appropriate tonality and words required when interacting with others by interpreting body language, tonality and context.
3	Consistent ability to identify appropriate behaviour to fit the situation.
2	Sincere acknowledgement and empathy but falling short in appropriate follow-up.
1	There is some ability to recognise that their action will impact on others but self-centredness and being lost in their own emotions overrule sensitivity to others. This results in an inability to respond with an appropriate intervention, words or style.

0	Lack of insight, inappropriate tone or wording. The focus on self is always back to self, whatever the topic; there is an inability to focus on others. There is no awareness of how self-absorption generates negative response from others.

	Giving Feedback
5	The intention of support and generosity is paramount: the positive is emphasised. The giver of the critical feedback offers it as though it were a precious gift. Ease is created to pursue the exploration of a way forward.
4	Factual, the recipient can identify measured steps for improvement, balanced, open to discussion with the strong intentionality for development and support of other.
3	Procedural, accurate and factual but some more specifics required.
2	Accurate, but includes subjective personal judgements of behaviour.
1	Opinionated, not objective, not balanced, not open for discussion, has 'attitude'.
0	Subjective, non-factual, can be with punitive intent, rather than the intent to help the person learn.

	Receiving Feedback
5	Actively soliciting feedback and creating ease for the feedback person to be comfortable enough to give difficult feedback with ease.
4	Reception with curiosity to consider the perception of another, and invitation as to what might be done differently in the future for a better outcome for both parties.
3	Calmly receptive: hearing the person out fully, trying to consider another's point of view.
2	Defensive: justifying the 'why I' approach.
1	Denial and counter-attack: verbally argumentative: may find something to accuse in retaliation.
0	Aggressively reactive: Physical assault (that is physically lashing out on hearing a perceived insult).

TRIAD skills practice

An easy way to begin to get team members to use some of the above skills in the way they work every day is to integrate the introduction of these skills into the Team Coaching Design and set up some team conversations around issues they are dealing with.

In order to get people to be able to be more consciously aware of their manner, the intention they convey, and the specificity with which they give feedback, as well as the practice of receiving feedback, it is recommended that discussions around some issues take place in groups of three, with people rotating the roles of the thinker (coachee), the thinking partner (coach/line manager/peer), and the observer. The TRIAD discuss the issue for a defined amount of time: the observer then gives feedback to the coach/line manager/peer on what they observed. The coach then gives feedback on their experience of receiving the feedback, its quality of specificity and the manner in which it has been offered. The speaker (coachee) then rounds off the TRIAD practice by stating their experience of the conversation and feedback.

It is not as complicated as it sounds. It generates high levels of energy, and huge learning, as people rarely have this opportunity to practise.

A checklist is useful for the participants to tick their observations, and to embed their awareness of the many aspects of a conversation that unfolds before their eyes.

What are you observing?	Tick as often as you notice	Record any specifics you want to give feedback on
Contracting		
Exploring		
Building rapport		
Empathy vs sympathy		
Defining outcome		
Defining next steps		
Accountability		

Recording		
Reflection		
Feed forward		
Listening		
Comfortable silence		
Open questions		
Leading questions		
Closed questions		
Giving advice		
Facial expression of interest		
Voice tone		
Eye contact		
Body language		

Feedforward is the one indicator most people are not familiar with and usually needs explaining. It differs from feedback (which focuses on past events and is thus rather limited and static) in that it deals with the future. Marshall Goldsmith,[29] one of the USA's top executive coaches, vigorously promotes feedforward. He has found that the successful outcomes of his coaching have increased dramatically since he introduced feedforward as part of his coaching model – since those who need to have buy-in to the success of the coaching intervention are included in the process. Goldsmith asks executives both to provide feedforward as well as receive it. In this exercise, people are asked to select a behaviour they would like to change because to do so would make a significant change in their lives. They describe this change to others, and ask for two suggestions for the future that might help them achieve the change. They listen carefully and make notes – this is 'receiving' feedforward. They thank the others for their suggestions without in any way being judgemental (not even in a positive way,

---

[29] Marshall Goldsmith is the founding director of the Alliance for Strategic Leadership and an authority on helping leaders achieve positive change. www.marshallgoldsmith.com.

like 'that's a good idea'). Then they ask others what they would like to change and provide two suggestions for them – this is 'giving' feedforward.

Goldsmith reports that participants find the exercise energising and even fun!

Using image cards to spark reflection

Marti Janse Van Rensburg

The set of cards I use is beautiful. They are created in a typical Chinese calligraphy style made up of black brushstrokes that form stylised images. These are neither entirely realistic nor totally abstract. This is the specific reason why I bought them and why I use them in a team setting or even as an opening in training sessions if the group is not too big.

The I Ching is regarded as the oldest of the ancient Chinese classic texts. It was also called the 'Book of Changes' and is a system of symbols that identifies order in change and is part of the cosmology and philosophy intrinsic to ancient Chinese beliefs. Part of the philosophy is the acceptance of change as being inevitable. Unfortunately in Western cultures and in modern East Asia it is regarded as a form of divination. Hence, and in spite of the explanation as to the use of the cards, this is NOT what I use them for.

The cards are laid on a flat surface – the floor or a table, depending on the circumstances. The group is then asked to identify the card that most speaks to them. I am usually asked by at least one person whether they can pick more than one card. That is fine, and it is interesting to note who asked and who followed suit when the question was answered. They are asked to identify said card(s) with their eyes and not to pick it up or point to it. From time to time I will ask them to consider more specific questions when they look at the cards, such as: 'Where am I in my life right now?' or 'What is important to me or relevant to me in my life right now?'

The rationale behind this is that it is often difficult for people to answer these questions directly, especially in a team coaching set-up where there might be friction within the team. Alternatively, if it is used as an ice-breaker in a new team or with a group of people who are attending a training session, it does not feel like a question that is inappropriately personal. Selecting a card creates a possibility.

Once everyone has selected a card, a volunteer is called for to start.

This person will pick up his/her card(s) and show it to the group while explaining why they picked the card. Once they have finished, they will put the card back as it might have been selected by someone else too. The group is urged to listen, not to make comments or ask questions, and especially not to interrupt the speaker.

It is a lovely exercise to ground the team and also to get them to respect where people are in their lives. Very often, group think starts showing up where several people will pick up the same card with a different reason and explanation. My experience has been that this happens with every group, except that, interestingly enough, it is not the same card(s) that are selected by more than one person from one group to another. The differing explanations for the same card is a very useful example within the team setting, or any other training scenario, of how we look at things differently and how the same thing/card/ word might have a different interpretation.

Any cards can be used for this exercise and they don't have to have the same design signature. I use the I Ching[27] cards because, sub-jectively, I find them beautiful and I like the symmetry in a set of cards with the same handwriting. I have seen semi-abstract pictures and/or photographs used in this exercise with no specific handwriting. The exercise worked equally well. You need to find cards that are not too realistic, though. If the cards are too realistic people will not be able to exercise their own fullest imagination.

---

[27] I bought the cards from a bookstore and the barcode is 9 783905 017137. It is listed as a product of AGMueller, printed in Switzerland.

The Power of Narrative

Helena Dolny

Telling our stories

It's Day 3 of a course with a group of bankers. It's a course called Leader as Coach. The MD Mpumzi Pupuma has commissioned his executive team to do this course alongside him. He is a role model; he is walking his own talk.

The group has been asked well in advance to stay on this evening for an early dinner. The course has included several individual analytical tools, the results of which we've drawn together to see what the composite team profile looks like. Each person has done the Reflected Best Self Exercise[36] and has also completed the Marcus Buckingham StrengthsFinder questionnaire that's included in the book, *Now, Discover Your Strengths*[37] and we've collated everyone's results and looked over the strengths of the team as a whole. We've done the Fred Emery/Robert Rehm work on the six criteria of productive work and people have a very good sense of each other in the workplace and what space they're in at present.

Tonight is being reserved for glimpses of people's personal stories. Our ideal setting for this work would be somewhere in the bush, sitting around a campfire. But here we are in the middle of the city, in a hotel meeting room. The hotel staff has done their best to rearrange the room attractively. The tables form a square and they've laid places for dinner, with candlelight, flowers and music.

The extended executive team comprises more than twenty people. They've been asked to be prepared to talk for five minutes each. The question they were given was: 'What is a challenge that you've faced in

---

[36] The exercise is based on an article, 'How to Play to Your Strengths'; Roberts et al; Harvard Business Review; January 2005. The premise is to ask colleagues and friends for feedback as to what you are good at and when you are at your best.
[37] Marcus Buckingham & Donald O Clifton (2001): *Now, Discover Your Strengths*. Simon & Schuster.

your life that you're proud of the way you handled it?'
The first person begins.

I was twelve years old. I was responsible to tend my father's sheep and goats. This he told me was my future; he would not consider the idea of my going to school. I resolved to run away.

I walked and walked and walked. I arrived in the town. I found the school. I wanted to talk to the headmaster. It was December 8th, but I was unaware of the significance of the date. I discovered that the school term had finished the day before.

I knew I could not go back to the village. If I did, I would always be watched. I would never again have the chance to run away.

I decided to walk to another town where there was a relative that I knew. I would ask for a place to sleep. I did so. I found work as a 'garden boy' and with the money I earned I paid my way through school.

Another person offered the following story.

I was thirteen years old. It was a very hot day. My friend and I decided to go swimming in the river. We left the village and decided to go to a pool in the river further away even though our elders forbade our going to this place. We were having a lot of fun, jumping, laughing, splashing, and teasing one another.

Suddenly I heard a noise, Ka, ka kah, ka, ka, kah. I thought it was an army helicopter. I jumped out on to the bank to look up at the sky. There was nothing in the sky. I heard the noise again, Ka, ka, kah. I looked around. I watched a crocodile swallowing my friend.

I wondered what to do. No one had seen us leaving the village. I could return home and say nothing, and no one would ever know we had broken the rules. No one would know how my friend had disappeared.

I decided I could not live with myself if I were to say nothing, that it was better for me to go to the village and own up to what had happened and take any punishment that was forthcoming.

I returned and told the story. Telling his parents was terrible. The village shaman took us all to the river pool and performed a ritual with special herbs to communicate with the river spirits. The ceremony allowed us to make peace with what had happened.

Another person told a story about dealing with racism in the country and having to claw their way into a career in banking through employment in South Africa's 'homelands' because blacks were not allowed to hold managerial positions in 'white' South Africa.

Another person spoke of falling in love while still a student, their wish to marry and their parents' total disapproval. They described their decision to go ahead, and their struggle to make a life without parental support. There were long hours of studying and part-time jobs, but they succeeded.

There were more than twenty stories. By the time the group parted company the air was palpably thick with emotion and respect for one another, every one of them awed by the challenges that their colleagues had successfully encountered.

The next morning was the last day of the course. When the day began with a check-in, the view was expressed that the sharing of their personal stories had shifted something among them. They reflected on all that they had learned about one another during the other team analysis exercises. They were unanimous that, while everything had been useful, it was the evening's storytelling that allowed them to see each other as truly human with deeply held values which manifested in the stories they told.

The power of storytelling is well recognised. As above, it is used as a tool for connecting. It is also often used as a tool for healing; the telling of a story can be therapeutic,[38] as was witnessed in the hearings of South Africa's Truth and Reconciliation Commission, when people's stories were heard and people's truths were told.

Stories are also used as a learning mechanism; we learn from fables, we learn from each other's stories. It's even said that an office machine company has written its maintenance manual in the form of a collection of stories, because this is more accessible to the technicians than traditional repair manuals.

---

[38] John McLeod (1997): *Narrative and Psychotherapy*. London: Sage Publications.

Journalling

Marti Janse Van Rensburg

Coaches often ask the people they work with to keep journals. They are trying to encourage people to reflect on their experience in order to be able to step back, analyse, consider doing something differently, and then committing to experiment with a new way of doing. It's doing the Reflective Observation part of Kolb's adult learning cycle in writing. It can be especially useful for people whose strengths lie in the doing, and they need to be very intentional in their efforts to make themselves sit back and reflect in order to work out how to do something differently.

Journalling therefore supports ongoing learning. It is not the same as keeping a diary of daily events because it calls for more than a recording of what happened, and it calls for reflection.

Khatija Saley describes the purpose of journalling as follows:
- The objective of keeping a journal is to create self-knowledge, reflections and learning as it provides access to the inner self.
- Journalling involves keeping personal records of observations and reflections about your thoughts, feelings, and actions.
- You can monitor your thoughts, feelings and behaviours, particularly in the context of learning new skills.

Benefits:
- Access questions and solutions more easily
- Develop new and broader perspectives on self and others
- Clarify goals, plan their intervention and track implementation
- Monitor new skills and behaviours
- Develop self-awareness of self-limiting beliefs
- Understand how you learn best
- Integrate life experiences

I always give all my coaching clients a journal, and endeavour to do the same with the teams that I work with. It is difficult for most results-driven executives to just reflect. I therefore suggest that the journal be used to assist with the learning cycle and process. I have found that the clients who escalate their learning the most are the ones who make good use of their journals. An example would be a client who never goes anywhere without his journal. If he is sitting in a meeting and has an idea or thought or emotion that he wants to explore, he will make a cryptic note in his journal and will reflect on it at a more suitable time. He will then (at the more suitable time) also consider what his theory or concept might be, and will plan what to do next, whether it be to get more information or to do something differently or perhaps it will just be a reflection and learning about himself. When he reads a book, he will jot down his thoughts, questions and reflections in his journal.

Another client used her journal in a similar way. After a period of time she reread it and used it to celebrate her journey and growth. Change is mostly incremental, much like a child growing up. If you see the child every day you do not notice the change and growth as vividly as someone who sees the child every couple of months or once a year. Using a journal can be a powerful celebration tool, especially when you feel that you have been working really hard and you have a bad day when you feel that the effort is not paying off.

I therefore ask clients to use their journals not only for reflection, but rather to write down anything they want to – observations of behaviours and emotions for later reflection, questions and ideas for later exploration, planning of changes and goals, as well as the tracking thereof and the celebration of achievement. Sometimes the journal is even used to clarify thinking. With my new generation and techno-geeky clients, I suggest that they create a journal on their computers. It does not always have to be in paper format.

Writing in your journal can open up new possibilities for creating meaning in your life. Writing helps us to crystallise our thoughts and makes action more likely. Some say that the best book they have ever read is the one they wrote for themselves.

The Effective Use of Video and Sound in Team Coaching

Michael Cooper

Haven't we all become video clip junkies in recent years? Every day someone sends me a clip of something by email. Youtube has become one of the fastest growing websites since it was founded in 2005.

I am constantly on the lookout for new, funny, interesting or motivational video clips. I like to try to find new ones as most people have seen the really good ones.

How can you use video clips to enhance your team coaching and training? I use them in a number of ways.

Energy

Use videos to create the right energy in the room. Sometimes you will find that people are tired or that the energy in the room is low. In my experience, this often happens after lunch or as the group returns from a break. At times like this I try to have a funny or inspirational video set up to run as soon as everyone has returned. I find this gets everyone's attention back in the room and away from the calls they have just made or the conversations they have been having. Having a really great laugh together is one of the most unifying things you can do.

At other times in the day if I sense that things have maybe got a bit too serious, or if people's attention is wandering, I will play a quick video clip (sixty seconds or less) to invigorate the group. If you look at the different learning styles of people you will see that many today have well developed visual learning styles. We like to *see* things. This may be driven by the high amount of visual stimulus most of us receive every day through the media. I feel that these short bursts of the visual throughout the day exercise different parts of the brain from those involved in listening and talking and so balance those with a visual learning style.

Motivation

There are some very powerful short videos available on the web if you are willing to spend time searching for them. I recently showed a class a video of a young American who was born with no arms or legs. He joined the school's wrestling team and won a number of competitions against able-bodied wrestlers despite his handicap. The video was less than four minutes long, but its message was incredibly powerful. I could have spent thirty minutes talking about not making excuses, or on making the most of what we are given, but the video accomplished this much more powerfully and elegantly than I could have.

Another video I downloaded from the web was about a young autistic boy who attended a 'normal' school as part of its special education programme. He loved basketball and served as their team ball boy, picking up things and cleaning up after the players. The coach decided to let him play as it was the last game of the season and the team was in the lead. In ten minutes he scored 21 points. The crowd went wild.

Now I could speak at length to a class or a team about teamwork and using opportunities when we get them, or about having unused skills, but I have never had people cry when I speak. This five-minute video had half the class in tears at the end. Such is the impact of video. It touches us at an emotional level that is very powerful. Also, each individual is able to take their own message out of it, so it always fits.

I have also used videos to help get people back into sessions if they seem to be taking a long time to return and settle down. I start playing some funny or inspirational video about three minutes before I expect the rest of the group back. People hear the noise and come in to see what is going on. Their curiosity drives them. They enjoy the video and by the time it is finished I have all the group seated and ready to begin again. If the video has been funny they are often laughing and so are relaxed and ready to continue.

How to use them

Keep videos short. If you are being paid a lot of money to facilitate a team coaching and you spend half the day showing funny videos, people tend to get irritated. I have found that funny videos should be two minutes or less. More inspirational videos that have a message and move the group towards their goal can be up to five minutes long, but never use more than two of these per day.

Be professional. Don't sit and fiddle with your laptop. Have the clips lined up and ready to go at the push of a button. Get yourself a good quality wireless mouse and learn how to use it efficiently. Buy a really good set of laptop speakers and take them with you. Most videos have sound and the speakers on the laptop are not adequate unless the group is really small. Many good conference centres have audio systems and it is easy to play the sound through them. Get there early and try it out. I have found some video projectors incompatible with my laptop. I always carry my presentation and video and sound clips on a memory stick which I keep separate from my laptop so that I can use the conference centre's PC if necessary. And if my laptop should be stolen or packs up I can quickly make another point.

Keep searching for new videos as they lose their impact if they have been seen before.

Always use videos judiciously. They are very powerful for getting a message across but lose their power if you overdo them or they are so long that the group loses interest.

I have often had people come up to me after a session to ask me to send them the videos so they can watch them again or use them with other team members.

Music

I also use music in all my sessions. I find that having a loud upbeat song to call people back to attention after a break acts as an anchor and gets their minds ready for work. Most of the people I have asked enjoy music played at a low volume during exercises when they are writing or thinking. I always ask if they mind if I play music and have never had a group that said no. Try to pick relatively modern and common music. This is not the time to break out your classical or heavy metal MP3s. If your music differs too much from what is mainstream it will distract rather then add to the sessions.

I would like to challenge you to play a little with video and music and see how it can transform team meetings, training and team-building. If you find any really great videos please email them to me.

Closing Words

Helena Dolny

This third section of the book has reviewed tools that allow individuals to take stock of themselves, to truly look at themselves. The tools include Journalling, The Enneagram, and Kolb's and Honey and Mumford's Learning Styles Preference.

There are other tools that begin with the individual, but then the results of the team can be collated and the team can consider who they are in relation to one another, and what the implications are of their combined skills, qualities and experiences. The Fred Emery/Robert Rehm work is very powerful in this sphere. Buckingham's Discover Your Strengths can be powerful if the team works out how it can leverage the information. Buckingham makes the all-important point that an innate talent doesn't come to fruition unless it's developed and that embedded practice turns it into a serious asset!

There are tools that are possibly more playful in their doing, such as vision boards, or painting images or compositions representing the future. These can help individuals clarify their own perspective, or the paintings/vision boards in combination can contribute to creating a shared team vision.

Other tools are both playful and serious in a different way. The team experience of building the Da Vinci Bridge, or the Nail Game and the Barnga Card Game are often both tense and humorous while teams jostle their way to a solution, or discover they have been making assumptions about the rules of the game which are not actually true. The facilitated discussion after the game of who took on what role in the team, or how it is that in real life we make assumptions about one another or the rules of the game, can be a powerfully revealing team learning experience.

In wrapping up the review of our section on tools, it's clear that coaches use a range of different tools in their team coaching work. They make choices according to the circumstances of the team and their own professional strengths to determine which tools are most comfortable for them to work with.

The metaphor of the coach as an artist can be extended if we consider that artists work in different media: oils, pastels, charcoal, collage and so on. Their choice is both situational and in alignment with their talent.

PART FOUR

Sustainability, Measurability and Design Generics

Introduction

Helena Dolny

Parts One to Three of this book were outcomes from the Quiet Mountain gathering. This last part is a post Quiet Mountain reflection on the issues that remain challenges for our profession. What can we as team coaches put in place so that our work is not 'an event' but has legacy, that its impact is integrated in the way of being of the team so that greater sustainability is secured. What about measurability, the return on investment, which must consider not just the direct costs of venue, travel, materials and so on, but the indirect costs of days out of the office of an entire team. Some of us have worked with teams of over twenty people for four days over a period of four months. A hundred-plus people days spent away from the activity of business is a huge investment.

And, lastly, once we reviewed all of the different case studies and the wide range of tools that we used (a range which we presented as premium favourites, tools we enjoy using and find effective, rather than trying to gather THE comprehensive collection), is there anything useful to be said about a generic approach to design?

The next three sections deal with these issues: sustainability, measurability and exploring the possibilities of a generic approach to designing a team coaching intervention.

1.   Sustaining Team Performance: the Teamwork Guide

Robert Rehm's guide,[39] adapted by Helena Dolny

Keep in mind that team design is never really finished. When you think you have your team organised just right, something changes. Maybe new people join the team, or the nature of your product or service changes, or the market changes your production requirements.

If Jon Katzenbach and D K Smith's definition of a 'team' is applicable then this teamwork sustainability guide might work for you – with adaptations, of course, by you and your team to suit the specificity of your situation. *'A small number of people with complementary skills, who are committed to a common purpose, performance goals and approach, for which they hold themselves mutually accountable.'*[40]

Robert Rehm's work suggests that a team should make explicit their expectation of the following areas of interface:

1. Team boundaries
2. Team goals
3. Team ground rules
4. Team information systems
5. Team coordination
6. Team skills development plan
7. Team work processes, and
8. Team space requirements

It is also suggested that periodically a team should revisit their scoring on the Six Criteria of Productive Work to check their progress. Rehm's

---

[39] Robert Rehm, *People in Charge: creating self-managing workplaces*, Hawthorn Press, 1999. Rehm's work is written primarily for a team that strips out the bureaucratic supervisory control layers, referred to as 'redundancy of function'. The team consists of people who work interdependently to contribute to the whole. The team leader position may be a rotating one. The delegation of responsibility and accountability is at such a level that the concept of the usefulness of hierarchy is challenged. In the adaptation of this work there is an acceptance of a prevailing status quo of hierarchy, and the team coaching process affirms the leader. Productive Work: the Six Criteria are used to take stock of a team and determine to what extent it is working optimally, and what can be done to optimise. Rehm's *Start Up Guide for Self Managing Teams* emphasises the desirable nature of adult to adult relationships in the workplace versus parent to child relationships which are more likely to proliferate in hierarchies.

[40] J R Katzenbach & D K Smith (1999): *The Wisdom of Team: Creating the High Performance Organisation*. London: Harper Business.

work was originally drafted for use by self-managing teams, but a great deal of what he covers is relevant to any team working on how to optimise its performance.

1. Team boundaries: decisions and tasks belonging to your team

Teams need clear boundaries defining what the team can and cannot control and coordinate. Boundaries are limits to the area of responsibility given to the team.

For example, there are some 'givens', such as organisation policies, government laws and regulations, and union contract limitations that your team cannot ignore. No team can decide for itself to ignore a law or regulation, or change the specifications the customer expects to see on the product or service they are buying.

So identifying your team's boundaries helps you understand what decisions you can make, and which decisions need to be negotiated with management or others in the organisation. Decisions may include production schedules and goals, hiring new team members, as well as assignment of team members to daily jobs.

You may also need to identify tasks that belong to the team. Tasks are the work activities your team performs every day to get the product out of the door or the service delivered to a customer.

Make the following lists to identify your team's boundaries.
- Decisions and tasks completely owned by the team
- Areas outside the team's control, such as legal obligations, organisation policy, or union contract
- Decisions and tasks shared between the team and management, and other teams
- Decisions the team is consulted on, but not responsible for making

You can do this list activity with management in the room, or negotiate with them later. Understand that management will do the same activity to be clear about their own boundaries. So you can expect some interesting discussions when you compare your lists.

2.   Team goals

Team goals answer the question, 'What is the purpose of this team?' Goals keep teams focused on what's important, the reason the team exists. Goals can also help teams continue to develop and learn on the job. Without setting its own goals, no team can be self-managing. There are three kinds of goals:

- Team production or service goals that focus the team on its output
- Team development goals that encourage the team to keep improving itself
- Individual development goals for each team member's desirable future

Here are examples of team goals:

- *We will produce x units by y date with z quality.* The production and service goals measure the number and quality of the product or service.
- *Development goals* focus on and identify measurable team growth and development over time. For example, 'We will have the competence within the team to learn and effectively use the new shared resources software.'
- *Individual goals* help each team member realise their desirable future at work. An example of an individual goal could be, 'Complete the research data module through the distance learning university to improve my capability to contribute to the impact assessment project.'

Begin *team goals setting* by agreeing on a few (3-6) key production or service goals. Make sure each goal is specific, clear, and that it has a time and quality expectation. Negotiate these goals with management. Remember, management might have different expectations from your team. Negotiating means listening, discussing, and being ready to compromise.

Then move on to team development goals and individual goals. Remember, the strategy in the area of individual goals is to provide each team member with a good job and a desirable future. But this does not necessarily mean anyone can do what they want. Your team needs always to balance the desire of the individual team member with the overall goals and available resources of the team.

3. Team ground rules

Teams are most effective when they agree on ground rules for behaviour.

In team meetings, for example, it may be useful to have ground rules that keep members focused on the discussion and respecting the participation of all members. Nancy Kline's Thinking Environment™: Transforming Meetings™ is a process, a set of skills and a way of being that can be learned and applied effectively.

- A more general ground rule might be: 'Arrange for someone to cover for you when you have a scheduled day off'. This kind of rule can help a team manage its consistency.
- Your team should pay attention to developing specific ground rules for managing conflict among its members. In traditional workplaces, managers and supervisors often intervene to take care of conflicts and disagreements. It is better if team members have the skills to manage their own conflicts.[41] Nancy Kline's Timed Talk process can be effective here. Stone, Patton and Heen's process, described in their book *Difficult Conversations*, is more complex, but also highly effective. A one-day workshop is offered to build the skills.[42]
- Be careful setting ground rules. There is a tendency sometimes to make a rule for every problem. Rules are often made to address a problem instead of dealing with the person who had the problem. Rule making can be a way of avoiding conflicts.
- Use the principle of the minimum critical specification as your guide. Minimum critical specification means identifying rules that are useful, their rationale is understood and has ownership; they are indeed essential.
- Make no more rules, limitations or procedures than absolutely necessary for the functioning of your team.

---

[41] Recommended reading on conflict resolution is the Arbinger Institute's 'The Anatomy of Peace: Resolving the Heart of Conflict'.

[42] Douglas Stone, B Patton & S Heen (1999): *Difficult Conversations*. New York: Penguin.

4.   Team information systems

Teams need timely accurate feedback so they know the results of their work. Feedback is information from people, like customers, or from technologies that tell us how we did – both mistakes and successes.

Feedback is timely and accurate when it comes directly to the team from the source, that part of the work process where and when the problem or success occurred.

Feedback and information systems allow teams to measure their own effectiveness so they know how they are performing against their own production or service goals.

Teams need to develop information management systems that help them coordinate their work. They require open, explicit documentation of goals, methods, and responsibilities. Typically, effective teams have charts, graphs, and schedules posted publicly on walls for all to see, or on computer programmes and email.

These are some of the key questions to answer as your team develops its information plan:
- What results do you need to measure?
- What information do you need to have in order to measure the results of your team's work?
- Who has this information now?
- How and in what form should this information be gathered?
- What systems or processes do you need to put in place to gather and analyse information?
- What documentation and publication methods will you use to communicate the results of your team's work? (Wall charts, email, etc.)

5.   Team coordination

A team that is well coordinated is a team that has everything and everyone working together, aligned in the same direction, towards the accomplishment of its goals, as well as the overall goals of the organisation.

Team coordination tasks might include:
- Keeping supplies flowing to the team
- Monitoring feedback system

- Representing team at organisation meetings
- Being the point of contact between the team and other teams and parts of the organisation
- Passing important information across shifts
- Being the point of contact for the team when a member is sick or needs help

The team identifies the tasks it needs to coordinate and decides how best to make sure this coordination is done. The team may either develop a coordination system or rotate coordinating tasks among its members so everyone can become skilled and no one person is overburdened with too much responsibility.

6.   Team skill development plan

It may be appropriate, especially in a service or processing environment, for a team to work out what are the essential skills the team members need to have between them in order to get the job done. The skills matrix is a barometer that tells people how deep and broad its skills are. Create a list of the essential skills, and then take stock of which team members have which skills, together with an indication of the level of competency. It may be that someone is very skilled at the legal part of lodging the home loan papers. Another person does not yet know this area of the work. A buddy system may be an appropriate way to support learning, or a mentoring match; both these will complement whatever formal learning the person has an opportunity to obtain.

To make a skills matrix, start by identifying all the skills and technical knowledge required to get the work of the team done. On a matrix, list these skills as shown in the example below. Place each team member's name across the top. Then compile a collective picture of your team's skill resources by using a simple scale:

- 0 for none of a particular skill
- One tick for an entry level of skill suggesting the person needs on-the-job support
- Two ticks for a sufficient level of skill
- Three ticks for the higher level of skill and experience and disposition, meaning that this person could teach the skill to others

Example matrix

Essential Skill	Tsepo	Justin	Rachmat	Angela	Mai-ene
A	√√	√√√	√	√	√
B	√√√	√	√	√	√√√
C	√√	√√	√√	√√	√√
E	√√	√√	√√	√√	√√√

The matrix indicates team strengths and areas in which it would be beneficial to deepen the strengths, and highlights the need for training so that there is more back-up for the team.

Your team should use the matrix to develop a team development plan. The plan specifies what training team members need to make sure the team meets its goals.

Consider the following questions when doing your team plan:
- Identify the strengths and weaknesses of your team. Where are you under-skilled?
- How much back-up skill does your team require to ensure that it gets its work done in a way that meets your team goals?
- Who needs training in what? List the names of the team members and what training they need.
- Where do you get the training? Can someone on the team do it, or should you go to an outside resource? How much will it cost, and how do you pay for it?

7.   Managing and improving your team's work processes

Teams need to monitor their work processes, continuously resolve problems and look for opportunities to improve the work system. The extent to which they do this will in some part be determined by where the team fits into the company, whether the process flow is a standardised one, without much elbow room being offered to the team, or whether the team is a unit that determines its own process flow to get its work done.

Completing the following task can provide the basis for reflection to consider how to improve the team's work system.

1. Map out your current work processes on chart paper so everyone has a clear understanding of how work moves through the team, from beginning to end. Work processes start with inputs to the team, like raw materials and customer orders, and end with outputs like products and/or services.
2. Brainstorm the process flow. Identify areas that you think can be improved upon. Process problems are any deviation from a quality standard, a malfunction, delay, foul-up, breakdown, or unplanned event that has a negative impact on schedule, quality, or cost.
3. Prioritise your list of potential process improvements, using criteria like impact on quality, cost, or customer satisfaction.
4. When you have identified the key areas of potential improvement, answer these questions for each one:
   • What's the technical issue?
   • What's the impact?
   • What are the causes?
   • How is the issue handled now, and by whom?
   • How might the problem be solved or prevented?
5. Develop an action plan for responding to each key problem. Include a clear description of your problem, your plan for solving or preventing it, and identification of who will work on it and when. Your plan may require fixing the problem or completely redoing the process.

Another way to do this activity is to bring the process to life through simulation, moving through the process step by step. This is particularly useful for teams that are made up of people coming from different parts of the process. In one instance, Robert Rehm found that when people acted out the steps involved in a request for a cheque in one banking institution that he worked with, so many signatures were required in order to reach the end stage of final approval that the absurdity of the process could not be denied.

A new team may have to design new work processes from scratch. This requires a 'clean sheet' approach in which the team maps out on chart paper each step of the 'to be' process, noting work activities and decision points along the way. You can start this process mapping by identifying the end product first. Start with the customer or stakeholder expectations for a quality product or service, then work backwards to identify each step it took to get there.

Regularly review changes and problems that occur in your team's work flow. It's the job of your team to constantly monitor and improve processes so that you can achieve your performance goals and optimise your team's effectiveness.

8.   Team work space and equipment needs

Your team may require some changes in the physical layout of your work space and additional equipment. Teams that pay attention to 'place'[43] as important to their thinking environment require:
- Face-to-face communication
- Opportunity for people to be specific about their personal preferences, for example, (a) 'I need to be able to sit with my back to people to be less easily distracted in an open plan set-up' (b) 'I need good light and a large monitor because of the work I do on tables or figures'
- A work space that has room for private work and team meetings

Carry out the following assessment:
1. Do a current inventory of all equipment, tools and technologies, and work space available to the team.
2. Brainstorm ideas for what work space and equipment to keep, get rid of, and add to make sure that the team has the resources that it needs.
3. Choose those work spaces, changes and equipment needs that are the highest priority for the team.
4. Develop cost assessments and justify the resource needs.

The work space design that fits best for the team's needs may challenge

---

[43] 'Place' is one of the ten components identified by Nancy Kline in *Time to Think* (Ward Lock, 1999) as contributing to creating an environment in which a person or team can do their best thinking. The other components are Attention, Ease, Equality, Diversity, Appreciation, Encouragement, Feelings, Information and Incisive Questions™.

the organisation's normal attribution of space according to status or hierarchy. It is up to the team to present its suggestions to management and negotiate for what the team needs.

Concluding remarks

When your team members are able to implement these guidelines as their default operating system you should be well on your way to optimising their performance sustainably! Remember that your team will continue to develop and evolve over the months and years ahead. The overall goal is for your organisation to become increasingly successful as a result of the increasing participation of its people. In the process, each member of your team strives towards their most desirable future at work.

The ability of your team to optimise their performance will not come about by accident. It will take hard work and diligence on the part of the whole team. Keep reviewing the team tasks on a regular basis, at least every three months, making changes as you go forward. Team learning and development require a good balance of action and reflection. Get into the habit of regularly taking time out to reflect. In team reflection you will discuss what you have been learning as a team, which also means being critical and demanding of yourselves and the organisation.

2.   Measurability: Team Coaching: Approaches to Assessing Business Benefits and the Return on Investment (ROI)

Khatija Saley

There is a paucity of information on the subject of measurability. Team coaching in the business world is in its infancy. How does it differ from other team interventions? Helena, Lloyd and I spent an entire morning talking about this aspect at the beginning. Soon afterwards, I attended a conference[44] at which international coaching doyen David Clutterbuck facilitated a session with the topic under discussion: 'How is team coaching different to facilitation and organisational development?' I am not sure if this one has been resolved in the last three years!

So, the leaders in the field were also still only beginning to dabble with this element of coaching. Team coaching, however, has gained momentum. We recognise that team coaching means many things to many people. Given the impact and scope of such an intervention, we chose to focus on engagement and co-creation of design so that we could establish its value through ensuring 'fit for purpose'. This approach to design would ensure the intervention met the needs of every team. Engagement and pre-work would also be the elements that would offer us the opportunity to measure the impact of the intervention.

Coaching takes place within a context; so too does evaluation. The question of coaching 'for what?' has to be answered. Assessing the benefits of the intervention supports business and the coaching community. Books written on team coaching have not evolved into the arena of evaluating the impact of team coaching interventions. We find ourselves again on the brink of something new. Our purpose in doing this piece is a need to show a comprehensive business rationale to help increase the credibility of coaching by being able to provide a compelling business case – both qualitative and quantitative. The implication of this work is the ability to speak the language of business, influencing the value business assigns to this work.

In researching the topic of evaluation, we have found the following:

---

[44] Oxford School of Coaching and mentoring Conference, Oxford, UK, June 2006

- Attempts at financial calculations. Studies show anything between 15 to more than 500 per cent of ROI, plus intangible benefits. Hard data is often repeated with a focus on process, for example CIPD 2003[45] or ICF 2004.[46] The data calculations would however be considered as tenuous by some, that is, my efficiency is up by 20 per cent as a result of the coaching intervention. As I earn X dollars per year, a twenty per cent efficiency enhancement can be considered to be worth Y dollars. The costs of the coaching intervention were Z, therefore Y/Z will give me the percentage ROI.
- There is not much credible data in the market on ROI, but there is a lot of data on tangible, identifiable qualitative benefits. Data found consists of anecdotal assertions; benefits, views, and case studies. For example, teams which adopted *Time to Think*'s meeting process had this to say:
- We rescued a multimillion dollar product design in 45 minutes (Global Pharmaceutical company)
- We jumped 32 per cent in the National League tables in four months (Creative consultancy)
- By running our meetings in a Thinking Environment™, we reduced by 44 per cent the cost of each decision (National Health Service Organisation)

But as the case studies in this book indicate it is very possible to work with identified outcomes which are measurable qualitatively. Michael Cooper's Meta Coaching described how you get a team to recognise different levels of listening and therefore benchmark the team's progress towards higher levels. Maryse Barak's work often focuses on 'How do you want this team to work differently? What would success look like? How would you know that you have reached there?' Helena Dolny's insert on goal setting provides similar qualitative benchmarking opportunities.

Gathering credible data on your clients is possible provided there is a strong focus on governance and ensuring a memorandum of understanding (MOU) is in place. An important element of the MOU is

---

[45] CIPD 2003 – Coaching Effectiveness Measures Most Commonly Used.
[46] International Coach Federation 2004 Internal Coaching Survey.

an understanding that pre-work must take place to establish baseline data. Just as it was important for Alice to know where she wanted to go in order for directions to be given, it is also just as important to know where you've come from to be able more consciously to recognise the changes and progress made.

The outcomes of a team coaching intervention are defined by the team; the coach often plays a creative and essential role in this process.

The model I chose to discuss here is the one that has outlasted all the others. It was developed by Donald Kirkpatrick[47] in 1959. Because it is well known, I used his four-step model as a starting point to see if it would meet our needs for evaluation.

Kirkpatrick four-level model:

    Level 1. Reaction to the training

    Level 2. Measuring what was learned: Post-training test scores

    Level 3. Is the learning being applied at work? Transfer of behavioural change

    Level 4. What were the results? Organisational results

Based on our research and acquiring a better understanding of how it was used and the results it yielded, we advocate a level before level 1. This level is the engagement/co-creation piece that was referred to earlier. It yields the baseline plus the desired outcomes and therefore the potential measurability of the intervention.

We need to establish a baseline in order to measure progress.

The main steps proposed to secure the possibility of a tangible evaluation are:

- Questionnaires done at pre- and post-intervention level to capture experiences and major impressions. The focus of these is personal efficiency, interaction with others and personal growth. Interviews are also considered where relevant. These could include a self-assessment (including a benchmarking exercise) as well as requesting direct reports and, where required, peer input. It is useful to use measures or interventions already used in organisations such a 360s and multi-raters.

- List the primary benefits that have been identified by the team at the two-hour engagement meeting. Interviews could be used to get a better picture and to include all conditions.

---

[47] Kirkpatrick, D L (1959): Techniques for evaluating Training Programs. *Journal of ASTD.*

- An analysis is done of benefits and costs. Typically, these would include variables of performance improvement, contribution by coaching, confidence in the estimations and the cost of the intervention.
- The last step would be a report. Typical contents would be the executive summary, value perceived by the manager and the team, the business benefits, further proposals and, finally, comments by the client. These are elicited by asking questions such as what is different or what is better since the intervention started.[48]

Additional evaluation approaches

Personal development plans as a consequence of team coaching
There is a common set of competencies and practices that can be developed and used by leaders in their role as 'leader as coach' that will support them in some of their leadership challenges. These are equally applicable to team members. As mentioned earlier, teams often identify, as part of their desired outcomes, the ability to communicate better and the acquiring of coaching skills. These are then expanded upon and defined in the first session. The ability of the team to assess and apply these in the intervention and back at the workplace is the result of an immediate benchmarking assessment that each team member does for themselves, offering an opportunity to reflect on what they want to do differently going forward.

During the three-month intervention (one day a month), attempts to monitor shifts in behavioural applications of learnings and integrate these culminate in a part of the programme that supports each individual to review their values, what shaped their lives, what supported them in achieving their outcomes and what are the identified barriers. The intended goal is to come up with a personal development plan with professional and personal outcomes that will support each one holding themselves accountable to achieving. Outcomes are sustained by individuals having acquired self-coaching skills.

The personal development plan in itself is a piece of evaluation, as

---

[48] Berg, I K & Szabo, P (2005): Brief coaching for lasting solutions. W W Norton & Company, New York.

it is a commitment by individuals. It is to be used for further discussions with reporting managers sustaining individual and team performance aligned to purpose and individual development trajectories.

Referrals and Feedback

Qualitative measures include immediate word-of-mouth referrals. A director and his senior team were engaged in a team coaching session. At the two-day away-break he contacted a colleague. He was aware of some challenges she was experiencing as a result of restructuring. She had a few new team members operating at senior levels, highly qualified and skilled, who were transferred from a strategic unit to an operational area. He texted her from his mobile to share the value his team was deriving from the session. The second engagement was for a director whose team was going through tremendous stress as a result of the economic downturn.

Subsequently I asked one of the directors what his most valuable take away was from the intervention. He said that because of the stress and pressures managers were under, and the constant pursuit of targets, team members rarely got to know one another. This further fuelled tensions as it often is a basis for conflict in teams. He remarked that we do not see each other as people with feelings, hopes and dreams. Organisational cultures require that we are interested in one another only at a cognitive level. The storytelling piece offers fellow team members an opportunity to touch each other at human level. It not only raised empathy for one another, but a humility and deep respect that we saw unfold during the rest of their days together. It took the intervention to another level where peers were more open to collaborate and support each other in a way that we had not seen before. The emotional intelligence (EI) quotient of the team quadrupled. There is a growing body of research on EI that demonstrates that groups can have levels of EI, and when they are explicit in acknowledging and manifesting EI, they perform more successfully.

3. Exploring the idea of a generic design

Helena Dolny, Khatija Saley, Marti Janse Van Rensburg

The experiences presented in this book confirm the need for professional coaches to have flexibility, versatility, artistry, and the imperative to think fast on their feet. As a team coach you may be given time to work with a team for one day only in order to achieve a specific objective. You may be invited to work with a sports team for as little as forty-five minutes, and then if you've succeeded in making a sufficiently good impression you may be invited back again – or not! It could be that the team coaching intervention that you are invited to support spans several months, that the work is holistic and includes business visioning, working out the strategy to implement the vision, and the organisational architecture and consequent team structure that will best serve the implementation. You may have the opportunity to work with a team to develop their awareness of themselves and their impact on others, their commitment to a way of being, and a possible code of conduct – all focused on optimising team performance.

What we've chosen to do here is to show you a generic approach that could be the basic design and checklist to be used with a team that wishes to make serious headway in thinking about how to work differently. We're assuming that there's commitment from the team leader and members to work together for a defined number of days over a period of, let's say, three to four months. The design presented below has a two-day start-up process, followed by three single days (one every month for three consecutive months). The design proposition is to have sufficient time to do foundational work with the team with follow-up days to secure and embed the new skills and their practice.

The design assumed that the generic objective is to enhance team performance, that shared clarity of purpose is essential to that. The team members' greater knowledge of themselves and one another in terms of their talents, the way their brains are wired, and how they are currently thinking and feeling about their work will further assist in creating a synergy of complementary effort. Finally, we are assuming that team members move, that teams in workplaces morph as a norm; the only certainty is change. We would therefore want team members to be equipped to step into their next role with the added skills that will enable self-coaching, as well as having acquired skills and practice of coaching as a leadership or managerial style.

There are several parts to the generic process being suggested:
- The engagement piece: clarification, co-creation, con-
    firmation and commitment
- Pre-work
- Generic proposition for the foundational start-up
- Building in the practice of coaching skills
- Securing sustainability – the team work guide
- The measurability question

The practice of coaching skills and the benchmarking thereof was discussed in detail on page 207, and the team work guide on page 232. The rest will be discussed in more detail in this section.

The engagement piece: clarification and co-creation

The prerequisite for any work we undertake is what we refer to as 'the engagement piece'. It's preferable not to walk in cold to work with a team you don't know. You may have met the team leader, who may be leading a team that's dragging its heels reluctantly into the session, resentful of the time being demanded from them when they are so busy, with so much to do, so many deadlines, and so many emails not yet answered, and more on their way. Winning the hearts and minds of team members to commit to investing time in the belief that they will save time and achieve better outcomes in the future is what the engagement piece is about.

The philosophy behind team coaching – as opposed to facilitation – is that we are also fostering adult-to-adult relationships. Holding to the integrity of the work we do requires that we do not engage only with the team leader. We do not want the team to necessarily follow the lead of the team leader. The team culture and leadership we hope to foster through the team coaching intervention means we want to engage all team members in what we do, how we do it, and what the shifts would be in the team and across the business unit as a result. It is this dialogue that will foster the outcomes we as coaches envisage for the team through the work we hope to do with them.

If the engagement piece results in a co-creation of a design for the team coaching intervention, where the team members know they were heard and have contributed, this will secure a more propitious start for a successful intervention. For example, the leader of one of the teams we worked with had a very different objective to what came out of the team. He wanted the team to focus on understanding one another better, to work on eliminating the internal competition in the team, as well as an explicit commitment to delivery. Team members wanted to work on crafting a vision for the team based on the broader group vision that they felt they had not fully understood. This part of the discussion resulted ultimately in the team, team leader and coaches co-crafting agreed outcomes.

Typically, we have found that teams have not thought much about how team coaching might be of benefit to them. A lot of teams have had 'away days': they may have taken on a challenging activity which meant they had to depend on the entire and diverse resources of the team in order to accomplish the challenge. They may simply have gone abseiling, river rafting, played golf, held a barbecue, played Thirty Seconds, or had a day of stress relief lectures and massage. These activities can contribute tremendously to the team's self-knowledge and the quality of rapport between its members. The company's expenditure on a pleasurable away-day activity can contribute to employees feeling rewarded and recognised.

The proposition here is somewhat different. The team leader has contacted the coaches, or the leadership development unit, expressing interest, and the coaches (or unit) have requested that time be reserved for a team meeting agenda so that the coaches can meet the team for the possibility to be discussed further. The exact nature of the team intervention design will depend on the outcome of the engagement discussion. It is worthwhile to note here that this initial part of the process, until a proposal is accepted, could either be done by the coaches who will deliver the intervention, or in some cases by the leadership development unit who will, depending on the nature of the intervention, then contract with the most suitable coaches. For ease of reading, the two possibilities will not be noted at all times.

The approach to the engagement meeting is diagnostic and, in assisting the team to reach their diagnosis, fidelity to the Kolb Adult Learning Model is retained. We need people to speak about their

Concrete Experience.

In terms of Reflective Observation, we want them to consider what it is that they have already experienced and identify perceived gaps, or simply what it is that they would like to be better at.

The third step requires Abstract Conceptualisation or, in Action Learning terms, this is the point where we as team coaches present our wares to the participants. We present, as simply as possible, the smorgasbord of what we have on offer, and initiate a debate about what the team thinks will most appropriately respond to their needs. The debate does not need to be resolved immediately. The agenda time allocated may well be up; agreement is reached on a way forward, that a draft proposal with costings will be submitted for consideration and iteration by a certain time line.

The fourth component, Active Experimentation, is the actual process of Team Coaching.

All of the above sounds very straightforward. The likelihood is that it won't be. The participants in the discussion are a diverse group of people with varied experience and opinions about coaching and mentoring, and differing opinions as to the hard benefits of investing in soft skills. The first part of the conversation, the drawing out of people's Concrete Experience seeks to begin the process of creating a common language so that we have a shared understanding of the difference between coaching and mentoring, and what experience and awareness there is, if any, that there are different kinds of coaching for different purposes. Getting people to talk about the coaching and mentoring experiences they have already encountered in their lives and getting them to identify what worked and why, and what didn't work and why, is an important step in this process.

The second step is getting the team to pool their ideas on what they would want as outcomes if they are to invest time in team coaching. A Thinking Pairs exercise to get people to drill down to their considered thoughts rather than top-of-mind brainstorming produces a better quality of suggestions. Doing a round and scribing the desired outcomes on to flip charts allows the team to review the range of suggestions being proposed. If the outcomes are hugely divergent then the task is to catalyse a debate that allows the team to work out what is most important to them.

At this point it will be possible for the team coach to describe, or even give handouts, various possible tools that could be fused into the composite design that best responds to the named outcomes. You can expect different responses and different levels of support for the various suggestions. Your aim is to reach a consensus that has a critical mass of support, and is, most importantly, unwaveringly supported by the team leadership.

If time allows, and if it looks as though it might be necessary to get further information on the team dynamics, then setting up one-on-one discussions with several team members can also be of great use. People are often more comfortable sharing their personal feelings in a one-on-one setting, especially if they know that the detail of the conversation will be kept confidential. Once trust is established in the team, and common issues have surfaced, these same team members are often much more comfortable discussing their views in an open forum. This also allows the coach(es) to adapt their design to accommodate or deal with team issues that did not show up in a team conversation.

From here we move to confirmation of what the process will entail and commitment to the process from all parties. This ideally should be described in an MOU (Memorandum of Understanding) and could also include agreement and commitment to pre-work being done by the team.

Confirming, contracting, pre-work, the MOU and governance

At this stage, the team leader indicates his/her required outcomes for the team intervention and the team engages in discussion to confirm these outcomes, or if need be to adapt them. The next step in the process is to confirm the design of the intervention and to contract specifics around time, structure and cost. Any pre-work that needs to be done by the team needs to be agreed to and an MOU drawn up to act as a measurable of the success of the intervention. The engagement piece has a twofold purpose: firstly, it elicits buy-in from the team, and secondly, it assists with the measurability of the intervention.

Confirming and contracting
The outcomes are defined as immediate high priority outcomes for the team, as well as outcomes that may affect the individual teams

headed up by each of the respective team members of the intervention being evaluated. Long-term outcomes that have a wider impact at organisational level may also be included. These outcomes have to be defined in a way that is measurable. Mike discussed nominalisation and goals that can be benchmarked in Part Two (page 81).

Immediate outcomes are defined at the team level. Common outcomes that have emerged in working with various teams are:

- Team climate, prevailing atmosphere and vision for a better model with a team code of conduct
- Acquiring leadership coaching skills
- Better communication at a team level (including better running of meetings)
- Surfacing and better understanding the skills, experience and expertise of each team member

This step is fundamentally important as it links the initiative to the requirements of the business; more specifically, it provides a baseline, not dissimilar to solution-focused scaling.[49] Solution-focused scaling is a very useful tool to quantify goals that are seemingly qualitative in nature in order to measure progress. An example would be improved communication. If the team can rate themselves on their current level of communication and then be specific (what will you see, hear, feel) in terms of their stated goal, progress can be measured. This is often a challenge.

The engagement piece has resulted in teams being proactive in linking their roles to the objectives or vision for the team and business. It forges a new/revised strategic direction. The intervention has resulted in reshaping the goals and way of working for the teams we have worked with. It offers an opportunity to hammer out and define tangible benefits rather than the quantitative measures that teams so often settle for. It is here that they are committing time and effort and it is opportune to get them to think about success measures. The measures then become meaningful to them. Introducing a second step of more generic measures as a complement has been met with a willingness, not as something we expected agreement on.

---

[49] Szabó, P: *About Solution-focused Scaling: Ten minutes for Performance and Learning* www.solutionsurfers.com

A proposal is sent to the team leader outlining the agreed outcomes, the suggested design of the intervention, costing, pre-work required to be done by the team and possible measures of the outcomes. If need be, the proposal is discussed and revised until it is accepted.

The MOU, pre-work and governance

Once the proposal is accepted, an MOU is drawn up and agreed between the team leader, the coach (and the representative from the company, if necessary). The MOU will state agreed outcomes, when and where the intervention will take place, costing, expected code of conduct from all parties, agreed pre-work for the team to do and possible follow-up sessions. What will not be in the MOU is often the breakdown and detailed measurement of outcomes that might only be determined in the first session, as well as the exact design of the follow-up sessions.

It is essential that the coaching has value-add for the team and the organisation. Defining measurable results is part of the process. Measurable results include the agreed outcomes of the team coaching intervention as well as the evaluation of the coaches delivering the intervention. Evaluating coaches following a defined process categorises coaches into their preferred niche and this information is available on the coach profile. Team coaching is complex and we have to ensure that coaches have the breadth and depth of business acumen and experience and the flexibility to work with a team of possibly highly complex individuals.

After the team coach and manager/leader of the team have explored and refined the coaching outcomes these are shared with the team at the two-day away-break for discussion. All the agreed outcomes are input for the subsequent measurability through a questionnaire process which is described in more detail later.

The following documentation can be designed to support governance and the tracking thereof:

- Proposal to the manager and team
- Coaching memorandum of understanding (MOU) / contract
- Portfolio with team coach profiles
- Evaluation documentation: questionnaires etc
- Pre-work assignments

It is tempting to want to jump in and assist a team without the necessary space and time for reflection and planning of the process. But this often results in teams enjoying a day out of the office but no real change happening in the workplace. Applying the discipline of the engagement and contracting process will result in a more successful intervention that can be measured, qualitatively and quantitatively.

The start-up overnight getaway

This may not be possible! But as a team coach you do have some elbow room of power to contract and to negotiate on the way you are going to work. You know what has worked really well for you. You know that you can say 'no' to the assignment. But let's say that you get an agreement for a two-day one-night getaway. Here is a suggestion of how that could be used, drawing on some of the tools presented in this book.

The start-up will be faithful to the overall underpinning design principles:

- Draw on prior experience
- Deliver on defined outcomes
- Build skills and access to tools for sustainability
- Create enhanced awareness of team strengths and diversity

Prior experience of being in teams: we all have it, and it provides a reference point for people to reflect and consider that should be capitalised on.

Outcomes: Generally, teams do want to work out how they might work better together in the future and thus optimise business performance. Outcomes may or may not include work on team business vision, or this is work that may already have been done. If it has not been done, it needs to be included in the outcomes because a team that does not know where it is going will not be able to figure out how it is going to get there.

Skills and tools: The analytical tools which show us snapshots of ourselves as a team are all very well, but so what? Unless there is an enhanced team relationship capability the work on increased self-awareness and awareness of others may be futile. Hence building in listening skills practice, questioning practice, the giving and receiving of feedback, and a model for issue exploring, and problem-solving conversations are the basis for sustainability of impact into the future.

Diversity is often restricted to awareness of very apparent differences between us: the colour of our skin, possibly our surname will indicate ethnic roots, our gender, and our religion and associated religious practices. These differences seem self-evident and relatively easy to be sensitive to – but even so we've known of teams that planned their overnight getaway for Friday to Saturday, ignoring the issues this would create for Muslim or Jewish members of their team.

In terms of optimising team performance we are suggesting the use of tools that reveal other diversities. In this proposed generic design we propose four: the learning styles inventory, the strengths-finder, the six criteria of productive work and personal narrative.

In terms of scheduling the two days, you are planning a cumulative build-up of shared information in order to arrive at an action-orientated, commitment session as the last part of the second day. You want people to commit to being at dinner together on the first evening and to be willing to share something of their personal story. This can even be done over dinner, if the dining space can be arranged appropriately. Personally, Khatija and I have a preference for doing the six criteria later in the process on Day 2, rather than earlier, which is Lloyd's practice. We prefer the more embedded climate of ease following the narrative evening to precede this piece of work. And what we are presenting is a skeleton framework to which coaches would inject their own signature additions: Ray would bring poetry, Tim would bring videos, Mike likes to use music, Marti might bring cards, Maryse, an appreciation; and then as we've all learned from each other, we all begin to borrow the best of each of us from one another.

Catering for difference in style: Marti's points raised in the section on Honey and Mumford (page 149) are important to keep top-of-mind. The design needs to embody all elements while keeping a certain pace for momentum: there should be enough 'doing' for the activists, enough data to analyse for the theorists, enough reflection time for the reflectors, and enough time dedicated to what to do as a result of reviewing all this information for the pragmatists to be satisfied.

Pre-work: You will have to decide on the appetite and capacity for pre-work. Suggestions are Buckingham & Clifton's StrengthsFinder (each participant needs to buy the book, get the scratch pad code, and do the on-line questionnaire), Kolb's Learning Styles Inventory, and

Kline's on-line Thinking Environment™ questionnaire. You may want to include some benchmarking questionnaires that will allow the team members to track their own progress on certain behavioural issues.

This is an example of a design that takes cognisance of the four principles stated above:

Description	Design	Desired Outcome
Introduction	Personal question related to work, values, something light	A safe non-threatening beginning. Nobody feeling as though they are being put on the spot
Expectations & agenda	Get them personally to state a desired outcome, and check this against the design	Confirmation that the design has the possibility of meeting expectations. If out of kilter, work out how to manage the disconnect
Contracting	Time, breaks, confidentiality, electronic interruptions	Get the group to create and agree their ground rules
Listening skills	Introduction to several of Kline's ten components, focus on listening skills, and types of listening	Greater awareness of the art of listening well, and the power of not interrupting
Prior experience	Thinking Pairs No. 1. When they've enjoyed being part of a team, what was it that worked well?	Identifying the positive on what's working well. If these are put on flip charts they provide a reference point for what the team would aspire to as its own way of working
	Thinking Pairs No. 2. Reflecting on what detracts from a team being at their best	Similarly, taking stock of experience in the room and drawing it out
	Thinking Pairs No. 3. What is one thing that would have to change in this team for you to feel more comfortable and to work more optimally?	This takes people to a more personal, edgy place because they have to name something in the present – whereas up to now they could have been talking generally – so you are creating the possibility of a level of sharing that will serve them

How are we different? What are our learning styles?	Do the Learning Styles Inventory (Kolb) or the Learning Styles Questionnaire (Honey & Mumford) and map out the team's positions on the four quadrants	Get the team to reflect on what their snapshot of themselves tells them. In a delivery team there is likely to be a skewed distribution: is there enough reflective and conceptualisation ability to rethink the way of doing things when necessary?
What talents do we have between us?	Buckingham & Clifton's StrengthsFinder	There is often too much focus on addressing weaknesses, whereas this work focuses on optimising strengths. The team can look at its overall profile and might reconsider their current roles against the mapping. It's interesting for teams to look at their overall weighting. The mapping might indeed show them that it's not surprising that they're having a problem communicating: there's no one among them with a talent for it!
Issue exploring, problem solving conversation model	Introduce the team to a coaching conversation model. We suggest CLEAR because of the focus on listening and exploring before getting action-orientated	This is a performance coaching conversation tool, but is equally applicable to peer conversations to explore issues. Setting up practice TRIADS will give the group the opportunity to practise listening, questioning, and giving and receiving feedback
Identify optimising points of entry	TRIAD work in which each individual identifies something that has emerged for them from the work that day as the subject matter for the conversation	A deeper shared understanding is one outcome. Practice skills is the second
Personal narrative	If possible this should be in the evening. You do not want a twenty-minute life story from everyone. The following has worked well: Tell us of a time in your life when you faced a challenge that you overcame; what were you assuming about yourself that enabled you to overcome this challenge. Four to five minutes is usually more than enough	This exchange brings the group to an intensely personal exchange, revealing each person's uniqueness beyond any typology tool that we can use. There is a personal history that no one person walking the earth shares identically. Asking people to talk of something that is positive, but about a challenge they faced, is revealing, but people can be depended upon to create their own boundaries with what they feel safe to share with others

How do we think and feel about our work and workplace at this point in time?	Six criteria of productive work (Rehm). Team work and learning satisfaction review	The team maps their individual results on to a shared chart. There is contracting for no judgement; how the person sees their own experience is theirs. But the overall review highlights issues that the team needs to be alert to, X is bored, Y sees no desirable future, Z feels a lack of elbow room, A is super content!
How is it that we want to commit to work in the future? Team work guide	Find a team work guide that the team can customise. Either design your own from scratch, or use one like Rehm's to work on as a team activity	Create the areas of teamwork around which the team agrees they would like to have a contract/guide/code of conduct. Create the debate, record the outcomes
What will I do differently to contribute to enhanced teamwork?	TRIADS using the conversation model. Instruction for the person to end up with a focus on Action & Accountability, and Reflect & Record	A personal commitment to what that individual will do differently, and will hold themselves accountable for. Doing this through a TRIAD exercise permits more skills practice. People voice their commitment and are witnessed
Looking back & looking forward	Review the two days. Check accomplishments against the expectations. Review the commitments going forward. Talk about the planned follow-up sessions	Close the loops. Get people to recognise the different parts of the design, and completion of it. Identify what it is that they had said they would still want to address in the future. Acknowledge issues arising which the team wants to pays attention to
Evaluation	Feedback forms may be part of the contracting process with the team. This is the time to complete them	Measurability is a challenging issue in the soft skills arena. Any questionnaire should be customised whenever possible to get the team to identify their progress on the issues they identified
CLOSURE	Ask people what was their most valuable learning out of the two days. Each person shares an appreciation of a neighbouring colleague they have worked with	

Post-work and follow up

This suggested design includes an agreement as to what each individual will commit to as well as agenda items for future sessions. These should be written up and available for all to keep track of. Any benchmarking done prior to this first session should be checked and adapted again to ensure measurability and progress on agreed outcomes. Ideally, the team should assign responsibility for regular follow-up on agreed goals and outcomes, typically weekly until the next session. The team coach should also elicit feedback.

Conclusion

In Part Four we have looked at defining a generic intervention that allows for enough design flexibility to meet the team's requirements. We also showed that measurement is possible if a structured way of identifying benefits is used early in the evaluation and a baseline measure is established. The methodology shown gives the team important feedback and recognition for their efforts. However, we suggest you follow the Keep It Simple approach. The more complex, the less likelihood there is of sustaining the research. Qualitative measures are as important as quantitative measures and we anticipate that even the most conservative quantitative estimate we can make, based on some of the qualitative feedback we already have, would be compelling.

Epilogue

Helena Dolny

Our prologue stated very definitively that this is not the definitive book on team coaching! But we believe the book is unusual in terms of the range that it presents for the reader to consider. We begin with very personal stories, very different ways of being, to writing up real life case studies in which different methodologies were applied. What is also different about the book is that we have unpacked the craft that team coaches work with. In doing so, what has emerged is the considerable diversity of the work, the skills, the tools and the situations.

Again, the tools that we chose to write about are wide-ranging, from very theoretical tools that have the potential of creating new individual and team insights to tools that are simply fun and energising. Laughter is part of creating an environment in which good team thinking can take place.

The last part of the book focuses on business concerns and the preoccupation with measurability, which is always a challenge when working in the arena of human interaction. The successful outcome, for example, of the cycle of reconciliation work done with the company team that was in a state of injury, is beyond doubt. How do you measure that? We know what the workshops cost, but what is the calculable return on the investment?

The more the work progressed, the clearer it was that the idea of a generic design, a one-size-fits-all approach, is problematic. We concluded that within a company it might be possible to plan a fairly generic start-up process, but the necessity for the work to emerge at its best requires flexibility.

The reader is asked to engage with the esoteric, the academic, the accountancy of this work. This might appear schizophrenic, but this is the reality of our work. We feel like artists when we are at work, crafting our design, selecting our different mediums (tools) as befits the occasion. And as this work is relational, involving real-time face-to-face interactions with human beings, there can be no 'paint-by-number' even when we have planned our canvas with great thoroughness. The ability to respond to what happens with the team, to be flexible, while maintaining focus so that the team achieves the purpose of the work is, at its best, seriously gifted artistry.

Recent Releases and other suggested reading

Marti Janse Van Rensburg

The following are brief reviews/summaries of books that we think may be of interest to team coaches.

The first two books are about team coaching, the next three about teams and how they are formed (or not) and the sixth book is a toolkit for teambuilding activities. The seventh book is written by two of the authors of this book, and the rest of them are a few, a very few, of our favourites.

1. Delani Mthembu: *Team Coaching* (Knowres Publishing, 2007)Delani Mthembu has a very impressive CV that is detailed in the introduction to the book. He is 'a shareholder, partner and director of People Capacity Solutions (a consulting and training company) and Change Partners (which specialises in internal, external and team coaching), as well as an associate partner of Franklin Covey – Southern and East Africa. He clearly has a lot of experience in Human Resource Development and holds an honours degree in HRD.

This book is rather small (about 90-odd pages) and is written as a facilitator's guide. Between 30 and 50 per cent of the book is devoted to questionnaires and little templates for answering questions. The first three chapters are geared towards the recipient of the coaching as they talk about the need for coaching, challenges for global leadership and the effect of team coaching on organisational effectiveness. The questionnaires and templates can be used by a facilitator to set up and explain team coaching. The book could probably also be of use to a leader/manager, but will more than likely be more useful for the facilitator.

The last three chapters of the book look at the 'how to' of a team coaching intervention, tools and techniques that can be employed and the learning that is derived. As much as Mr Mthembu talks about individualised design, he gives a very specific and involved process as a model without detailed description as to its working. Much of his work is influenced by the Change Partners' coaching model and the Stephen Covey work that he is accredited to do. The book uses icons, in the way made popular by Tom Peters. It is useful as a basic overview and selling point for the work Mr Mthembu and his organisation does. Facilitators might find it useful and practical as a guide.

2. David Clutterbuck: *Coaching the Team at Work* (Nicholas Brealey International, 2007)

David Clutterbuck has twenty-five years' experience in coaching and mentoring and is visiting professor at Sheffield Hallam and Oxford Brookes Universities in the UK. He co-founded the European Coaching and Mentoring Council and heads up an international consultancy specialising in mentoring.

This book is written for HRD professionals and coaching practitioners. It is written very comprehensively but in an easy-to-read and rather non-academic style. Clutterbuck gives detailed definitions of coaching, starting with individual coaching. He contrasts coaching with mentoring and counselling and also touches on how to coach. He then moves on to similar detailed descriptions and definitions of teams, different types of teams and diversity in teams.

The rest of the book looks at how team coaching can create a coaching culture within organisations, as well as the process of learning, the skills needed to be a team coach, the role of the members of the team and the role of the organisation in assisting the team's functioning, effective or not so.

He clearly sees teams as 'highly complex social entities' and the book is written to support that. He contrasts individual versus team coaching as well as the team coach versus the team facilitator and team coaching versus team building.

Clutterbuck says in the introduction to the book: 'Research into team effectiveness suggests that limited collaboration (where everyone does their own thing, with clear guidelines and occasional liaison) often delivers better results than trying to get everybody to work together.' That is what I like about this book. He talks about how useful and necessary well-functioning teams are and the role of team coaching, but he doesn't advocate it as the solution to all corporate problems.

This book would be very useful for practitioners and maybe for the occasional leader/manager who is prepared to work through all the details for a better understanding. There are some short case studies in the book. This is not a 'how to' book but rather a book that illustrates the need for and complexity of team coaching. Some people might find it a bit dry. It doesn't have icons and checklists.

3. Deborah Ancona & Henrik Bresman: *X-Teams* (Harvard Business School Publishing Corporation, 2007)

Deborah Ancona is the Seley Distinguished Professor of Management at MIT Sloan School of Management and Henrik Bresman is Assistant Professor of Organisational Behaviour at INSEAD. This is a book written by academics and is based on research done over a period of time mainly through MIT Sloan School of Management. The book proposes the theory that happy teams are not necessarily successful teams and looks at why bad things happen to good teams or why good teams fail.

In short, the book looks at what the authors define as X-teams, with the 'X' being derived from 'externally focused'. Their theory is that successful teams manage internally and externally, as opposed to just internally. They define when X-teams are needed and when not, and then, lastly, look at how to build X-teams through three basic principles that they define as External Activity, Extreme Execution, and Flexible Phases.

They state that: 'Evidence now exists suggesting that teams' success at leading, innovating and getting things done means managing both inside and outside the team.' They emphasise that their suggestions are for teams that need to innovate and create change and for teams with exchangeable membership. They clearly specify that X-teams are not needed when team goals and organisational goals are aligned, information is freely available and not changing and there is little to no interdependency.

This book is very useful for anyone who needs to put together and manage or lead a team, especially a team that continuously needs to change and innovate, or practitioners who want to understand the dynamics of teams.

4. J Richard Hackman: *Leading Teams* (Harvard Business School Publishing Corporation, 2007)

J Richard Hackman is the Edgar Pierce Professor of Social and

Organisational Psychology at Harvard University. He has a degree in mathematics and a doctorate in social psychology. He taught at Yale before moving to Harvard.

This book is similar to the previous one. It is written for the leader/ manager who needs to put together a team or teams. It similarly questions certain assertions; for example, that teams with internal harmony perform better than teams with some internal conflict, or that team dynamics are dependent on the behaviour of the team leader. It is an extensive book with many case studies and examples that look at various types of teams and when what type of team is needed.

Hackman starts by contrasting two airlines: one doing international and the other doing domestic routes. The international airline has very clearly defined rules and procedures and the domestic airline is more flexible and adaptable. He concludes this story by indicating that effective teams 'always serve their customers well, are increasingly capable performing units over time as members gain experience and discover new and better ways of working together' and that they provide settings in which individual members can find personal learning and fulfilment in their teamwork.

He defines a team as having four essential features: 'a team task; clear boundaries; clearly specified authority to manage their own work processes and membership stability over some reasonable period of time'. The book has a thirty-page section dealing with the issue of when coaching within a team context is appropriate.

If you like lots of stories and examples then you will like this book.

5. *Harvard Business Essentials: Creating Teams with an Edge* (Harvard Business School Publishing Corporation, 2004)
This book has a singular focus – 'Teams with an Edge'. It defines and contrasts teams versus workgroups. Workgroups are defined as a group of people who work for the same boss or manager but are not necessarily linked in what they do. Typically, they work mostly independently of one another. The book defines several types of teams and asserts that two are relevant today: Self-managed Work Teams and Project Teams. It discusses when teams are necessary and/or needed and when not.

The book then looks at the essentials for an effective team (being mainly a clear goal and commitment to this goal); the forming of the team and potential challenges facing a team. It looks comprehensively at all aspects of a team, from the difference between a team leader/manager and a team coach to the role of each member as contributing to and benefiting from the team. It even touches on virtual teams.

The book gives a broad overview of all aspects of an effective team. None of the aspects is discussed in great depth. It will probably be useful for the team manager/leader who wants to read up on teams fairly quickly.

6. Drikus Kriek: *Team Building Activities for South African Organisations* (Knowres Publishing, 2007)
This is a toolkit for anyone doing team building. It lists fifty potential activities with about two pages per activity as a description. The activities are all explained under the following headings: Introduction to the activity; 'In a nutshell'; Objectives; Materials Required; Procedure and, lastly, some Tips. An example would be an activity where participants are invited to look at the night sky and journal their reflections. The objectives of this activity are stated as: 'to illustrate multiple realities; to allow creativity to emerge; to generate shared narratives; and to allow opportunity for reflection'. Any facilitator of team building events and activities will find this useful.

7. Michael Cooper and Tim Goodenough: *In the Zone with South Africa's Sports Heroes* (Zebra Press, 2007)
This book is half a collection of condensed and focused sports biographies and half a textbook explaining the fundamental building blocks for high performance in sports and in life. The seventeen interviews are with prominent sportsmen and women from Gary Player, Natalie du Toit and Sherylle Calder to Jonty Rhodes and Lucas Radebe, asking the question: What is happening mentally when you are at your very best? Surprisingly, thirteen unique skills commonly occur in all these great athletes, and around those thirteen skills the book explains, teaches and explores what these skills are and how they might apply to you.

8. Lucas Derks: *Social Panoramas: Changing the Unconscious Landscape with NLP and Psychotherapy* (Wales, UK: Crown House Publishing, 2005)
Reviewed by Tim Goodenough

This book explores the concept of social panoramas, how we as human beings create rich and meaningful maps in our minds of how we represent people, concepts and important aspects of our life pictorially. Derks explores how the inter-relatedness and the meanings we give to our panorama is the key to understanding our own thinking and emotions as well as being the first clue to reshaping our own panoramas into more empowering vistas.

9. Sue Annis Hammond: *The Thin Think Book of Naming Elephants –*
   How to surface undiscussables for greater organisational success
   (Thin Book Publishing Co., 2004)
   Reviewed by Maryse Barak
'An undiscussable is a taboo subject, something that people don't talk about in an open forum.'

Successful team coaching is founded on a healthy relationship between team members as well as productive conversations. This 'thin' book – it is indeed very short – lays out in a very clear and animated way how to enable people to name fearlessly what is unsaid in the group so that genuine learning and productive interaction can continue. The authors use the story of the tragic Columbia orbiter disintegration in 2003 to illustrate what occurs when people do not say what they see and the more insidious and dangerous impact caused when they do not notice what is in front of them because of unspoken assumptions.

The authors offer simple and direct tools to create a discipline to actively surface and examine assumptions so that teams can courageously debate multiple perspectives and realities.

10. William Isaacs: *Dialogue and the Art of Thinking Together* (New York: Doubleday, 1999)
A lot of what we discuss in our team coaching book is about how we interact with one another and how we can create shared thinking that will lead to better results and more understanding. Bill Isaacs is a lecturer at Sloan School of Management and is also president of DIAlogos, a leadership education firm. The essence of this book lies in the word dialogue, which derives from the Greek *dia* (through) and *logos* (meaning), or flow of meaning. *Logos* can also mean to gather together. Isaacs therefore defines dialogue as '*A shared inquiry, a way of thinking and reflecting together*' as opposed to thinking alone and

talking to convince others of one's own point of view.

In building a capacity for dialogue, he advocates fours skills: listening, respect, suspending and voicing. He then uses examples to make the application of dialogue practical in a business environment, adds closed and open systems to the mix and finally expands the process to the economy and democracy.

11. Margaret Wheatley: *Leadership and the New Science* (San Fransisco: Berrett-Koehler Publishers Inc., 1999)

The 'New Science' Meg Wheatley refers to is any new theories in biology, chemistry and physics, not only the popular quantum mechanics, that are changing the way we think and way we view the world. She looks at self-organising systems and chaos theory and how these changes in what we know about our world change, or should change, how we view leadership, our thinking and our behaviour.

In between the chaos and complexity, she looks for a simpler, or more elegant, way of being that still honours complexity. *'To live in a quantum world … we need to change what we do. We need fewer descriptions of tasks and instead learn how to facilitate process. We need to become savvy about how to foster relationships, how to nurture growth and development.'* (p39)

In embracing chaos and change we create the capacity for transformation and lives rich in meaning.

12. David Whyte: *Crossing the Unknown Sea* (New York: Berkley Publishing Group, 2001)

Reviewed by Ray Sher

We recommend this book to team coaches because it refers to the requirement of being alert and sensitive to one's inner voice, enabling creative conversations with others. His exploration of the meaning of work, the connection of our inner and outer worlds and the possibility that work holds for us and our clients provides a context for coaching that is rich with potential.

In this gracefully written book David Whyte, poet and Fortune 500 consultant, explores work as an opportunity for the deepest discovery of one's life. Whyte invites the reader to enter into an imaginative conversation about life and work. He draws from his real-life personal experiences, utilising the metaphor of a sea voyage to demonstrate one's journey through the world of work. Whyte's imaginative use of story to illustrate how we engage with each other and the world is inspiring, practical and models a potentially powerful style of coaching.

Referring to conversations, Whyte writes: 'Conversation is good; conversation can be good work; conversation is an absolute necessity; meetings must meet, but all of our verbal conversations depend on a continuous conversation with the real patterns forming in an unspoken way at the center of our work. We need this intensely personal, private conversation with what we do, or none of the other outer conversations make sense.'

About the Authors

Maryse Barak was born in Alexandria, Egypt, and came to South Africa as a child. She graduated from the University of Cape Town with a degree in psychology in 1969 and has lived, studied and worked in Paris, London, the United States and Canada. She is a veteran corporate trainer and facilitator who believes deeply that everyone holds the answers to their own challenges. Passionate about her work, Maryse lives out her sense of purpose and calling by assisting in the creation of work environments where men and women may discover and express their own unique identity – and so create excellent results. She received her Postgraduate Certificate in Coaching from Middlesex University (United Kingdom) in 2003 and is an accredited Thinking Environment™ Consultant and Coach by Time To Think, Inc. and has recently joined its faculty. Maryse is presently discovering the richness of the 'second half of life'!

Lloyd Chapman is an executive coach, organisational architect and certified personal fitness trainer. He has twenty-two years' business experience in leading, managing and implementing strategy, large-scale organisational change, mergers and acquisitions, business process re-engineering and workflow implementations, and various other IT-related projects. He is a founding director of the Manthano Institute of Learning (Pty) Ltd, a consortium of executive coaches delivering integral, experiential coaching grounded in work-based learning and research.

Lloyd completed a doctorate in Professional Studies in Executive Coaching through Middlesex University and the National Centre for Work Based Learning in the United Kingdom. (He was the first person in the world to qualify with a DProf in Executive Coaching.) He holds an MBA degree and degrees in marketing and theology and a diploma in personal fitness training.

He has been a guest lecturer at the Graduate School of Business of the University of Cape Town, the University of Stellenbosch Business School, and the Department of Industrial Psychology of the University of South Africa. His postdoctoral research interest is the issue of how high levels of stress affect an executive's heart rate variability, which in turn inhibits optical cortical (logical) functioning.

Lloyd is fortunate enough to live in Cape Town, South Africa, with his wife, daughter and son.

Michael Cooper is an executive coach who works with individuals and teams from senior executives and management teams to elite athletes and sports teams. He is an internationally Certified Meta-Coach and is President of the MCF in South Africa. Michael's background is in IT and management and he has worked for years as a freelance facilitator and trainer for most of South Africa's large corporates. He is much in demand as a speaker at conferences and functions.

Michael is the co-author of *In the Zone with South Africa's Sports Heroes* which is currently enjoying its second print run. He is a partner in the company Coaching Unity and is presently working on a research project on highly effective teams.

Helena Dolny is a freelance coach, consultant, facilitator and founder member of Grey Matters. Her interest in personal and institutional transformation was sparked when she was managing director of the Land Bank of South Africa and she embarked on a major career shift. In 2005 she was awarded her MA (cum laude) from I-Coach Academy, Middlesex University, United Kingdom. She is a Time To Think consultant and faculty member. In March 2009 she completed a three-year commitment to building a coaching and mentoring programme and team at Standard Bank's Global Leadership Centre.

Helena has traversed the roles of agricultural economist, civil servant, doctoral researcher on land markets, development facilitator and agricultural banker. Her consistency is a commitment to enabling others to develop themselves and purposefully shape and reshape their lives in an ever-changing society. Her focus is on creative thinking environments and leadership. She enjoys writing. She is the editor of *Joe Slovo the Unfinished Biography*, and the author of *Banking on Change*.

Tim Goodenough coaches corporate executives and managers as well as elite sports people on an individual and team level. He is an internationally recognised executive coach using the Meta-Coach methodology, and is a Neuro Linguistic Programming (NLP) and Neurosemantic (NS) Trainer. Tim's career history includes working as the mental coach of the 2008 Super 14 Sharks rugby team and looking after the mentoring and executive coaching portfolios at Standard Bank's Coaching and Mentoring Unit. While at Standard Bank, Tim co-developed and trained coaching and mentoring workshops and was part of a team that assessed external executive coaches for fit and expertise to work with the Bank's top talent. Tim is in demand as a public speaker, and his cutting edge articles and blogs are highly sought after.

Tim is the co-author of *In the Zone with South Africa's Sports Heroes* which is currently enjoying its second print run. He and Michael Cooper, his business partner at Coaching Unity International, are currently working on their next book, *Raising Talent*.

Marti Janse Van Rensburg has a background that ranges from scientific research to fashion design, and from teaching to corporate management. She has often, in her varied career, found herself mentoring and guiding colleagues and employees and in 2000 she decided to make this her full-time vocation.

She has coached, and is coaching, at various corporations as well as on the Emerging Leaders Programme, a joint initiative of the Southern Africa-United States Centre for Leadership and Public Values at the University of Cape Town and Duke University. In addition to one-on-one coaching, she also does team coaching (or group facilitation) and leadership development for some of her clients. She designed a company-wide training programme for Standard Bank for all their managers on how to give and receive feedback. She also designed a Performance Coaching for them in conjunction with their Leadership Development team and was asked to start their Leader-as-Coach Programme at the Global Leadership Centre. In 2003 she was involved in a groundbreaking Action Reflection Learning (ARL) programme with one of the partners at the MIL Institute in Sweden. Twenty-two final year students at CIDA City Campus were taken through a three-month intensive ARL programme normally done with middle to senior managers in companies.

She is a founder director of Coaching and Mentoring Southern Africa (COMENSA), a coordinating body for coaches and mentors that aims to be inclusive of all types of coaching and mentoring and also to provide ethics and standards for the industry as a whole. She is a member of the Worldwide Association of Business Coaches (WABC) and was on their Expert Certification Panel. In 2007 she was invited to join the Global Convention on Coaching (GCC) work group on research in the field of coaching.

She has a degree in chemical engineering from the University of Pretoria and an MBA from the Gordon Institute of Business Science (GIBS) where she did her research project on coaching. She was involved in research at the Council for Scientific and Industrial Research for five years before moving into the high fashion industry where she worked as a designer and was the owner of a training facility for designers. She did some contract teaching and consulting and spent ten years in fashion retail which gave her experience in conducting business in Asia. She was a South African Breweries divisional director before deciding to change to a full-time career in coaching and leadership development.

Her work as a coach during the past eight years has seen her work with various local and international associates. She has coached across Africa and in the United Kingdom.

Khatija Saley was born in Mpumalanga and grew up and received her schooling in Lenasia, south of Johannesburg. Passionate about animals, her early dream was to become a veterinary surgeon. However, because of the strictures imposed by the apartheid regime, her application to the University of Pretoria met with rejection. Instead, she completed a BA degree, majoring in psychology and philosophy. She worked part-time in a bank while doing her undergraduate studies and was offered a full-time position in human resources on graduation. She then moved into the systems environment and completed an MBA at the Wits Business School. She later headed the transformation unit of the bank for which she was working. The realisation that change needed to be effected at an individual level drew her to the profession of coaching. She completed her initial qualifications in the area of executive coaching and is currently working on a master's degree in coaching at Middlesex University. Her dissertation deals with 'The Return on Investment on the Acquisition of Coaching Skills by Managers'. She is also training as a Time to Think consultant.

Through her work as a coach, Khatija wants to offer others the support to be able to make the best possible choices they can make, in whatever circumstances they find themselves.

Raphael Sher brings his lifelong interest in personal growth to his coaching practice as he skilfully guides clients to find their own solutions. He has the ability to make relevant links using poetry and story.

Believing that everyone has a gift and a purpose, he asks penetrating questions, listening deeply as the ability to think expands. His clients appreciate his ease and humour as he inspires and encourages them in an atmosphere of safety.

His philosophical view that people are inherently intelligent, powerful and capable of change, has catapulted many to new heights.

Recently accredited as a 'Time to Think' coach/consultant he has spent the last sixteen years coaching and facilitating for global and blue chip companies as well as government departments, small business owners and private individuals.

Index

Ancona, Deborah 54,127
Archetypes 129,174-179
Authors' personal stories 7-49
Axes of change 83-86

Baba Ram Dass 14,232
Barnga Card Game 129,191-193,227
Bates, Marilyn 159,162
Beck, Martha 132,139
Belbin, Meredith 135
Belbin Test® 163
Benchmarking 81-83
Bodenhamer, Bob 27
Boon, Mike 47
Bresman, Henrik 54,127
Briggs, Katherine 157,162
Briggs-Myers, Isabel 158,162
Briggs-Myers, Peter 162
Buckingham, Marcus 57,109,227

Clifton Strengthsfinder 109
Clutterbuck, David 242
Conflict resolution 128
Containers 63,131,144-148
Conversation skills: 207-216; awareness of impact on others 210, 212-213; coaching conversation models 208; feedback 210,213; listening 207,210-211; questioning 210,211; self-awareness 210,212
Covey, Stephen 47
Creating Dynamic Tension Model 67-69

De Bono, Edward 59
Duval, Michelle 32,78,86

Emery, Fred 181,182,227
Emery, Merrelyn 181
Emotional Intelligence (EQ) 60,246
Enneagram 58,129,164-173,174,227
Esalen Institute 45

Feedback 183,236
Feedforward 138,215-216
Five Fingers 83
Flaherty, James 47
Four Fields of Knowledge 24
Frames 63

Games for team building: 194-206; Count to Six 205-206; Da Vinci Bridge 202-205,227; Mr Potato Head 195-197; Nail Balance 197-201,227
Games, use in team coaching 58
Generic design for team coaching 247-259
Goals 134-139,183
Goldsmith, Marshall 138,215-216
Goleman, Daniel 60
Gurdjieff, George Ivanovich 165,166

Hall, Michael 27,28,32,78,86
Harmonic groups 168,169
Harri-Augstein, Sheila 24
Heart Maths 186-189

Honey, Peter 149,150
Hornevian groups 168,169
Horney, Karen 169
Hudson, Russ 166,167,169

Ichazo, Oscar 166
I Ching cards 7,58,129,217
I-Coach Academy 18
Integral-Experiential Coaching
    Model 24,99-112

Jacques, Elliot 23
Joint Enrichment Programme 47
Journalling 131,222,227
Jung, C J 56,157,158,162,174,177

Katzenbach, Jon 232
Keirsey, David 159,162
Kinsey-House, Henry 47
Kirkpatrick, Donald 244
Kline, Nancy 1,7,11,42,66,71,88,
    189,235; Meeting Process 92;
    Council Process 92. See also
    Thinking Environment™,
    Thinking Pairs,
    Transforming Meetings
Kolb, David A, 57,91,100,150-
    152; Experiential Learning
    Model 24,102-105. See
    also Learning Styles Inventory
Kraybill, Ron: 117; Cycle of
    Reconciliation 117-119,128

Learning Conversations 24
Learning style preferences 149-156
Learning Styles (Honey Mumford)
    152-156,227
Learning Styles Inventory (Kolb)
    57,60,129,150,151,227
Learning Styles Questionnaire

(Honey Mumford) 57,60,149-
    150
Lewin, Kurt 181,182
Liberating Assumptions 90
Listening in Pairs, types of
    listening 90
Look Again Foundation 18,47

Maslow, Abraham 28
Mayer, John D 60
Memoranda of Understanding
    3,243,251
Mental development for coaching
    140-143
Meta-Coaching 32,33,78-87,243
Meta-Levels 140,142
Mumford, Alan 55,149,150
Music, use in team coaching
    129,226
Myers-Briggs Type Indicator®
    57,58,129,157-163

Naranjo, Claudio 166
Neuro-Linguistic Programming
    27,28,30,31-32
Neuro Semantics 27,28,32,78

Optimising team performance 127-
    128,181
Owen, Harrison 4,72

Painting, use in team coaching
    131,227
Personology 110-111
Poetry, use in team coaching 129
Preparation for coaching inter-
    ventions 70-72,78-79,123,
    145-146

Reconciliation, facilitating 114-122

Rehm, Robert 23,106,129,181,182, 227,232
Renew, Anne 32
Revans, Reg 55
Riso, Don 166,167,169
Rose, Colin 60

Salovey, Peter 60
Sandahl, Phil 47
Schumacher, E F 24
Senge, Peter 17,47
Six Criteria of Productive Work: 106-107,180-185; self-rating 180,232-233
Smith, D K 232
Smuts, Jan 110-111
Sports teams, coaching interventions 63-69
Sternberg, Robert 60
Storytelling: 110-111; power of 7,219-221
Stress 186-190

Team alignment 130
Team coaching, assessing business benefits and ROI 242-246
Team, definition 232
Teamwork Guide (Rehm): 232-241; managing and improving team work processes 238; team boundaries 233; team coordination 236; team goals 234-235; team ground rules 235; team information systems 236; team skill development plan 237-238; team work space and equipment needs 240
Thiagarajan, Sivasailam 191
Thinking Environment™: 1,11,88,93,186,235,257; Incisive Questions 1,90; ten components 1,11,89-90,189
Thinking Pairs 66,92,116,207
Thinking Partnership 90
Thomas, Laurie 24
Thomas, Lewis 182
Thorsrud, Einar 182
Tools for coaching interventions 127-228
Transforming Meetings 88-98,235
Triads 168
TRIAD skills practice 214
Trist, Eric 181

Video clips, use in team coaching 58,129,224-226
Vision Boards 132-133,227
Von Franz, Marie Louise 177
Vulindlela Network 47-48

Well Formed Outcome 135-136
Whitworth, Laura 47
Whyte, David 129
Wilber, Ken 23,100; integral philosophy 100-105
World Café work 121-122

'Zoning Pyramid' 28